SCOTLAND DECIDES

SCOTLAND DECIDES

The Devolution Issue and the 1997 Referendum

David Denver • James Mitchell
Charles Pattie • Hugh Bochel

FRANK CASS
LONDON • PORTLAND, OR

First published in 2000 in Great Britain by
FRANK CASS PUBLISHERS
Newbury House, 900 Eastern Avenue
London IG2 7HH

and in the United States of America by
FRANK CASS PUBLISHERS
c/o ISBS, 5804 N.E. Hassalo Street
Portland, Oregon, 97213-3644

Website: www.frankcass.com

British Library Cataloguing in Publication Data

Scotland decides: the devolution issue and the 1997
referendum
1. Scotland. Parliament 2. Decentralization in government –
Scotland 3. Referendum – Scotland 4. Scotland – Politics and
government – 20th century
I. Denver, D.T. (David Trodden), 1944–
320.9'411

ISBN 0-7146-5053-6 (cloth)
ISBN 0-7146-8104-0 (paper)

Library of Congress Cataloging-in-Publication Data

Scotland decides: the devolution issue and the 1997 referendum /
David Denver ... [et al.].
    p. cm.
Includes bibliographical references and index.
ISBN 0-7146-5053-6 (cloth) – ISBN 0-7146-8104-0 (pbk.)
    1. Referendum–Scotland. 2. Scotland–Politics and
government–20th century. 3. Elections–Scotland. 4. Political
participation–Scotland.
5. Scotland. Parliament–History–20th century. I. Denver, D.T.
JF497.G7 S26 2000
320.1'5'09411–dc21   99-088817

Printed in Great Britain by
Creative Print and Design (Wales), Ebbw Vale

Contents

List of Tables and Figures

TABLES

FIGURES

Foreword

September 11 1997 was a turning-point in the history of the United Kingdom. By three to one the Scottish electorate opted to institute a Scottish Parliament. The changes reverberating from that decision will alter the politics of Britain for ever, even if we do not yet know how.

In 1979 a similar attempt at innovation fell at the referendum hurdle. The rules of the political game as well as the public's attitudes to central government have been much modified over the last twenty years. David Denver and his colleagues chronicled the Scottish disappointment in 1979; they have now chronicled its reversal twenty years on in a book that shows a penetrating understanding of the forces, both in haute politique and mass electioneering, which produced the volte-face.

The study of politics in these islands has been greatly enriched by well-written, detailed research into individual events, composed with an appreciation of their wider national and international context. This book is a notable example of the genre.

Dr David Butler
Nuffield College
Oxford

Preface

On 16 January 1707 the independent Scottish Parliament ratified the Treaty of Union with England by 110 votes to 67. On 25 March the Parliament adjourned and on 28 April it was formally dissolved (see Ferguson, 1977: ch. 4). Throughout the session popular opinion had been clearly opposed to the Treaty, with pro-Union members being manhandled by the mob in Edinburgh, anti-Union riots in Glasgow and the Articles of Union being ceremonially burned by 300 armed Cameronians in Dumfries (*ibid.*). The Union was 'carried by the Parliament against the country' (p. 266) and 'to the popular mind the treaty seemed nothing but a base betrayal and its negotiators traitors' (p. 230). In the immediate aftermath of Union 'the mood of most people was sombre if not sullen' (p. 270).

Eighty-five years later the event was still being lamented by Robert Burns. The Union had made Scotland 'England's province' and his verdict on the passage of the Treaty was:

We're bought and sold for English gold;
Such a parcel of rogues in a nation!

During the nineteenth century, although Scots retained a distinct identity and culture within the United Kingdom, the Union came to be widely accepted. Towards the end of the century the Scottish Office was established to provide some administrative devolution but although home rule sentiment was never quite eliminated, political devolution was not of great interest to most Scots. This changed from the 1960s onwards and 292 years after the original Scottish Parliament dissolved itself, on 1 July 1999, in the Church of Scotland Assembly Rooms in Edinburgh, the Queen opened the first session of a new Scottish Parliament.

This book examines the process by which the new Parliament came to be established. We trace the origins and history of the demand for home rule, paying special attention to developments following the failure of the first referendum on the issue in 1979. These culminated in a second referendum which was held in September 1997. Referendums have been rare events in United Kingdom politics but this one produced a decisive result and led directly to the creation of a Parliament in Scotland for the first time in almost 300 years. Such a major event merits detailed consideration and provides the focus for most of the book. The penultimate chapter looks at developments in the politics of devolution in the aftermath of the referendum and provides an appraisal of prospects for the new Parliament. We also include a postscript which summarises and discusses the implications of the results of the first elections to the Scottish Parliament.

The research on which this book is based was made possible by an award from the ESRC (ref. R000237374) which we gratefully acknowledge. We are also grateful to Mark Stuart who acted as research assistant on the project and whose meticulous attention to detail and capacity for hard work did much to ensure its success. Michael Cavanagh of the University of Strathclyde also provided valued assistance, particularly in relation to the chapter on the Scottish media, and we would like to record our thanks here.

We would also like to thank the officers of the political parties in Scotland and referendum campaign group leaders who were willing to be interviewed; John and Dorothy Bochel for analysing local newspapers; Susan Anderson, Stephen Dunstan, Brent Collins and Ritchie Denver for envelope stuffing and coding; and the 2,335 Scottish voters who returned completed questionnaires. The poem from *The Herald* is reproduced with permission.

This is a genuinely co-authored book. Although individuals took responsibility for the initial draft of specific chapters and sections, all of the authors read and contributed to each of them. We are, therefore, jointly responsible for any errors of fact and for the interpretations offered.

It should perhaps be recorded that, although all four of us now work in English universities, we are all Scots (having travelled the same path as many in previous generations). Like most expatriates we remain strongly attached to our country. Nonetheless, the account offered here is as detached as we can make it.

David Denver
James Mitchell
Charles Pattie
Hugh Bochel

May 1999

1

Scottish Devolution: The Historical Context

INTRODUCTION

The referendum on Scottish devolution held in September 1997, less than five months into the new Labour government's term in office, was the second to be held on this issue. Eighteen years before, in the dying days of the previous Labour administration, the Scottish electorate was asked to decide in a referendum whether, as proposed by the government, a Scottish Assembly should be established. A narrow majority of those who voted agreed that there should be an Assembly but this was not enough to overcome the qualification (that 40 per cent of the eligible electorate had to support the measure for it to be passed) which had been imposed by Parliament at Westminster. The change in the use of language between 1979 and 1997 is itself significant. By the time of the second referendum the debate was about creating a Scottish 'Parliament', not an 'Assembly'. There were other changes which were more than symbolic, however. A substantial change of attitude had occurred among Scots although few home rulers could have anticipated this in 1979. Shortly after the first referendum, a cartoon appeared in a Nationalist newspaper. It showed a picture of a boy reading a book about 'EVOLUTION' with a picture of dinosaurs on its cover while his father was reading a newspaper with 'DEVOLUTION LATEST' on the front page. The caption below summed up the feeling of many supporters of Scottish devolution at the time. 'No son – they're not the same thing – devolution takes longer!', the father explained.

Although it was not until the 1970s that Scottish devolution became a serious possibility, it could be argued that it was indeed a long time in coming. A Scottish Home Rule Association (SHRA) had been set up in 1886 and Scottish home rule was part of Keir Hardie's platform when he contested the Mid-Lanark by-election, as the first independent Labour candidate, in 1888. Hardie was supported by the SHRA although this later proved controversial within the organisation, as its secretary argued that the SHRA had been mistaken in backing Hardie (Mitchell, 1996: 71). This was only the first difficulty Labour was to have in a long history of relations with umbrella groups campaigning for a Scottish Parliament, up to and including the 1997 referendum. During the late nineteenth and early twentieth centuries, however, Scottish home rule was not an important issue in British politics. The Irish question was far more pressing and divisive and it had a considerable impact on Scottish politics. The issue split the Liberals to the great advantage of the Conservatives. The Scottish Unionist Party, initially a coalition of Conservatives and Liberal Unionists, was the official title of the Conservative Party in Scotland until 1965. Such was the relative importance of Scottish and Irish home rule, that the unionism expressed in the name of the party referred to the union between Ireland – later Northern Ireland – and Britain rather than to the constitutional position of Scotland. At the same time, while Labour in Scotland attracted strong support among Irish Catholic immigrants and there was much sympathy for Irish nationalism in Labour's ranks, this was not translated into support for Scottish nationalism. Indeed, Scottish Unionists and Conservatives often portrayed Scottish home rulers as in some way connected with Irish nationalism while Labour supporters, in the west of Scotland, often associated Scottish nationalism with the Orange Order and Irish unionism.[1]

Despite these inauspicious beginnings, home rule sentiment in Scotland did not disappear. Throughout the first half of the twentieth century the idea was sustained and promoted in a variety of ways – through pressure groups, constitutional conventions, petitions, parliamentary action by Scottish MPs, direct action (including removal of the Stone of Scone from Westminster Abbey in 1950) and the founding (in 1934), and subsequent electoral activity, of the Scottish National Party (SNP). As a result of these sorts of activities the issue intermittently crept on to the political agenda. Moreover, there is evidence of extensive support for some form of home rule for Scotland over a long period of time. From the 1890s to the 1920s, on 11 occasions a majority of Scottish MPs voted in favour of resolutions or private members' bills advocating the creation of a Scottish Parliament. In 1945, out of 84 Scottish parliamentary candidates who replied to a request by the Scottish Convention for their views on home rule only three declared themselves opposed to the idea. In July 1947, the *Scottish Daily Express* published the results of an opinion poll showing that 76 per cent of Scots approved of the establishment of a Parliament dealing with Scottish affairs while only 13 per cent disapproved and 11 per cent had no opinion. During 1949–50 a petition calling for a Scottish Parliament, known as the Covenant, circulated in Scotland and was signed, the organisers claimed, by 1.7 million people.

Nonetheless, it was not until the 1960s that Scottish home rule became a politically significant issue first within Scotland and then in British politics. The catalyst for this change was the electoral success (in both local and national contests) of the SNP. The effect was that the 1970s became what Andrew Marr has dubbed 'The Devolution Years' (Marr, 1992) culminating in the first referendum. To account for the transformation of home rule from an issue at the fringe of politics to one that dominated Scottish political debate for almost 30 years we need to look in more detail at the development of the parties' attitudes on the issue.

THE POLITICAL PARTIES AND HOME RULE

For each of the political parties in Scotland, the 1997 referendum was the culmination of years of internal debate. Past experiences and memories, some bitter, were important in the internal debates in each party as they decided how they would campaign. Most prominent, of course, were memories of the 1970s and the previous referendum. But the referendum also evoked old themes which have been present throughout the century of campaigning for a Scottish Parliament – cross-party pressure groups for home rule, the changing policies of existing parties and the relationships between different parties on the issue. In this section we trace the development of the policies of the major parties on the question of Scottish devolution.

Labour

As we have seen, the Labour pioneer Keir Hardie was a supporter of Scottish home rule and, from its inception, Labour had a commitment to home rule in its programme. In the inter-war period the 'Red Clydesiders' were staunch supporters of the policy. After 1945, however, Labour's position changed as a centralist ethos came to dominate Labour thinking on the economy. Gordon Brown, later to become Chancellor of the Exchequer, wrote in his doctoral thesis on the Scottish Labour Party that, 'No theorist attempted in sufficient depth to reconcile the conflicting aspirations for home rule and a British Socialist advance. In particular, no one was able to show how capturing power in Britain – and legislating for minimum levels of welfare, for example – could be combined with a policy of devolution for Scotland' (Brown, 1981: 527). This tension proved important over much of the post-war period.

Home rule agitation during the Attlee government's period in office (1945-51) proved embarrassing for Labour. In a confidential cabinet memorandum in 1947, Arthur Woodburn, the Secretary of State for Scotland, identified four groupings within Scotland at that time (see Mitchell, 1996: 44). The first, 'extreme home rulers', were a 'small, picturesque and articulate' group but it was 'difficult to say whether there is any considerable support for their view'. The second, the Scottish Convention, was a body demanding a separate Parliament in Edinburgh while retaining Scottish representation in the 'British Parliament for British affairs'. This group, according to the Secretary of State, was 'certainly strong, though its numbers are difficult to estimate, as during elections its vote is not recorded because of stronger loyalty to the main political parties'. Nonetheless, it had a 'large number of supporters in all parties'. The third group, not formally organised, was 'by far the largest' ('almost universal') and had 'strong emotional feeling behind it in Scotland'. It wanted Scottish affairs to be given more time and to be dealt with by Scots themselves 'within the British Constitution and the unity of the two countries'. The fourth group was one calling for a 'fact-finding enquiry' into the constitutional, economic and political relations between Scotland and England including the possibility of some form of devolution.

Woodburn's memorandum serves as a useful benchmark against which subsequent events and developments can be analysed. It is difficult to gauge the state of public opinion in Scotland at that time with a great deal of confidence but the memorandum gives a confidential and, one would assume, well-informed interpretation by one of Scotland's senior politicians of the period. He quoted the *Daily Express* poll referred to above, noting that 80 per cent of Socialists were in favour of a Scottish Parliament, as were 75 per cent of Tories and 70 per cent of Liberals. The memorandum also highlighted reasons why support for some kind of change had arisen. It seemed clear to Woodburn that this demand was not solely a product of national sentiment. Government policies had provoked a backlash. The nationalisation of industries was thought to take control of Scottish industries out of Scotland. A 'contemptuous suppression of Scottish initiative' had been attacked in transport policy. Of course, the Conservatives in opposition had played on these feelings. There was, warned the Secretary of State, a 'smouldering pile that might break through the party loyalties and become a formidable national movement'. In particular, he thought that this was becoming a more likely possibility as the Labour programme was fulfilled and the 'great dividing issues are settled, leaving the cleavage between the parties less deep and intense'. Woodburn was raising the possibility of a new cleavage emerging, based on national identity, and the prospect of a decline in party identification associated with class. In addition, he was signalling the contingent nature of national identity. Each of these predictions was, to some extent, prescient. However, he was wrong in thinking that a period of relative social tranquillity and economic improvement, marked by a consensus across the two main parties, would see the eruption of Scottish nationalism.

To tackle the mounting pressure for some form of home rule, Woodburn recommended changes in parliamentary procedure and other administrative reforms, falling far short of devolution or even an enquiry into it. Attlee's government eventually agreed to establish a committee to consider the financial and economic relations between Scotland and England but more immediately two sets of proposals were recommended. It was suggested that certain bills and Scottish Estimates should be transferred for debate in the Scottish Grand Committee and that there should be greater co-ordination of economic affairs in Scotland itself. These proposals were published in a white paper in 1948 (Scottish Home Department, 1948). A Scottish Economic Conference should also be established which would meet regularly under the chairmanship of the Secretary of State for Scotland. It would have members from the Scottish Council (Development and Industry) representing all sides of industry plus business and commerce, the nationalised industries and government departments. These were measures designed to appease any feelings of neglect among the Scottish public and to reinforce the government's commitment to Scotland as a distinct entity. In many respects, these moves were very similar to proposals which emanated from John Major's Conservative government in the 1990s in response to home rule agitation (see Scottish Office, 1993). Devolution had not been formally abandoned by Labour under Attlee but that was what had happened in effect. By the late 1950s, even the paper commitment to Scottish home rule was abandoned (Keating and Bleiman, 1979: 147). Labour had entered a period of staunch unionism. Devolution continued to be supported by some party members but it was neither a salient issue nor one which carried much support amongst activists. By the early 1960s Labour was unequivocally a unionist party hostile to Scottish home rule.

The rise of the SNP in the 1960s changed all that. The early optimism and success of the new Labour government elected in 1964 gave way in the late 1960s to a period of relative economic decline and crisis. As a consequence Labour became deeply unpopular among the voters and in Scotland this benefited the SNP. The Nationalist advance in local and by-elections forced the issue of Scotland's constitutional status to the forefront of Scottish politics. Initially Labour remained hostile to making any concession to Nationalist demands. William Ross, Secretary of State for Scotland under Harold Wilson, was vehemently opposed and his views found an echo among many activists in the constituencies, who came to regard the SNP as an enemy posing a serious electoral threat. In 1969, however, Wilson set up a Royal Commission on the Constitution, expecting that it would 'spend years taking minutes'. Instead of buying time for Labour, however, this gave the Tories an excuse for prevaricating when they came to power the next year. In addition, when the Commission finally reported in late 1973, recommending devolution in its majority report (Kilbrandon, 1973), it helped to fuel the very demands which it had been set up to douse. In the interim, North Sea Oil had been discovered and the SNP had found a new lease of life, capitalising on the vast wealth lying beneath the sea off Scotland's coast. Adding grist to the SNP mill, the British economy was once again in trouble and the government was plagued by serious industrial relations problems.

The change in Labour policy came in 1974, a year in which the SNP made spectacular advances in two general elections. In August, a special conference was held at which the trade unions forced through a change in Labour Party policy. Devolution became official policy in time for the October 1974 general election. Many party members remained sceptical, however. Devolution was seen as a dangerous sop to the Nationalists which was inconsistent with both core values such as equality of service provision and traditional policies such as central economic management. The party's official endorsement of devolution in the late 1970s was superficial as became clear in the referendum in 1979. John Smith, charged with piloting the devolution legislation through the House of Commons, was among those who had spoken against devolution in the past and he had argued in a newspaper article in May 1974 that the cost of devolution was 'too high' (McSmith, 1994: 76). Smith reiterated this point at Labour's special conference in August and argued that anyone claiming that Scotland could have an Assembly without losing its Secretary of State and some MPs in the House of Commons was guilty of dishonesty (McSmith, 1994: 76). These were matters to which Labour was to return in the 1990s. Smith later (in 1992) became leader of the Labour Party. He was the only Labour leader in modern times to be associated with strong support for Scottish home rule but he had once been, like his party, opposed to the idea. He had come round to it rather reluctantly at first before becoming an enthusiast for devolution.

Although Labour's switch to a pro-devolution stance was opposed by some in the party, for others it did not go far enough. In July 1976 some of the home rule enthusiasts broke with Labour to launch a new party – the Scottish Labour Party – which tried to marry socialism and nationalism. The Scottish Labour Party was created by Jim Sillars. Sillars, MP for Ayrshire South from March 1970, when his chief by-election opponent was the SNP candidate, had been a leading figure in the Labour Party in Scotland but had become disillusioned and left with one other Labour MP (John Robertson who represented Paisley) to form the new party. With much journalistic support, but experiencing the vehement denunciations of all political apostates, Sillars and his party were built up with the same hype and suffered the same fate as that of Scotland's international football team in the 1978 World Cup. Great hopes and expectations were succeeded by contemptuous dismissals, sometimes written by the same people. Sillars and the SLP, however, (unlike the 'tartan army') had an enduring effect. The SNP came close to adopting the programme of the party a decade later when it moved more decisively to the left and embraced membership of the European Community. By then Sillars himself had joined the SNP.

The Conservatives
The Conservatives, long known as 'Unionists' in Scotland, supported the setting up of the Northern Ireland Parliament following partition in 1922, but have traditionally been staunch opponents of Scottish devolution. In opposition after the Second World War they 'played the Scottish card' to embarrass the Labour government but stopped short of supporting devolution. Between 1945 and 1951, Scottish Conservatives attacked the Attlee government's nationalisation programme, on the grounds that it would take control of Scottish industry out of Scotland, and gave implicit support to those then campaigning for a Scottish Parliament. When they returned to office in 1951, the Conservatives set up a Royal Commission on Scottish Affairs and appointed an additional junior minister at the Scottish Office but they had no intention of satisfying home rulers, with whom they had temporarily been allied while in opposition. The 1950s was a decade of relative consensus and prosperity for Britain as a whole and it was also a lean time for home rulers. In 1959, the *Glasgow Herald* looked back on the excitement which had been provoked by the agitation for home rule a decade before and noted the withering of the movement since then (8/9 July 1959). Scottish nationalism's obituary, it appeared, had been written. In fact, it was around this time that the seeds of discontent were being sown which would yield a sharp revival in its fortunes.

The success of the SNP in the 1960s had a major impact on the Conservatives. Edward Heath, the party leader, announced a dramatic change of policy at the Scottish Conservatives' annual conference at Perth in 1968. Heath startled party members when he made his 'Declaration of Perth' in favour of a Scottish Assembly. There was much disquiet in the party and little enthusiasm for the new policy. Even those in favour had been taken by surprise and acknowledged that the policy had been imposed by the centre against the wishes of party members (Mitchell, 1990a: 56). As was to happen in the Labour Party six years later, a devolution policy was imposed on the Scottish party by the London party leadership. The issue receded in importance, however, following the 1970 general election at which the SNP failed to make the breakthrough which many commentators had predicted (although they did advance from their position at the previous election) and Heath, now Prime Minister, quietly abandoned any intention to deliver a Scottish Assembly. The revival in SNP fortunes in 1974 placed the Conservatives in a weak position to respond. Having had the opportunity to deliver while in office, they lacked the necessary credibility to go into the 1974 elections as a home rule party. Conservative policy remained officially in favour of devolution but the party was now outflanked by both the SNP and Labour.

Heath's defeat in the two 1974 elections was followed by Margaret Thatcher's successful challenge to his leadership in the following year. Thatcher accepted the policy on devolution that she had inherited but gradually changed it. By this time a pro-devolution element had emerged inside the Scottish party. In December 1976, the Conservative Shadow Cabinet decided to oppose Labour's first devolution bill thus signalling a change in party policy. Alick Buchanan-Smith, Shadow Scottish Secretary, and Malcolm Rifkind, his junior, resigned from the front-bench in protest. Both voted for Labour's devolution proposals in the 1979 referendum with the former campaigning vigorously in favour. Both later became ministers under Margaret Thatcher but Buchanan-Smith never made it to the cabinet and resigned from the government to sit on the back-benches after 1987 while Rifkind accepted the party line and rose to become Secretary of State for Scotland, Defence Secretary and finally Foreign Secretary. By 1979, Conservative policy was to support all-party talks or a 'constitutional convention' in which Scottish representatives would discuss and agree Scotland's constitutional status. In principle the party remained committed to devolution but in practice they were opposed. This was hardly surprising. Devolution sat uneasily with a party whose leader was committed to a free economy and a strong (centralised) state (Gamble, 1994).

The Liberals
The Scottish Liberal Party has been consistent in its support for a Scottish Parliament since the time of Gladstone. Scottish home rule, as part of 'home rule all round', was favoured in the 1880s as much as a means of overcoming the problems inherent in giving devolution to only one part of the United Kingdom, at that time to Ireland, as it was a means of achieving land reform and other parts of the Liberals' radical programme in Scotland. As with Labour and the Conservatives, however, the Liberals never quite got round to implementing their commitment to home rule when in office, although there was a real possibility of Scottish home rule being implemented just before the First World War. Among the strongest advocates of this policy in Asquith's cabinet was Winston Churchill, then a Liberal MP for Dundee. In their last years in office, however, the question of Ireland dominated all the Liberal government's thoughts and time on constitutional matters. Out of office since the demise of Lloyd George, Liberals have supported and often initiated calls for Scottish home rule. They were active, along with the more numerous and vociferous Clydesiders, in the reconstituted Scottish Home Rule Association between the wars and were active in the campaign for a Scottish Parliament in the late 1940s. John MacCormick, who had earlier been a leading member of the SNP, joined the Scottish Liberal Party at that time, becoming its vice-president for a period, and was a leading home rule campaigner.

Even before the rise of the SNP, the Liberals were taking the issue of Scottish home rule seriously. At the party's 1961 joint assembly of British Liberal Parties, a motion was passed in favour of Scottish self-government. In the 1960s, Russell Johnston and other Scottish Liberals sponsored home rule bills and bills proposing referendums in the House of Commons. Also in the 1960s, there was talk of a pact being formed between the Liberals and the SNP in order to advance the home rule cause. Though this never came to anything, the Liberals had long been involved with support for cross-party campaigning in the home rule movement and they continued this tradition through the 1970s and after. The Scottish Liberal Party – like the Liberals in the rest of Britain – had been reduced to a rump in the 1950s, but from the 1960s it started to pick up support in the peripheral areas of Scotland: the Highlands, Islands and Borders. In time it became clear that support for devolution was relatively weak in some of these areas. Significantly, however, the party never wavered from its commitment and remained overwhelmingly in favour of home rule.

The SNP

The *raison d'être* of the SNP is Scottish self-government. While that can mean either complete independence or devolution within the United Kingdom, it has generally been interpreted within the SNP as meaning independence. The objective of 'self-government' had been written into the party's constitution from the outset as a compromise, satisfying hard-liners who wanted nothing less than independence, and moderates who would have accepted devolution, at least as a first step (Finlay, 1994). The tension between fundamentalists and gradualists or pragmatists has endured throughout the party's history (Mitchell, 1990b). During the Second World War, in 1942, there was a split in the SNP. Although there were a number of issues behind the split – including the question of conscientious objection to the war and the personalities of the people involved – the basic division was between home rulers and those who insisted on independence. The smaller grouping, the home rulers, broke away and set up what was to become the Scottish Convention, a pressure group that was active in the 1940s. The SNP came under the leadership of Robert McInytre, who became the party's first MP after winning a by-election in Motherwell in April 1945, largely because of the wartime truce which existed between the established parties (he lost the seat at the general election which followed in July). McIntyre was convinced that pressure group politics alone would not succeed and that the SNP needed to contest elections in order to put pressure on the other parties. His view was that the party should remain loyal to its ultimate goal of independence but needed to be pragmatic in its attitude towards devolution.

During the 1950s the SNP remained in the electoral doldrums. In the 1960s, however, the party suddenly emerged as a serious player in Scottish politics and transformed the political landscape. Having obtained just 0.8 per cent of the Scottish vote in the 1959 general election, the SNP advanced to 2.4 per cent in 1964 and 5 per cent in 1966. A series of good performances in parliamentary by-elections culminated in Winnie Ewing winning the formerly safe Labour seat of Hamilton in 1967 and this success was underlined by sweeping gains in local elections. A new and highly successful party logo was adopted and party membership soared from 2,000 to 30,000 in the four years from 1966 (Mitchell, 1996: 200). As we have noted, the 1970 general election proved a disappointment to the SNP – they increased their share of the vote to 11.4 per cent and won one seat – but this was below heightened expectations and the by-election gain was lost. In the two elections of 1974, however, SNP support increased dramatically. In February they won 21.9 per cent of the vote and seven seats and in October leapt to 30.4 per cent of votes (coming a fairly close second to Labour on 36.3 per cent) and 11 seats. It was these SNP successes that made the 1970s 'the devolution years'.

In the late 1970s, when the Labour government lost its majority and needed the support of minority parties in the House of Commons, the SNP had an opportunity to push for significant constitutional change. It gave support to the government's policy of devolution but faced in different directions on other matters, notably the nationalisation of steel and shipbuilding. A new cleavage based on national identity may have been emerging in Scottish politics but it was not replacing the old class-based politics. The SNP proved incapable at this time of creating an image and strategy which took account of both cleavages simultaneously. Unmistakably Scottish, it was not always clear where it stood on social and economic matters. Its policies were decidedly left-of-centre but its rhetoric and the voting of its MPs in the House often suggested more right-wing sympathies. Similar problems existed in local government where SNP councillors were frequently divided over issues such as housing policy. Labour's problems with the emerging cleavage around national identity were mirrored in the SNP's difficulties with class-based politics.

The SNP supported Labour on devolution throughout the 1974–79 government even though a minority in the party expressed doubts about the wisdom of this strategy. If Labour's August 1974 special conference on devolution was a historic turning point, the SNP conference in Motherwell in 1976 was in some respects similar. The party decided to back devolution and the Labour government's proposals. Those opposed to this strategy reluctantly accepted the party line and some were later to regret bitterly not speaking out more vehemently against it. The SNP, they felt, came to be too closely associated with devolution at the expense of arguing for independence. The party had made too many compromises and suffered accordingly in terms of popularity. Interpretations of the events of this period became important in future SNP strategic thinking and debate.

SOCIAL CLEAVAGES AND POLITICAL PARTIES

Having described the development of party policies on devolution it is useful at this point to make a brief excursion into political science theory. The work of Lipset and Rokkan (1967) on the underpinnings of party systems provides a general framework within which the emergence of devolution as a significant issue for the parties can be located. In their path-breaking and influential study, Lipset and Rokkan argued that four major social cleavages underlay modern European party systems. These cleavages were created by two successive revolutions which were critical to the modernisation of society. Two were associated with the 'National Revolution', the process of state formation and nation-building in the eighteenth and nineteenth centuries (although this process began much earlier in the British case). The first was a centre–periphery cleavage involving conflict between a central state-building, dominant culture and the subject cultures of ethnic, linguistic or religious minorities frequently located on the geographical peripheries of the state. Secondly, a church–state division also developed from this process. New claims made on behalf of the authority of the state collided with the traditional claim of the (Catholic) Church to spiritual authority and hence to control of important aspects of national life, as typified by bitter disputes between church and state in France throughout the nineteenth and early twentieth centuries. The Industrial Revolution, originating in Britain in the latter part of the eighteenth century created two further cleavages. The first was a land–industry division, as groups with interests associated with agriculture and the land came into conflict with the interests of the burgeoning industrial and urban classes. Secondly, the Industrial Revolution created a class conflict between workers and their employers, or the owners of the means of production.

According to Lipset and Rokkan, the interaction between these cleavage structures formed the basis of party systems throughout Europe and created political divisions that are still manifested in the modern party system. Until recently, however, the orthodox view among political scientists was that the continuing modernisation of society – involving the development of mass media, and further urbanisation, industrialisation and secularisation – would almost inevitably lead to a decrease in the relevance of the land–industry, religious and centre–periphery cleavages. In the latter case, sub-state identities would be eroded. As a consequence, the class cleavage and class politics would predominate. These processes were thought to lead towards an 'ultimate integration of societies' (Black, 1966: 155) and it was also thought that this was irreversible (Huntington, 1971: 289–90).

There was more to the integration of society than economic and social forces, however. Institutions also played a part, including the political parties themselves. Parties were involved in the modernisation process which scholars had identified as contributing to the integration of societies. Based on an appeal to class, dominant parties cut across other divisions, including the centre–periphery divide. They both reflected and maintained the importance of class over ethnicity or region. In this way, parties were thought to have an integrative function for the nation-state (Lipset and Rokkan, 1967; Rose and Urwin, 1969, 1975).

In Britain, for example, in an era of two-party politics during which each party alternated in power, and of relative economic stability and growth, the integrity of the state was not threatened, nor was there much pressure for radical constitutional reform. The real divide, as manifested in political debates at elections, was between different social classes and not based on where voters lived. The Conservatives and, even more so, Labour in Scotland played a significant role in integrating Scotland into the United Kingdom. With party appeals being based mainly on class, or at least without an explicitly territorial dimension, politics in Scotland was conducted in broadly the same terms as elsewhere in Britain.

The re-emergence of regionalism and sub-state nationalism in different parts of the world in the 1960s and 1970s, especially in Western Europe, challenged this orthodoxy (Mitchell and McAleavey, 2000: ch. 3). In Scotland, the rise of the SNP from the late 1960s suggested a revival of the centre–periphery cleavage. While this interpretation is convincing, it is worth noting that divisions between Scotland and the centre had never entirely disappeared. Scotland had not been assimilated but rather accommodated within the United Kingdom. Scottish distinctiveness had been catered for in a number of ways, including specifically Scottish governmental machinery at both central and local levels which produced distinctive policies. All of this amounted to what Kellas ([1973], 1989) referred to in his seminal work as a 'Scottish political system'. Although the idea that there was a separate Scottish political system was challenged (Rose, 1982; Midwinter *et al.*, 1991; Moore and Booth, 1989), few doubted that Scottish politics had elements that distinguished it from 'British' politics. Nonetheless, the Scottish dimension was filtered through the class cleavage in Scottish politics. Although Labour and the Conservatives had distinctive Scottish features they remained traditional class parties (Keating and Bleiman, 1979; Mitchell, 1990a).

To be successful in Scotland, political parties needed to take account of and accommodate the centre–periphery cleavage in their rhetoric and policies in Scotland. Suggesting that a political opponent failed to represent and advance Scottish interests adequately was a regular theme of political discourse. All parties had to 'play the Scottish card' to some extent. This did not, it should be stressed, amount to supporting devolution until quite late in the post-war period. As a study published in 1966 observed:

> The widespread existence of Scottish loyalties provides support for the activities of the Home Rule movements but also – and to date more important – it buttresses the autonomy of the Scottish sections of the two major parties and provides a favourable environment for the growth of distinctive pressure groups and the survival of autonomous legal and administrative institutions. (Budge and Urwin, 1966: 133)

The four cleavages identified by Lipset and Rokkan offer a useful way of making sense of the development of public and party attitudes in Scotland towards home rule and help to place the 1997 referendum in an historical context. The class cleavage ensured that the Labour Party remained dominant while the growing importance of the centre–periphery cleavage resulted in increasingly strong feelings of Scottish national identity (Bennie *et al.* 1997). There is also evidence that, at least until the 1960s, religion was a cleavage of considerable importance in some parts of Scotland (Budge and Urwin, 1966; Bochel and Denver, 1970). This was not a church–state divide but involved political divisions between Protestants and Catholics. An urban–rural cleavage is also discernible although it has been expressed as a division between the densely populated central Lowlands and the more sparsely populated peripheral areas to both north and south. Opponents of devolution often argued that a Scottish Parliament would be dominated by politicians representing the interests of the central belt to the detriment of people living in peripheral parts of the country.

The relationships between these different cleavages are as important as each cleavage is individually. The nature of these relationships has changed over time and these changes, in turn, are important in understanding both the changing fortunes of the political parties and also the growth in support for devolution. The central issue, of course, is the centre–periphery cleavage. How it relates to the others tells us much about changing attitudes and the contemporary scene. It has been the relationship between class and national identity, however, that has been most important in understanding the changing attitudes to home rule among Scots. Changes in the attitude of Labour supporters, traditionally the party of the working class, have been most significant in the evolution of the debate, especially over the last two decades. In crude terms, for much of the post-war period most Labour politicians thought that a working-class identity was in conflict with support for a Scottish Parliament and a strong Scottish *political* identity. Although there is evidence that many Labour supporters wanted a Scottish Parliament, the attitude of the party itself was, at best, ambivalent. This continued to be the case up to the 1979 referendum. After that date, however, things changed. Again expressed in crude terms, class identity and Scottish national identity began to reinforce each other.

The changing influence of the religious cleavage is illustrated by the fact that in the 1970s there was evidence that those of Irish Catholic descent in Scotland were less likely to support Scottish nationalism than non-Catholics. By 1992 this had changed, with young, male, working-class Catholics being among the strongest supporters of Scottish independence and older, middle-class Protestants being among those least likely to support constitutional change (Bennie *et al.*, 1997: 108–19).

For most of the post-war period, then, there was agreement between the Labour and Conservative parties on how Scotland should be governed. Although each party attacked the other for neglecting Scotland, neither proposed anything other than minor changes in the institutions of government. While serving to integrate Scotland into the Union, however, the parties also helped to preserve what made Scotland distinctive. From the 1960s changes in the structure and salience of cleavages relating to class, national identity, religion and geography led to a change in public attitudes towards devolution and hence forced the parties to reconsider their positions on the issue.

THE FIRST DEVOLUTION REFERENDUM, 1979

We noted above that memories of the 1979 referendum played an important role in conditioning the attitudes and actions of the parties during the 1997 referendum. The experience of the 1970s was also fresh in the minds of many voters – at least among those who were old enough and who cared about the question. The 1979 referendum was, therefore, an important pre-cursor to that of 1997 and we provide here a brief account of its main features (for a comprehensive treatment see Bochel *et al.*, 1981).

The road to the first referendum
Labour won the October 1974 election with a small overall majority in the House of Commons and was committed to legislating for a Scottish Assembly. This proved difficult, however, given the divisions

within the parliamentary Labour Party and, in time, the absence of an overall majority after seats were lost in by-elections, which meant that Labour remained in office only with the support of the smaller parties. In late 1976 Labour back-benchers opposed to devolution forced the government to concede that there should be referendums on the government's proposals for Scotland and Wales. Despite this concession, the Scotland and Wales Bill fell in February 1977 when the government lost a guillotine motion, presented in order to ensure that the Bill was not filibustered in the House of Commons. A formal pact with the Liberals followed this failure of Labour's first attempt to legislate for Welsh and Scottish Assemblies.

A second attempt was made later in 1977 when separate bills for Scottish and Welsh Assemblies were introduced. Even with the support of the Liberals, the Welsh and Scottish Nationalists and a few Tory devolutionists, however, the government's devolution plans ran into difficulties. In November, the Scotland Bill passed its second reading and the government won a guillotine motion two days later. However, it lost a number of votes at the committee stage (taken by the House as a whole). The first clause of the Bill, declaring that the unity of the United Kingdom and the supreme authority of Parliament to make laws would be unaffected by the measure, was lost. This did not substantially alter the Bill but it was a symbolic defeat, signalling that a majority of MPs believed that devolution would indeed undermine the sovereignty of Parliament.

The most significant defeat for the government came on Burns night (25 January) 1978 when the 'Cunningham amendment' was passed by 168 votes to 142. The amendment, which came to be known as the '40 per cent rule', was proposed by George Cunningham, a Scot representing a London constituency for Labour. It was, as Cunningham wrote some years later, a 'delayed-action bomb that later blew up devolution' (Cunningham, 1989). The amendment stipulated that for the devolution proposals to go ahead they would have to be supported in the referendum by at least 40 per cent of the eligible electorate.[2] Its effect was to introduce what is known as a 'qualified majority' condition into the referendum and it meant that well over 50 per cent of those who actually voted would need to vote in favour of devolution. The origins of the 40 per cent rule are disputed. Some Conservatives claimed that it was their idea but believed that the amendment had a better chance of being passed if it was moved by a Labour MP. On the other hand, Cunningham insisted that it was his own idea (Mitchell, 1990a: 84–5). What is not at issue is the significance of the condition imposed by the amendment.

The focus of the devolution debates in Parliament was quite different from that within Scotland itself. In Scotland, the question was simply whether or not having an Assembly would be in the interests of Scots. For many Parliamentarians the issue was how devolution would affect government of the United Kingdom as a whole and the role of the Westminster Parliament in particular. The attitudes of many MPs were typified by Tam Dalyell, Labour MP for West Lothian. Dalyell had been in favour of devolution at the October 1974 election but later changed his mind and became the most persistent critic of the policy in Parliament, coming to be known as the 'uncrowned leader of the opposition' in the Commons. He frequently raised concerns about the implications of devolution for Parliament. In a debate on the Queen's Address, he asked the Prime Minister James Callaghan, himself a Cardiff MP:

> Shall I still be able to vote on many matters in relation to West Bromwich but not West Lothian ... and will my Right Honourable Friend be able to vote on many matters in relation to Carlisle but not Cardiff? (Hansard, vol.938, col.31)

This question came to be known as the 'West Lothian Question' in recognition of the frequency with which Dalyell asked it (or some variation on it). There was no neat or simple answer to the West Lothian Question. It pinpointed an issue which was likely to have greater resonance with MPs than with the Scottish public but it ensured that anti-devolutionists were able to build up a credible opposition in Parliament to devolution.[3]

The Scotland Bill received the royal assent in late July 1978 and the date of the referendum was fixed for 1 March 1979. The passage of the Bill had been tortuous and there were three reasons for this. Firstly, the government had no overall majority and there was a substantial minority of Labour MPs who opposed the measure. Secondly, it was a lengthy piece of legislation, with devolved powers enumerated in great detail. One legal commentary observed that the definition of the powers of the Assembly was so complex that it was 'unlikely to be understood by most Assembly members and the electorate' (Bradley and Christie, 1979: 51). Thirdly, since it was a matter of great constitutional significance, the Bill had been debated on the floor of the House of Commons rather than in a smaller, more manageable standing committee. In addition, the legislation included numerous over-ride powers and safeguards, regulating relationships between the Assembly and Westminster, further complicating and lengthening it.

In many respects, the referendum campaign had begun during the passage of the Scotland Act. The fact that (unlike in 1997) the devolution legislation was debated in Parliament before there was a referendum to determine whether there should be a Scottish Assembly meant that the debates were conducted with an eye to the forthcoming referendum. As the prominent devolutionist MP John Mackintosh had warned, the 'overhanging thought' in the minds of MPs would be whether an amendment would help defeat or carry the proposals at the referendum (Hansard, vol.925, col.1719). Amendments were moved and votes cast with a view to the referendum campaign.

Campaign organisations

An official 'Yes for Scotland' (YFS) campaign, designed to involve people from all parties and none, was launched in January 1978, chaired by Lord Kilbrandon who had also chaired the Royal Commission on the Constitution which reported in 1973. On the following day, Helen Liddell, Labour's Scottish general secretary issued a statement explaining why the party would not participate in a cross-party referendum campaign. Labour would not, as she put it, be 'soiling our hands by joining any umbrella Yes group' (Macartney, 1981: 17). The 'Labour Movement Yes Campaign' was the official Labour Party and trade union campaign. The party had decided it would go it alone and a circular to Labour constituency parties explained the reasons. Labour, it claimed, was alone in believing in devolution for its own sake while others supported it as a step on the path to 'separation' or federalism. Devolution would prevent separation and it would undermine that position to be associated with the separatists. Labour would be able to claim full credit for creating the Assembly and it would be wrong to let opponents take any credit.

The SNP also ran its own Yes campaign although some of its senior members and many activists on the ground were involved in YFS. The SNP leadership left the decision as to whether to campaign under the YFS umbrella, or under the party banner, to individual branches and constituencies. The message which went out from SNP headquarters was simple: 'Balance your impulse to make short-term propaganda against the need to maximise the "Yes" vote.' (Macartney, 1981: 19).

While there was no doubting the commitment of the Liberals to a Yes vote the party was undecided about how to campaign. In the end, typically, the party decided to leave it to the constituencies to decide whether to work with an umbrella group or to campaign on their own. There was no national Liberal campaign to speak of but some leading lights were prominent in umbrella groups – Donald Gorrie was on the executive of YFS, for example.

There was also a small 'Conservative Yes Campaign', but this had little support and primarily attempted to convince Conservative pro-devolutionists to vote 'Yes' despite Lord Home's call for such people to vote 'No' in anticipation of a better scheme of devolution to be introduced by an incoming Conservative government (see p.22).

'Yes for Scotland' was the main cross-party grouping and members of all parties were involved as well as – at national level – actors, prominent clergymen, authors and broadcasters. Nonetheless it was dominated by the SNP and the SLP under Jim Sillars and failed to project itself as a genuinely all-party group. Partly as a consequence, a rival all-party campaign, 'Alliance for an Assembly' (AFA), was launched in November 1978 with Alick Buchanan-Smith from the Conservatives and Russell Johnston of the Liberals joining with James Milne of the Scottish Trade Union Congress and Donald Dewar from the Labour Party as leading figures. The group intentionally avoided having a member of the SNP in its leadership. Working with a well-known member of the Communist Party, as was Milne, was less of a problem for Buchanan-Smith than association with the SNP. However, AFA proved 'more important to its founding MPs, as representing a unionist-devolutionary position, than it was to the voters' (Macartney, 1981: 16).

Given the preceding account it need hardly be said that the campaign for a Yes vote in the 1979 referendum was very fragmented, riven as it was by party jealousies. The opponents of devolution were better organised and presented a more coherent message. 'Scotland Says No' (SSN) was launched on St Andrew's Day 1978 to replace an organisation previously called 'Scotland is British' (SIB) which had been established to oppose the Labour government's first devolution bill. It became the main anti-devolution campaign group in the referendum – and the best-financed of any campaign. Although SIB had contained a sprinkling of Labour members, the establishment of a separate 'Labour Vote No' (LVN) campaign left SSN as a Conservative-dominated organisation with the strong support of leading figures in Scottish business. A number of prominent businessmen were active in the 'No' campaign and some firms made their opposition to an Assembly public. The Clydesdale Bank, for example, issued a statement to each of their customers urging them to vote No. Through these activities an impression was created that there was overwhelming opposition to devolution among the Scottish business community.

The official Conservative No campaign was established against the backdrop of Conservative divisions on devolution and an official position of opposing the measure on offer but being in favour of devolution in principle. As Russell Sanderson, Scottish Conservative President explained to constituency parties in an official letter in December 1978:

> Let me make it quite clear that in campaigning for 'No', the Party will not be campaigning against Devolution for Scotland but only against the type of devolution contained in the Act. In the event of the 'No' campaign being successful, the Party is committed to the establishment of an all-Party Conference to discuss better forms of Devolution. (Macartney, 1981: 22)

The letter urged constituencies to co-operate with SSN who would supply Conservative associations with free campaign material. In effect, SSN was an unofficial wing of the Conservative No campaign.

The 'Labour Vote No' campaign stemmed from a meeting of anti-devolution Labour MPs in the Commons when it became clear that a referendum would be conceded by the government. Its leading figures were the indefatigable Tam Dalyell and Brian Wilson, then a journalist but later a junior Scottish Office minister during the 1997 referendum. The main objective of LVN was to convince Labour voters that it would not be disloyal to the party to cast a No vote. This was, according to Miller (1980: 113) an 'audacious and successful bid to associate the Labour name with an anti-Labour policy'.

Rules of the referendum
The 1979 Scottish referendum (along with a contemporaneous one in Wales) was only the second 'national' referendum to be held in the United Kingdom, the first having been on the question of United Kingdom membership of the European Community in 1975.[4] Rules and procedures for the conduct of the 1975 referendum had been drawn up in a largely *ad hoc* way but nonetheless established some precedents. Thus the same arrangements for counting votes were adopted in 1979 – on a regional or island basis in the first instance with the result for the whole of Scotland being the responsibility of a chief counting officer. Similarly, given the constitutional doctrine of parliamentary sovereignty, it was stressed in both cases that the referendums were consultative and their results could not be regarded as binding. On the other hand, the 1975 precedents were not followed in four significant ways. Firstly, in 1975 the government used public funds to pay for the distribution of three leaflets to every household in

the country – one from each side and one putting the government's case – whereas no such arrangements were made in 1979. Secondly, in 1975 umbrella campaign organisations were each granted £125,000; in 1979 no public funds went to either side. Thirdly, and most notoriously, the result of the 1979 referendum was subject to the 40 per cent rule whereas in 1975 there was little debate over whether anything other than a simple majority should determine the result of the referendum. This rule excited a great deal of controversy – being seen by some as an attempt to rig the result – and, since the electoral register is not an accurate and up-to-date record of those eligible to vote, it required the government to make (much criticised) adjustments to the size of the electorate. The fourth difference between the 1975 and 1979 referendums relates to political broadcasting.

Broadcasting problems
Although rules about broadcasting during election campaigns are not prescribed in detail by government (in addition, that is, to general rules requiring balanced coverage) how the broadcast media cover any political campaign is clearly a matter of considerable importance. We will deal with the question of broadcasting in the Scottish referendums in more detail in Chapter 4. Here it is worth noting that during the 1975 referendum, party political broadcasts were abandoned and, instead, each side in the debate was allocated four (free) television broadcasts of ten minutes each. The fragmentation of campaigning groups in 1979 meant that this precedent could not be followed and so the broadcasters planned to transmit four scheduled party political broadcasts. This would have been contrary to at least one interpretation of what the rules about 'balanced coverage' demanded. The broadcasters' plans were challenged in the Court of Session on behalf of LVN by Brian Wilson and Tam Dalyell. Delivering his judgement, Lord Ross concluded that a referendum was quite different from a general election: 'Voters are not being invited to vote for members of political parties but to answer the question: "Do you want the provisions of the Scotland Act of 1978 to be put into effect?"' (Fowler, 1981: 125). The LVN petition was upheld. As a result, no broadcasts straightforwardly advocating a Yes or No vote were transmitted.

The campaign
Largely because of the plethora of campaigning groups and parties, the 1979 referendum campaign was confused. The various organisations held press conferences, issued press releases, organised public meetings and advertised in the press and on hoardings to get

their messages across. Leading politicians, including the Prime Minister, made special visits to Scotland. All of this was reported in the press and on television but the differences between groups which were supposed to be on the same side and the variety of messages involved (and the absence of partisan broadcasts) made for a sharp contrast with general elections when the choices involved are clearly and vigorously put before the electorate. Local campaigning too compared poorly with what is normal in general elections, being lacklustre, unexciting and, in many places, barely visible. Labour campaigning in particular – at both national and local level – appeared to lack urgency. This might be attributed to the fact that the SNP threat appeared to be waning. During 1978 the SNP had failed to make much impact in three parliamentary by-elections and also lost ground in local elections. The principal motivation behind Labour's adoption of devolution had been fear of the SNP and that now seemed to have been exaggerated.

One account of the campaign (Macartney, 1981) identifies three key events, all of which were detrimental to the Yes cause. The first was the decision of the Church of Scotland to reverse its previous intention to have ministers read out a statement from their pulpits calling for a Yes vote. The second was the decision by Lord Ross referred to above which banned 'partisan' broadcasting. The third, and probably most significant, was the intervention of Lord Home, a former Conservative Prime Minister. Home maintained that he was still a committed devolutionist but challenged the view expressed by Prime Minister Callaghan that the referendum offered a last chance for devolution and outlined five defects in the scheme which were to be significant in debates over the following 18 years. He argued that the Assembly should be able to raise a proportion of its own revenue; that the West Lothian Question remained unaddressed; that the proposed Assembly was too large; that no machinery existed to define whether a bill was purely Scottish, which would lead to trouble if a measure was later deemed to be *ultra vires*; and that there was no element of proportional representation in the electoral system for the Assembly. An increasing number of people, according to Home, were 'concerned to get the matter right even if that means more time' (*Scotsman*, 15 February 1979).

It is difficult to be certain about the extent to which Home's intervention affected the outcome of the referendum, but its purpose was simple: to encourage supporters of devolution to vote against the measure.

The result of the 1979 referendum

The actual question on which Scots were asked to vote in the 1979 referendum appears almost abstruse. The ballot paper contained a statement – 'Parliament has decided to consult the electorate in Scotland on the question of whether the Scotland Act 1978 should be put into effect' – followed by the question: 'Do you want the provisions of the Scotland Act 1978 to be put into effect?' Nonetheless, after years of debate, relatively few voters could have failed to understand the main point of the question. The results of the referendum are shown in Table 1.1.

As can be seen, over Scotland as a whole turnout in the referendum was 63.8 per cent which compared well with the 1975 referendum when 61.7 per cent turned out in Scotland. However, only a slim majority of those who voted (51.6 per cent) supported the government's proposals and this fell well short (32.9 per cent) of the 40 per cent of the electorate required by the Cunningham amendment. No area managed to overcome the 40 per cent rule and four mainland regions – Borders, Dumfries and Galloway, Grampian and Tayside – voted against, as did Orkney and Shetland. The fact that devolution would not go ahead despite being backed by a majority of those who voted led some pro-devolutionists to think that they had been cheated out of an Assembly and reinforced the views of those who believed that the rules were rigged against them.

Table 1.1: The 1979 Scottish devolution referendum results by region

Regional/Islands authority	Turnout %	% of votes		% of electorate	
		Yes %	No %	Yes %	No %
Borders	67.3	40.3	59.7	27.0	40.1
Central	66.7	54.7	45.3	36.4	30.2
Dumfries & Galloway	64.9	40.3	59.7	26.1	38.7
Fife	66.1	53.7	46.3	35.4	30.6
Grampian	57.1	48.3	51.6	27.9	29.9
Highland	65.4	51.0	49.0	33.3	32.1
Lothian	66.6	50.1	49.9	33.4	33.2
Strathclyde	63.2	54.0	46.0	34.1	29.1
Tayside	63.8	49.5	50.5	31.5	32.2
Orkney	54.8	27.9	72.1	15.3	39.4
Shetland	51.0	27.0	73.0	13.7	37.1
Western Isles	50.5	55.8	44.2	28.1	22.3
SCOTLAND	63.8	51.6	48.4	32.9	30.8

Note: turnout figures include spoiled ballots

The relationship between party supported and voting for an Assembly, according to pre-referendum opinion polls, is shown in Table 1.2. The story told is fairly consistent and clear. SNP supporters were overwhelmingly in favour but only around two-thirds of Labour supporters were. Intention to vote Yes declined steadily among Conservatives as the referendum drew nearer and it may be that the steep decline suggested by the last two pre-referendum polls was a consequence of Lord Home's intervention on 14 February. By the end of the campaign Conservatives divided four to one against the government's proposals. In interpreting these data it should be borne in mind that not only was the proportion of Conservatives intending to vote No increasing during the campaign, so also was the proportion of Conservative supporters in the Scottish electorate. For reasons quite unconnected with devolution – mainly industrial unrest – Labour's popularity was sliding. In November 1978 System Three reported Scottish voting intentions as Conservative 25 per cent, Labour 48 per cent and SNP 21 per cent; by February 1979 the figures were Conservative 37 per cent, Labour 40 per cent, SNP 18 per cent. The parties most strongly advocating a Yes vote were losing ground. With some justification the *Scotsman* headline on 19 February asserted 'Tories hold the key to March 1 vote'.

Table 1.2: Percentage intending to vote Yes in the 1979 referendum by party supported

	Con	Lab	SNP	All
*January 8–20	46	68	95	64
*January 29-February 6	32	58	91	56
**February 12–14	35	70	92	64
**February 20–21	24	69	94	60
*February 23–25	21	66	91	52

Source: * = System Three Scotland; ** = MORI.
Notes: Percentages are calculated after excluding 'Don't knows'. 'Party supported' is indicated by voting intention for the next general election. There were too few Liberals for separate analysis but 'All' includes these as well as other respondents not intending to vote for one of the three major parties.

Although later campaign polls correctly predicted a close result in the 1979 referendum, the outcome was nonetheless something of a shock to home rulers. A great deal of evidence had suggested, after all, that a solid majority of Scots had favoured some degree of constitutional change for a very long time. Explanations focused, therefore, on short-term factors – more coherent campaign organisation on the No side, Lord Home's statement, divisions within the Labour Party and Labour's decision to stand aloof from a joint-party effort, complacency in the Yes camp and so on. The best explanation is probably that it was a matter of unfortunate timing. The electorate was asked to vote on proposals made by a Labour government and Labour – although normally the dominant party in Scotland – was at the end of a long and hard period in office. At the time of the referendum the party was experiencing a period of extreme (if temporary) unpopularity. Given that voting in the referendum was structured by current party preferences – as it was to be, in different circumstances, in 1997 – this probably explains why the Yes majority was so slim.

CONCLUSION

The referendum of 1979 is important in two ways for understanding the 1997 referendum. It allows us, of course, to measure the extent to which public opinion changed over the intervening 18 years. In addition, however, the experience of 1979 proved important in subsequent debates. The long shadow cast by the 1979 experience was an important backdrop for both supporters and opponents of home rule. The idea that the Scots had been cheated in 1979 was something that supporters of devolution felt deeply and there was a suspicion of referendums and of qualified majorities in particular. As the Conservative period in office was drawing to a close in the 1990s, opponents of devolution turned once more to a referendum in a last ditch effort to halt the establishment of a Scottish Parliament. Many of the criticisms of the 1978 Act were addressed during these 18 years, including each of the five criticisms made by Lord Home. The proposals which emerged in 1997 contained substantive and symbolic changes as compared with what was offered in 1979 and this was due to the perception amongst home rulers that the 1979 proposals were deficient and could be improved. Lord Home's call for more time was certainly a cynical exercise but, ultimately, the White Paper which was put to the Scottish people in 1997 was generally regarded as an improvement on the Scotland Act, 1978 and met his demand to get it right, even if that meant taking more time. In addition, pro-devolutionists consciously learned from the strategic and tactical errors made in 1979 with regard to legislating for a Scottish Parliament, timing the referendum and campaigning for a Yes vote.

Many themes and issues which emerged in the 1970s and before were evident in the 1997 referendum. John Major's government responded to the increased demand for constitutional change with proposals which were remarkably similar to those put forward by the Attlee government almost 50 years before. The positions taken and roles played by the political parties, how the scheme on offer was perceived by different groups in different parts of Scotland and the role of the mass media all proved significant in 1997. The relationship between class, national identity and support for constitutional change was critical in shaping the referendum outcome, but in a way that was very different from what had happened in 1979. The rules of the game and the nature of the campaigning organisations again proved important in the short, intense campaign leading up to the vote. Before turning to the referendum itself, however, we first consider the evolution of the devolution debate over the 18 years following the first referendum in Chapter 2.

NOTES

1. A few colourful figures on the fringe of Scottish Nationalist politics have provided each side with ammunition to back up their respective, contradictory claims. In the inter-war period, for example, it was common for supporters of a Scottish Parliament to refer to the Irish Free State (as it then was) Stormont or the Manx Tyndwald as models for a Scottish Parliament. Fact-finding trips were made to each in an endeavour to understand the workings of these systems. During the 1960s and 1970s, however, there was a marked reluctance to look at other models, especially that of Northern Ireland after the outbreak of 'The Troubles'.
2. The text of the amendment (Scotland Act, 1978, Clause 85) is as follows:
   > If it appears to the Secretary of State that less than 40 per cent of the persons entitled to vote in the referendum have voted 'Yes' in reply to the question posed in the Appendix to Schedule 17 to this Act or that a majority of the answers given in the referendum have been 'No' he shall lay before Parliament the draft of an Order in Council for the repeal of this Act.
   > If a draft laid before Parliament under this section is approved by a resolution of each House Her Majesty in Council may take an Order in the terms of the draft.
3. An amendment attempting to tackle the West Lothian Question was passed but it did not solve the question and raised further problems (including simple practicality). It provided that bills going through the House of Commons which did not concern Scotland but which would, if it related to Scotland, have been under the legislative competence of the Scottish Assembly, would be subject to a second vote at the second reading stage if they had passed only by virtue of the votes of Scottish MPs.
4. There was also a referendum in Northern Ireland in 1973, on the constitutional status of the province, but it was boycotted by Nationalists and was not, therefore, very significant.

2

The Politics of Devolution
1979–97

The question of Scotland's constitutional status within the United Kingdom grew in importance during the 18 years between 1979 and 1997, a period of uninterrupted Conservative government. Our discussion of this period is located, firstly, within the framework of social cleavages discussed in Chapter 1. In addition, the position of each of the parties and their responses to pressures for change are considered and the process which led to another referendum being held on the issue is analysed. The experience of 1979 made home rulers suspicious of the device and in the 1990s opponents of devolution proposed a referendum as a means of attempting to stall the establishment of a Scottish Parliament. It is easy to understand, therefore, why supporters of a Scottish Parliament were seriously concerned when, in 1996, the Labour Party under Tony Blair's leadership proposed holding another referendum. As we shall see, however, the circumstances which led to this proposal were significantly different from those which had led to the first referendum.

The 1979 referendum and the subsequent general election cast a long shadow over Scottish politics. Different lessons were drawn by those involved. Pro-devolution Labour supporters blamed the SNP for impetuously bringing down the Labour government in the aftermath of the referendum. Having failed to force the government to have a vote in the House of Commons on whether the devolution legislation should be implemented, the 11 SNP MPs voted with the Conservatives and Liberals on a motion of no confidence in the government. The motion was carried by one vote on 28 March 1979 and the government was forced to call an election. Labour lost the election, Margaret Thatcher came to power and the SNP lost nine of their seats. As Prime Minister James Callaghan had presciently remarked during the debate on the no confidence motion, the actions of the SNP MPs resembled 'turkeys voting for an early Christmas' (Hansard: HC 965 col.472). On the other hand, the SNP accused Labour of duplicity in failing to deliver devolution. Labour MPs had helped to impose the 40 per cent rule, the Labour campaign during the referendum had been lacklustre and a significant segment of the party had actively supported a No vote. Now the government refused to allow a vote on repealing the Scotland Act (for fear of demonstrating divisions within the party). Distrust between Labour and the SNP was intense and it would be difficult for co-operation to develop between the two parties in the years after 1979.

For Conservatives, the lesson of the 1979 referendum was that devolution could be successfully resisted. Although the Tories had campaigned on the basis of opposing the particular measure on offer and not the principle of devolution, the result was soon interpreted within the party as a victory for anti-devolutionists. Conservatives who favoured devolution were marginalised as the party swung behind hard-line opposition to any measure of home rule. A number of pro-devolutionists in all parties concluded that there was a need to build bridges between parties supporting some measure of home rule but, in the aftermath of the events of 1979, this was an unpopular position inside both the Labour Party and the SNP.

At the start of this period, class and (Scottish) national identity appeared to be in conflict (at least as suggested by relations between Labour and the SNP) but in time a quite different relationship between class and national identity developed. Over the 18 years of Conservative rule, the events of 1979, and the different interpretations of them, greatly influenced the debate on Scotland's constitutional status and Scottish politics more generally. At the outset, bitter recriminations within the various parties supporting some measure of self-government made cross-party, anti-Conservative campaigning difficult. As the Thatcher era began, devolution was off the agenda and the Conservatives were the most optimistic of the parties in Scotland. They had played the major role in defeating devolution and in the subsequent general election their share of the vote in Scotland rose from 24.7 per cent to 31.4 per cent and the number of Conservative MPs increased from 16 to 22.

Over the next 18 years, however, the popularity of the parties in Scotland changed dramatically. Table 2.1 shows the shares of the vote and seats won in Scotland in general elections from 1979–97 – the electoral backdrop to the politics of devolution. Perhaps the main story told by the figures is one of steady Conservative decline except for a small recovery in 1992. Very much the same sort of thing happened in local government. In 1982 Conservatives comprised 22.2 per cent of all Scottish councillors; by 1995 the figure was 7.5 per cent. After the 1997 general election the Conservatives were utterly demoralised. They had no MPs and no Euro-MPs and controlled no local councils. In this situation, devolution was catapulted to the top of the Scottish political agenda.

Table 2.1: General election results in Scotland 1979–97

	1979	1983	Share of Votes 1987	1992	1997
	%	%	%	%	%
Conservative	31.4	28.4	24.0	25.6	17.5
Labour	41.6	35.1	42.4	39.0	45.6
Lib Dem	9.0	24.5	19.2	13.1	13.0
SNP	17.3	11.8	14.0	21.5	22.1
			Seats Won		
Conservative	22	21	10	11	0
Labour	44	41	50	49	56
Lib Dem	3	8	9	9	10
SNP	2	2	3	3	6

Notes: 'Lib Dem' refers to the Liberals in 1979 and the Alliance in 1983 and 1987. Figures for vote shares do not total 100 as 'others' are omitted.

HOME RULE AND WORKING-CLASS POLITICS

Despite the experiences of 1979, Labour anti-devolutionists failed to take the initiative and made no attempt to return the party to the anti-devolution position that it had abandoned five years before. The argument that devolution was divisive, that working-class Scots had more in common with working-class English people than with Scots of a different class, had frequently been voiced by Labour anti-devolutionists but it failed to find any significant resonance in the 1980s.[1]

The Labour Party went through a period of recrimination and soul searching after the general election defeat. The rise of the Labour left in response to the defeat (Seyd, 1987) had serious implications for Labour's constitutional policies. A more interventionist economic strategy, the 'alternative economic strategy', was developed which would have involved highly centralised policy making while, at the same time, the party gave fulsome support to devolution. Rarely were Gordon Brown's comments on the conflicting aspirations of home rule and a British Socialist advance (see p. 3) more apt than during the early 1980s. The proposed economic strategy clearly sat uneasily with a policy of devolution. However, before the 1983 election an 'alternative regional strategy', was developed, under the leadership of John Prescott, which attempted to reconcile these conflicting aspirations. Labour devolutionists hitched support for devolution to a radical interventionist economic policy, arguing that a devolved Scottish Parliament would provide a democratic institution willing and able to pursue such a policy.

As Scots in general increasingly came to believe that Thatcherism was being imposed on Scotland, a growing number of Labour politicians came to conclude that a Scottish Assembly, even one as weak as that on offer in 1979, would have had responsibility for policies in areas in which the Conservatives were passing legislation to which they were deeply opposed. Labour's hostility to the Conservatives and Margaret Thatcher made a Scottish Parliament look increasingly attractive to party activists, despite their suspicions of the SNP. While the Assembly would have had few powers to develop radical alternatives, it might have been able to block many Conservative-inspired policies, especially those affecting local government. As early as November 1981, the *Financial Times* (5 November 1981) commented that Scotland had become a 'test bed for the Government's offensive against local authority spending'. This culminated in the legislation, just before the 1987 election, which provided for the introduction of the poll tax in Scotland a year before it would be started in England and Wales. Ironically, this policy was urged on the government by Scottish Conservative MPs fearing a loss of support following a controversial rating revaluation (see Butler *et al.*, 1994). Senior Labour councillors had been amongst the most vehement opponents of devolution in the 1970s but in the 1980s they came to view a Scottish Parliament as a means of protecting services. The perception that Scotland was being treated as a guinea-pig for unpopular measures was developing.

The first stirrings of Scottish disenchantment with the Conservative government were reflected in the results of the 1983 general election. In England, capitalising on Labour's internal problems, a booming economy and the success of the Falklands War, the Conservatives advanced from 306 to 362 seats; in Scotland (Table 2.1) their share of the vote declined by three percentage points and they lost a seat. During the 1983-87 Parliament, the link between the class and national dimensions in Scottish politics started to emerge more clearly. For example, threats to the steel industry in Scotland provoked well-publicised campaigns against the Tories. The closures of the Gartcosh and Ravenscraig steel plants were long drawn-out affairs which were kept at the forefront of Scottish politics to the disadvantage of the Conservatives. One senior Scottish Tory, who had been a leading anti-devolutionist,[2] defected to the SNP on the day that Gartcosh finally closed (28 March 1986). More significantly, the SNP was prominent, alongside Labour and the trade unions, in campaigning on behalf of a number of other threatened Scottish businesses and industries.

The Conservatives were re-elected in 1987, with a slightly reduced majority, on the basis of their support in England. In Scotland (Table 2.1) they lost more than half of their seats and had less than a quarter of the votes. This increasing dependence on English voters for control of the Scottish Office (and on English MPs to pass Scottish legislation) exacerbated the Conservatives' problems. A conscious effort had been made by Labour devolutionists and left-inclined Nationalists to develop the notion that the Conservatives were 'anti-Scottish'. As SNP vice-convenor for publicity, Alex Salmond, later leader of the party, launched a campaign in the mid 1980s attempting to pin this label on the Tories. In retrospect, this appears to have been one of the most successful propaganda campaigns waged by the Nationalists. It was a campaign with which Labour politicians, especially pro-devolutionists, were tempted to align themselves, since it made it easier to link class and national identity, to the benefit of supporters of constitutional change and the detriment of the Tories. The Conservatives were portrayed as not only class enemies but as enemies of Scotland. Just before the 1997 general election an ICM poll found that 73 per cent of Scots respondents agreed with the statement that 'The Conservative Party is a mainly English party with little relevance in Scotland.'

The poll tax was a significant issue in the 1987 election in Scotland. The idea for such a tax had originated in an effort to find an alternative to domestic rates (local property taxes). Ironically it was introduced first in Scotland in response to vociferous complaints over a rating revaluation which had taken place in 1984–85 and which would have resulted in steep increases in rates for many, especially middle-class, voters. Scottish Tories urged the government to take speedy action in Scotland in order to prevent a sharp loss of support. This was a serious miscalculation as the poll tax issue came to encapsulate the emerging link between the class and national dimensions of Scottish politics. Although exceptions were made for groups such as students and the very poor, the basic premise of the tax was that each elector should pay the same amount, regardless of income, making it an extremely regressive form of taxation. It found few friends in Scotland and proved a potent symbol and powerful agent for political mobilisation. It was exploited fully by supporters of constitutional change although it did create tensions and show up divisions between Labour and the SNP, since the latter advocated non-payment while Labour urged opponents of the tax to demonstrate their feelings through legal means of protest.

The ease with which the SNP and Labour could portray the Conservatives as anti-Scottish was aided by the Conservatives them-selves. The government, on a variety of issues, appeared insensitive to

Scottish opinion. After the 1987 election, the two Scottish Conservative vice-presidents wrote a report in which they noted that the party was perceived to be 'English and anti-Scottish' and that this was a 'feature of (let's be honest) an over-centralised London-dominated country and of Scots having very sensitive nerve endings (*Scotsman*, 10 September 1987). The particular brand of Conservatism associated with Mrs Thatcher was especially abhorrent to many Scots and Mrs Thatcher herself was deeply unpopular. At the time of the 1987 general election, she was thought to be 'extreme' by 75 per cent of Scots voters, 'looking after the interests of one class' by 72 per cent and 'uncaring' by 54 per cent. While 96 per cent thought that she was 'capable of strong leadership', this was a negative characteristic when viewed alongside the other traits attributed to her (Mitchell and Bennie, 1996). Thatcherism, as she herself was to concede, was 'rebuffed' in Scotland where there was 'no Tartan Thatcherite revolution' (Thatcher, 1993: 618).

Personified by Mrs Thatcher and encapsulated in the case of the poll tax, Conservative government of Scotland lacked popular legitimacy by the late 1980s. The combination of right-wing policies with a perceived anti-Scottish prejudice created a powerful tide of opposition to the Conservatives in Scotland and supporters of constitutional change could take advantage of this by merging national and class appeals. Far from cutting across each other, these two cleavages were now mutually reinforcing. This was a very different situation from that which had prevailed in 1979.

THE CONSTITUTIONAL CONVENTION

The 1987 general election was a watershed in Scottish politics. Prior to the election there had been much media speculation on the likelihood and consequences of a Conservative victory across Britain while other parties made advances in Scotland, the so-called 'Doomsday scenario'. *Radical Scotland*, a left-Nationalist magazine founded in the 1980s, had articulated the need to devise a strategy in response to continued Conservative rule and had given strong support to the idea of a Constitutional Convention. This idea had a long history in the home rule movement – Conventions had been established in the 1920s and 1940s but, while they drew public attention to the home rule question, they failed to achieve any significant progress. There were no sanctions which these Conventions could apply in order to force governments to take notice of their wishes and, indeed, they embodied the very principles to which home rulers are opposed being unrepresentative of, and lacking any mandate from, the Scottish people (see Mitchell, 1996). Despite these discouraging precedents, the Campaign for a Scottish Assembly (CSA), a cross/non-party pressure group established in 1980 to build bridges amongst supporters of constitutional change in different parties, issued a document entitled 'Claim of Right for Scotland' in July 1988 in which setting up a Constitutional Convention to agree a scheme of devolution and campaign for its implementation was proposed.

After the election, the 'Doomsday scenario' appeared to have arrived and the Conservatives, with only ten Scottish seats, were in a vulnerable position. Although Labour won 50 seats they were put on the defensive by the SNPs high-profile mass civil disobedience campaign in relation to the poll tax. The SNP outflanked Labour on the issue and Scottish Labour MPs were branded as 'the feeble fifty' as the poll tax campaign increased the temperature in Scottish politics. In November 1988, Jim Sillars, the former Labour MP, won a parliamentary by-election for the SNP in Glasgow Govan putting more pressure on Labour and the Conservatives. In this new context, constitutional and socio-economic politics became intertwined. Labour's response was to agree to participate in a Constitutional Convention. Having considered the options proposed by a committee established by the CSA, Labour's leadership concluded that it would be safer to become involved in a Convention in which its members and supporters would have a clear majority than to stand aside. On the other hand, having been early advocates of a Constitutional Convention, or at least of a directly elected Convention, the SNP reached the opposite conclusion, fearing that Labour dominance of such a body would be used to attack the SNP's recently developed policy of 'independence in Europe'. The Convention was launched in 1989 with Labour, Liberal Democrats, Greens, trade unions, local authorities, churches and other 'civic' bodies involved but without the participation of the SNP. The Scottish media gave it considerable backing with the two main broadsheets, the *Scotsman* and *Herald*, rarely being critical. This episode demonstrated the difficulty of getting Labour and the SNP to co-operate in a single campaign effort and there were other examples of friction between the two parties around that time with campaigns against the closure of steel plants and in opposition to the poll tax exposing serious tensions between them.

The Convention attracted a great deal of media attention but it was largely of interest to political elites. Its public deliberations were largely concerned with projecting an image of unity and consensus while in its private sessions the details of a scheme of home rule were discussed. In the event, a scheme of broad principles was agreed but there were significant unresolved matters and some aspects of the scheme were left deliberately vague as agreement could not be reached. In large measure, the agreed scheme followed the provisions of the Scotland Act, 1978 and was very similar to a bill proposed by Donald Dewar on behalf of the Labour Party in autumn 1987. There were a number of launches and re-launches of the Convention proposals prior to the 1992 election. More progress was made after the 1992 election when a committee was established to consider questions which had not been satisfactorily resolved. The extent to which the Convention's devolution scheme reflected progress made since 1979 can be considered by comparing it with the proposals which formed the subject of the 1979 referendum focusing, in particular, on Lord Home's five criticisms of the latter (see pp. 22).

Home's first criticism had been that a Scottish Assembly should be able to raise a proportion of its own revenue. Under the proposals of the 1970s, the Assembly would have been funded entirely through a block grant from London. Initially, the Convention suggested that certain revenues should be assigned to a Scottish Parliament and that it should have the power to vary the income tax rate within an unspecified range. An equalisation grant was also foreseen. Later, the 'own resources' element proposed was watered down to allow the Parliament to vary the rate of income tax by three pence in the pound with the bulk of its funding coming from a central government grant. Although the proposed tax-varying powers later proved to be highly significant politically, they were fiscally feeble. Lord Home's criticism was hardly met, but the attacks on revenue raising powers which were made in the 1990s were exactly the opposite from those made in the 1970s. Whereas Home had attacked the legislation in the 1970s for *not* allowing the Assembly to raise its own finance, Conservatives criticised the new proposals because they *would* give tax-varying powers to a Parliament.

Home had also argued that the 'West Lothian Question' remained unanswered. It was, he suggested, intolerable that Scottish MPs at Westminster would be able to make decisions about health, housing and so on in England whereas in Scotland these matters would be the preserve of the Scottish Assembly. The Liberal Democrats' response to this problem was to propose a federal system, which had the advantage of providing a symmetrical solution, but they made little effort to define anything more than the vaguest outline of a scheme. The response of the Convention and of Labour was to ignore the matter. There were, it was suggested, plenty of asymmetries and anomalies in the British system of government as it was and these had been accommodated and accepted. The anomalies arising from devolution could also be accommodated. The third of Home's criticisms was that no machinery existed to define whether a bill was purely Scottish which, he maintained, would lead to difficulties if a measure was later deemed to be *ultra vires*. The Convention proposed that matters to be devolved would be defined in the legislation and that all other matters would remain at Westminster. However, this was treated as a fairly technical matter and was not deemed to be politically sensitive during the Convention's deliberations.

Finally, Home made two interlinked criticisms – that the proposed Assembly, with about 150 members, was too large, and that the absence of an element of proportional representation in the electoral system was a weakness. In the context of the Convention, the executive of the Scottish Labour Party decided in 1990 that it would support an electoral system that 'fairly rewards parties with representatives broadly equal to the number of votes cast'. This was a major step forward and although agreement could not be reached initially on an appropriate system some broad principles for the electoral system were agreed by the Convention:

1. that it produces results in which the number of seats for various parties is broadly related to the number of votes cast for them;
2. that it ensures, or at least takes effective positive action to bring about, equal representation of men and women, and encourages fair representation of ethnic and other minorities;
3. that it preserves a link between the member and his/her constituency;
4. that it is as simple as possible to understand;
5. that it ensures adequate representation of less populous areas; and
6. that the system is designed to place the greatest possible power in the hands of the electorate (Constitutional Convention, 1990: 12).

These principles are difficult to reconcile and it is not surprising that the Convention found it difficult to agree on an electoral system for the Parliament. Following the 1992 election, therefore, a 'Commission' was established by the Convention which concluded in favour of the Additional Member System (AMS) with each voter having two votes – one for a constituency MP based on the existing Westminster constituencies plus another vote for a party or group list. These additional seats would provide a proportional element to representation in the Parliament which would have 129 members. The principles listed above also placed the issue of the representation of women and other 'minorities' on the political agenda but, since candidate selection has traditionally been an internal matter for political parties in Britain, it proved difficult to devise a system which would achieve this. Related to the question of women's representation there was also the problem of what to do about the more sparsely populated areas of Scotland. In the 1979 referendum, fears had been expressed that the Assembly would be dominated by politicians from west-central Scotland (Glasgow and Strathclyde, in particular) to the disadvantage of rural and peripheral areas. The agreement on a new system, it was believed, went some way towards meeting these fears. Significantly, the change in the electoral system was as much the result of internal Labour politics as intra-Convention politics. Many Labour home rulers became convinced that an alternative electoral system would not only lend a Scottish Parliament greater democratic legitimacy but would also be a means of creating a new, more consensual type of politics.

Overall, the devolution scheme agreed by the Convention was broadly similar to that on offer in the referendum in 1979. The new body would have very limited independent tax-raising powers and the most significant difference of substance was in the electoral system which was agreed. The most significant difference of all, however, was symbolic. A Scottish *Parliament*, not an Assembly, was being proposed. Its tax-varying powers may have been very limited but at least it was now agreed that such powers were appropriate. The long discussions during the years of Conservative rule may not have produced a complete and detailed set of proposals, but there was now at least a framework in place, which was much more than existed when Labour had come to power in 1974. More importantly, the experience within the Convention deepened Labour's commitment to devolution. Devolution was now not some 'add on extra' to Labour's basic policies but was seen within the party in Scotland as a central part of its platform. Much remained unresolved and some aspects of the policy changed after Labour came to office. Nonetheless, it would have been difficult, given the preceding years in the Convention, for Labour, had it so desired, to abandon its devolution commitment. In any event, by the 1990s Labour in Scotland had no such desire.

THE CONSERVATIVE RESPONSE

Despite promising in the 1979 referendum that a 'No' vote would not be interpreted as signalling opposition to the principle of devolution, the Conservatives had no intention of legislating for a Scottish

Assembly when they won the subsequent election and came to power. In June, the Commons repealed the 1978 Scotland Act, and George Younger, the new Secretary of State for Scotland, offered all-party talks to consider alternatives. These resulted in a few minor changes in parliamentary procedure. Later, Margaret Thatcher claimed that the Conservatives had actually provided devolution by 'rolling back the state rather than by creating new institutions of government' (Thatcher, 1993: 36). There appeared little need for anything more radical at the time. The Conservatives had improved their position in Scotland at the election and pro-devolutionists were deeply disillusioned.

As the issue returned to the forefront of Scottish politics in the late 1980s, however, the Conservatives were in a weak position to respond. The party was on the defensive and the emphasis was on convincing Scots that Tories were not anti-Scottish rather than attempting to take the initiative on the constitutional question. Under Thatcher the best hope seemed to be damage limitation. Thatcher's demise as Conservative leader and Prime Minister in 1990, and her replacement by John Major, offered the Conservatives an opportunity to regain the initiative. Major had had little association with Scotland and was much more popular among Scottish voters than Margaret Thatcher had been. Table 2.2 shows that by 1989 Mrs Thatcher had acquired an unenviable reputation among Scots. Few thought that she had Scotland's best interests at heart and large majorities believed that she thought Scotland unimportant and treated Scots as second-class citizens. In 1991 John Major had a better reputation on each of these questions. This personal popularity did not translate directly into support for his party, however. On becoming Prime Minister in 1990, Major's appointment of Ian Lang as Secretary of State for Scotland initially appeared to offer an opportunity to break with the recent past. Lang was a new face and had been an advocate of devolution in the 1970s (as had George Younger and Malcolm Rifkind, the two Secretaries of State under Thatcher) but the opportunity was not taken. He made little effort to change either the party's policy or its image. As the 1992 election approached, there was much speculation as to the likely fate of the Conservatives in Scotland and the prospect that the Tories would lose all of their seats – rendering the country 'a Tory-free zone' – was seriously mooted. During the campaign Major heavily emphasised the need to maintain the unity of the United Kingdom – despite advice from campaign managers that this was not an issue which greatly appealed to the voters. In a series of speeches he returned to the theme – 'The United Kingdom is in danger. Wake up my fellow countrymen! Wake up now before it is too late!' (quoted in Butler and Kavanagh, 1992: 130). In the event, the election results appeared to vindicate Major's insistence on campaigning on the issue. The Conservatives, somewhat surprisingly, won the election and in Scotland the party gained a seat and marginally increased its share of the vote (see Table 2.1). Given that the rest of the country moved against the Conservatives, the Scottish result was hailed as a great victory – which it was when measured against the expectations of many commentators. Set against the party's performances historically and not just against the previous election, however, and taking account of the fact that the party was unencumbered with Mrs Thatcher as leader, it was actually a rather poor result – a temporary staunching of the flood of votes away from the Conservatives in Scotland. Nonetheless, politics is as much about perceptions of reality as it is about reality itself and the perception that the Conservatives had had a major success in Scotland allowed them an opportunity to grasp the initiative.

Table 2.2: Perceptions of Margaret Thatcher's and John Major's attitudes to Scotland (percent agree with statements)

	Thatcher %	Major %
Has the best interests of Scotland at heart	10	26
Regards Scotland as unimportant in his future political plans	68	40
Treats the Scots as second-class citizens	77	41

Source: Glasgow Herald 20 September 1989; 19 June 1991.
Note: The poll relating to Thatcher was conducted in August 1989 and that relating to Major in June 1991.

During the 1992 election campaign, the Prime Minister promised that the government would 'take stock' of the situation in Scotland, implying the potential for new initiatives. This became a formal process after the election, when the 'stock taking' exercise was launched by Major and Lang. If the Conservatives had far surpassed the expectations of commentators in the general election with very modest gains, they failed to live up to the expectations that they themselves created with the 'stock taking 'exercise by offering only very modest changes. The high point in the consultative process was a breakfast meeting in Edinburgh attended by the Prime Minister and a few barely known and mainly Conservative-inclined Scots. The publication of a White Paper, 'Scotland in the Union – a partnership for good' (Scottish Office, 1993) in March 1993 failed to inspire enthusiasm for the party. Its proposals followed a familiar pattern of responses to demands for Scottish home rule – some alteration to parliamentary procedures and the transfer of some functions to the Scottish Office – which had been established by the Attlee government.

In 1995, Ian Lang was moved to the Board of Trade in a cabinet reshuffle and was replaced as Secretary of State for Scotland by Michael Forsyth. Forysth had been a controversial chairman of the Scottish Conservatives a few years before and had served as a junior minister at the Scottish Office. He was an enthusiastic Thatcherite with a reputation in Scotland as something of a political bruiser. Forsyth brought an unaccustomed (in recent years) vigour to his office and, in a sharp reversal of previous form, attempted to project a more strongly Scottish image. In keeping with the growing sense of Scottish national identity, he wore a kilt at the Scottish premiere of the film 'Braveheart' (the story of the fourteenth-century Scottish patriot, William Wallace). On St Andrew's day (30 November), Forsyth made a speech setting out projected reforms in the government of Scotland which took the spotlight away from the (re-)launch of proposals from the cross-party Constitutional Convention.

His most audacious initiative came in the following summer (1996), however, when he announced that the Stone of Destiny would be returned to Scotland. The symbolism surrounding this Stone was significant. According to legend, it was the one of the stones which, in Old Testament times, Jacob had used as a pillow (see *Genesis* 28 v.11). Somehow it found its way to Scotland and kings of the Picts, and later the Scots, sat on it to be crowned. In the fourteenth century it was captured and taken to London by the English to be used in the coronations of subsequent English and British monarchs. In 1950 a group of Nationalist students removed the Stone from Westminster Abbey and returned it to Scotland, causing much merriment in Scotland and considerable anguish among the London establishment (Mitchell, 1996: 259–66). The Stone was eventually returned and the episode became a part of Nationalist folklore. Immediately after the return of the Stone to London, the government considered placing it officially in Scotland, at least for part of each year, but decided to postpone making a decision until the excitement generated by 'the Pinch' had died down. The 1951 election intervened and the incoming Conservative government decided against such a move.

Sir Walter Scott's translation of a Latin prophecy (quoted in Mitchell, 1996: 260) which had been appended to a cabinet memorandum after the Stone was removed almost 50 years before, might have given Forsyth warning:

Unless the fates are faithless found,
And prophet's voice be vain,
Where'er this monument is found,
The Scottish race shall reign.

On its return in 1996 significant crowds turned out to observe the progress of the Stone through Scotland. Designed to appease rising Nationalist sentiment, the decision to return the Stone appeared to have fuelled it.

Forsyth's St Andrew's day speech outlined a number of proposed reforms in the government of Scotland, which were similar to those put forward by his predecessor but were presented more skilfully. There were also remarkable parallels with the Attlee government's response to home rule agitation. The 1948 White Paper, as discussed in Chapter 1, proposed reforms in parliamentary procedure and the establishment of the Scottish Economic Conference. Lang and Forsyth too focused on these institutions. More meetings of the Scottish Grand Committee were to take place and it was to be permitted to meet in Scotland (suggestions revived from the early 1980s). Forsyth proposed that in addition to the Scottish Secretary other Cabinet Ministers should appear before the Committee to answer questions. He claimed that under his proposals there was 'nothing which a Scottish Parliament could do which could not be done by the Grand Committee except raise a Tartan Tax' Scottish Conservative and Unionist News Release, 30 November 1995 (STUC). He also intended to revive the Scottish Economic Council, an idea suggested to him by Campbell Christie, general secretary of the Scottish Trade Union Congress, during consultations. This proposal allowed Forsyth to present himself as listening to the ideas of those unsympathetic to the Conservatives and reviving an institution established largely for the same purpose by a previous Labour government.

These efforts attempting to manage symbolic politics to the advantage of the governing party failed. At the 1997 election the Scottish Election Study survey asked respondents how much they trusted each of the parties to work in Scotland's interests. The results are shown in Table 2.3 and it can be seen that more than half replied 'almost never' for the Conservatives, compared with 3 per cent for Labour, 4 per cent for the SNP and 8 per cent for the Liberal Democrats. Within the Conservative Party there was a view that Forsyth's strategy of making symbolic concessions had played into the hands of advocates of constitutional change. The attempt to move on to the political territory of his opponents, a strategy which had after all worked well for New Labour, failed for the Scottish Conservatives. However, the immediate problems which afflicted the Scottish Conservatives as the 1997 election drew near were the same as those damaging the party across Britain as a whole – perceived weak leadership, economic incompetence, party divisions, sleaze and so on. It is impossible to know whether Forsyth's strategy would have succeeded had it been launched at some time in the 1980s or had the Conservatives been generally more popular across the country as a whole.

Table 2.3: How much parties are trusted to work in Scotland's interests (1997)

	Con %	Lab %	Lib Dem %	SNP %
Just about always	2	14	4	59
Most of the time	8	57	43	26
Only some of the time	38	26	44	12
Almost never	52	3	8	4
(N)	(828)	(817)	(735)	(806)

Source: Scottish Election Study survey, 1997.
Note: Respondents who answered 'Don't know' have been omitted from the table.

What is clear, however, is that Forsyth's strategy was very similar to that pursued by the 1945–51 Labour government when it came to appeasing Scottish nationalism. While remaining unequivocally opposed to home rule, symbols were used in an effort to demonstrate the government's sympathy for Scottish national identity and a few institutional reforms, again largely of a symbolic nature, were introduced. Even the symbols and institutions involved were largely the same. However, the context had changed and that made all the difference. Labour in the 1940s had considerable support in Scotland whereas the Tories in the 1990s did not. Home rule was a more pressing issue and the stakes were higher. Symbols would no longer suffice.

THE TARTAN TAX AND DECISION TO HOLD A REFERENDUM

In the 1990s the Conservatives did have one major success so far as devolution is concerned and that was in forcing Labour to accept that a referendum should be held on the issue. In 1995, when the Conservatives' prospects of winning the next election looked bleak, a few Scottish Tories concluded that supporting a referendum might be the best strategy to thwart devolution. Prominent among these was Brian Monteith, who had led the Student Campaign Against Devolution in 1979 and was to be a leading figure in the No campaign in 1997. The idea had a number of merits. Firstly, there was a precedent and the view that major constitutional changes required popular approval through a referendum was widespread. Secondly, it would allow the Conservatives to present themselves as consulting the people directly and thirdly, it offered possibly the best hope of stalling devolution. It would have been difficult for the Conservatives to have demanded that Labour should hold a referendum before implementing devolution as this could have been interpreted as an admission that Labour would win the general election. Consequently, those who supported the strategy found it difficult to win support for it within the party. Nonetheless, the idea gained currency amongst a few anti-devolutionists before Labour officially endorsed it as policy. Tam Dalyell, the Labour MP and inveterate opponent of devolution, urged his party to agree to a referendum but this was ruled out in February 1996 (*Scotsman*, 11 February 1996).

It was the controversy over Labour's proposal that a Scottish Parliament should have tax-varying powers which eventually led to the decision to hold a referendum. Forsyth had coined the phrase the 'tartan tax' to focus attention on the issue and he attacked this aspect of the devolution plans at every opportunity. He had identified what he saw as the weak link in Labour's policy and hoped to damn the entire package by focusing on it remorselessly. This issue was given particular relevance (and Forsyth's strategy was particularly adroit) because Tony Blair's Labour Party was intent on getting rid of its image as a 'tax and spend' party. For the first time in almost two decades the Conservatives were on the offensive on the issue of Scotland's constitutional status. Labour's difficulties with the 'tartan tax' campaign soon became evident and the party's response was confused for a number of months. In quick succession it was suggested that the tax-varying power would exist but might not be used, that it would be used only if Labour had an explicit electoral mandate, including a manifesto commitment and that it would not be used at all. None of these responses seemed to clarify Labour's position or reassure the public and the Conservatives continued to make the running on the issue.

Eventually, the Labour leadership decided that the best means of defusing the issue, and getting the party through the general election campaign, was to offer a referendum with two questions – one on whether Scots wanted a Parliament and the other on whether they wanted it to have tax-varying powers. The logic behind this strategy was that Labour could respond to 'tartan tax' jibes by arguing that the decision on whether the Parliament would have this power would be taken by the people. This argument proved effective in the election campaign but caused considerable difficulties within the Labour Party. As the Conservatives were not slow to point out, Labour shifted its position on a number of occasions. In February 1996, George Robertson, Labour's Shadow Scottish Secretary, stated that there were no proposals for a referendum (*Scottish Daily Mail*, 12 February 1996). In June, a group of senior Labour politicians – including Donald Dewar, George Robertson, Robin Cook and Gordon Brown – assembled to announce that after the election of a Labour government there would be a two-question referendum. Among those who opposed the idea of having a referendum and were incensed at the unilateral manner in which the new line had been declared were the Liberal Democrats and the Scottish Trade Union Congress, Labour's partners in the Constitutional Convention. Senior Scottish Labour figures also spoke out against the need for a referendum. John McAllion MP, Labour's Scottish constitutional spokesman, had not even been consulted on the matter and resigned from his front-bench position. Lord Ewing, who as Harry Ewing had been a Scottish Office Minister in the 1970s and played a prominent role in the first referendum, resigned as co-chair of the Constitutional Convention. A number of Scottish Labour MPs and senior officials spoke out against having a referendum. George Kerevan, a former senior Labour councillor, resigned from the party and joined the SNP.

The Scottish Labour executive met in late August 1996 to resolve the disputes within the party. By this time, those previously opposed now accepted that there should be a referendum but wanted only one question relating to the entire devolution package but at the executive meeting, a motion to this effect was defeated by 21 votes to 18. An alternative motion, put forward by Labour's parliamentary candidate in Glasgow Govan, Mohammad Sarwar, proposed that, in addition to a two-question referendum, before legislation was passed on devolution, there should also be a separate referendum before a Scottish Parliament could use its tax-raising powers. This was passed by 23 votes to 16. This new position was defended by Robertson who argued that the people of Scotland should be consulted twice on the issue (*Scotland on Sunday*, 1 September 1996). In fact, at this stage, Labour was proposing to put the question on tax-varying powers in one form or another more than twice. A devolved Parliament with tax-varying powers would be part of Labour's policy put to the people in the general election campaign. If elected there would be a two-question referendum. If that was successful, legislation for a Scottish Parliament would be passed and elections to that Parliament would be held at which, presumably, the party would draw up a manifesto which included some commitment to increase taxes if that was thought necessary and desirable. This would be put to the people in the elections to the Scottish Parliament and finally, before the tax-raising powers could be used Labour was proposing that there should be another referendum! This was a barely credible position and within six days the policy was changed again. Tony Blair decided that there would be no need for a second referendum.

These changes in policy damaged Labour's credibility and that of George Roberston in particular. Michael Forsyth turned attacks which were usually made on the Conservatives against the Labour Party in Scotland, accusing it of being impotent and under the control of Tony Blair and the London leadership. These proved difficult months for Labour in Scotland but as the election approached no leading party figure wanted to be seen as giving comfort to opponents by exposing internal divisions. Nonetheless, the experience had taught New Labour's leadership that there were potential problems ahead, with a number of senior members likely to disagree publicly with policy decisions taken at the centre. In early 1997, almost all of the executive members who had opposed the leadership's line were defeated in party elections and trusted New Labour members took their places. One of the few figures to retain his place was Bob Thomson, the party's Scottish treasurer but other key figures including Bob McLean, convenor of Scottish Labour Action, lost their seats on the Scottish executive: the Nationalist wing of the Labour Party had been defeated. Dissent within the party was silenced, at least temporarily, and the tax issue had been sidelined through the proposal to have a referendum. Blair's Scottish problem had been handled in a typically New Labour manner – ruthlessly, with electoral considerations foremost and by tackling Conservative criticisms head on. Critics of the U-turn within the party had been removed. The idea of having another referendum on devolution, which had originated in Conservative circles, had been adopted by Labour to the latter's advantage.

Devolution was certainly an issue in the 1997 election campaign in Scotland but it was not the only one, or even a dominant one. Although John Major ended his campaign with the slogan '72 hours to save the Union' and visited Northern Ireland, Scotland and Wales in one day to drive the message home (see Butler and Kavanagh, 1997: 111), the key issues in Scotland were the same as those elsewhere. A poll published in the *Scotsman* (17 March 1997) reported that devolution ranked seventh among Scottish voters' concerns, after the economic situation, unemployment, taxes, welfare, education and the National Health Service. Labour's safety first approach meant that constitutional questions, perhaps the most obvious area on which there were clear differences between them and the Conservatives, were played down. Constitutional reform was presented by New Labour in terms of creating a 'New Britain'. Tony Blair gave a controversial interview to a *Scotsman* journalist in which he said that even after devolution 'sovereignty rests with me as an English MP and that's the way it will stay' and went on to say that 'once the [taxation] power is given, it's like any parish council, it's [the Parliament] got the right to exercise it' (*Scotsman*, 4 April 1997). These remarks were interpreted (in a rather cavalier way) as showing that Blair equated the tax-varying powers of the proposed Parliament to those of an English parish council (see Brown, 1997: 157). This was blown up by sections of the media into a serious gaffe on Blair's part but it could equally be interpreted as part of a strategy of portraying Labour as a moderate, modernising force with no intention of ripping up the constitution as its Conservative opponents charged. Despite efforts to raise the issue of devolution, the Conservatives found it difficult to get away from defending themselves over accusations of sleaze, divisions over Europe, privatisation and the health service. The SNP, meanwhile, had difficulty in engaging with Labour. The latter had identified the Tories as their main opponents and focused all of their attention on them. The general election in Scotland was very much a 'British affair' with the SNP apparently squeezed out of the debate (see Mitchell and Bennie, 1997).

As we have seen (Table 2.1), however, the SNP made a small advance in terms of vote share, taking it to second place in Scotland, and won six seats. The geographical distribution of party support and the quirks of the electoral system resulted in the Liberal Democrats gaining more seats on a smaller vote share than the SNP but across Scotland, with 44 second places, the Nationalists were now the main electoral threat to Labour. The Conservatives were routed. All seats, including that of Michael Forsyth who campaigned impressively in Stirling, were lost. Apart from a few local councillors Scotland was indeed now a 'Tory-free zone'. Ironically, the election which brought to power the government which would finally establish a Scottish Parliament was fought primarily on 'British' issues and brought to power a Prime Minister known to be less than enthusiastic about devolution. However, after 1979 the best hope of achieving devolution always rested on Labour winning a majority of seats in the House of Commons and not just in Scotland. This had now been achieved.

To some, Labour's huge overall majority and the loss of all Scottish Tory seats made a referendum seem unnecessary, but it had been part of the new government's manifesto commitment and they were determined to implement it. In forming his government, the new Prime Minister appointed Donald Dewar as Secretary of State for Scotland. George Robertson, who had shadowed the post in opposition but whose performance had been heavily criticised, was made Defence Secretary. Dewar was acknowledged to be a consistent supporter of devolution and accepted the description of himself as a 'cultural nationalist'. It was expected that he would be more willing and able than Robertson to co-operate with the SNP in a referendum. Preparations for holding the referendum began as soon as the government took office.

THE REFERENDUM (SCOTLAND AND WALES) BILL

The Referendum (Scotland and Wales) Bill was the first public bill of the new Parliament. It was introduced on 15 May and had its second reading a week later. It was a short, five-clause piece of legislation setting out who could vote and the questions to be put and authorising expenditure to cover the costs of administration. These were to be pre-legislative referendums. In other words, they would be held before the actual devolution legislation detailing the nature and powers of the new representative institutions was passed. This was in sharp contrast to the 1978 Act which provided for the establishment of a Scottish Assembly and a referendum in one highly complex piece of legislation. In 1997, Scotland and Wales were taken together for the purpose of legislating for referendums but would be treated separately when it came to the devolution legislation itself. The pre-legislative nature of the referendums was criticised by the Conservatives. Michael Howard claimed that this was 'designed to pre-empt parliamentary debate' (Hansard, vol.294, col.736). From the Labour side, Tam Dalyell maintained that the sole purpose was to 'put pressure on Government Members' (col.746). Although there was some truth in what they said, these critics failed to attract very much support.

In 1979 eligible voters had been defined as those entitled to vote in a parliamentary election plus peers. Under the 1997 legislation, those eligible to vote in the Scottish referendum were those normally entitled to vote in local government elections. Thus peers would be able to vote as would EU citizens resident in Scotland, the former numbering 123 and the latter amounting to around 12,000 voters. The provision allowing EU citizens to vote was based on an agreement made in the Maastricht Treaty which gave voting rights in local and European Parliament elections to EU citizens resident in any member country. While the referendum was not a local election, the government was ensuring that the result would not be open to legal challenge on the grounds that it was a regional or local poll. Scots serving in the armed forces outside Scotland would have had the opportunity to make a service declaration stating the place of normal residence. Other Scots living outside Scotland would not have a vote, however, giving rise to what opponents saw as anomalies. Tam Dalyell publicised the 'Gary McAllister Question', which had been raised earlier in the letter columns of *The Times* (28 May 1997), referring to the captain of the Scottish international football team who played for Coventry City and lived in England. Despite his manifest Scottishness and the position he held, McAllister would not be able to vote on Scotland's future while assorted Europeans would. Nonetheless, in conformity with notions of citizenship and the normal rules about voting, place of residence (or previous place of residence in the case of citizens living abroad) rather than a subjective sense of nationality, was to be the basis of the right to vote in the referendum.[3] A spoiling amendment, proposed by Bill Cash, the Euro-sceptic Tory MP, sought to extend the referendum to people throughout the United Kingdom on the basis that the future nature of the state was a matter of concern to all citizens but it was heavily defeated.

The two questions to be put to the Scottish people were also the subject of debate. The SNP wanted to have three options – independence in Europe, devolution and the status quo – in a referendum in which voters would order their preferences. As the SNP reminded him, Donald Dewar had supported this view after the 1992 election when he was shadow Secretary of State for Scotland, stating that the case for a multi-option referendum should be 'shouted from the rooftops' (*Scotsman*, 23 April 1992). There was little support in the Commons for this suggestion, however. The Liberal Democrats attempted to remove the second question and have a one-question referendum but despite receiving some back-bench Conservative support this too was defeated. The final decision was that each voter should complete two ballot papers, the first asking whether they agreed that there should be a Scottish Parliament and the second asking whether they agreed that a Scottish Parliament should have tax-varying powers (see Figure 2.1).

No government financial support was to be given to any campaign groups or organisations but an explanatory leaflet was to be delivered, at public expense, to every household in Scotland and the legislation made no reference to rules governing broadcasting. Nor was the date for the referendum set by the Bill (although it was set for 11 September in the final version of the Act). A Chief Counting Officer for Scotland would be appointed and he or she in turn would appoint counting officers for each local government area in Scotland. The counting of votes was to take place in each of these areas separately with the total for Scotland being announced by the Chief Counting Officer. Finally, no qualified majority was to be required – a simple majority of voters rather than some fixed percentage of the electorate would be an adequate basis on which to proceed.

The legislation for the referendum was short, simple and deliberately designed to be able to pass through Parliament quickly and easily. It differed markedly from the provisions made for the 1979 referendum, not least in being pre-legislative. Indeed, the actual proposals on which people in Scotland were to be asked to vote were not published until July, after the referendum legislation had been passed into law. More significant politically, however, was the very different context in which the preparations for a referendum were made. In 1997 Labour had a massive Commons majority and the government and the Prime Minister were enjoying an unprecedented level of popularity among the electorate at the start of a new Parliament. This augured well for a positive endorsement of devolution in Scotland.

CONCLUSION

The years between 1979 and 1997 were tumultuous ones in Scottish politics. After the failure of the 1979 referendum pro-devolution forces were dispirited, dejected, fragmented and pessimistic. For 18 years the majority of Scots perceived themselves as suffering unduly under a series of governments which they had not elected and which showed no interest in constitutional reform. By 1997 sentiment in favour of home rule had greatly strengthened and, after the election, Scotland was on the verge of a historic change in the way it had been governed for almost 300 years.

We have suggested that the key to understanding this change lies in the structure of social cleavages in Scotland. Formerly, the dominant class cleavage cut across Scots' sense of national identity. Working-class solidarity across Britain was in conflict with Scottish national solidarity. In this period, however, thanks in no small measure to the policies and actions of successive Conservative governments, working-class identity and national identity came to reinforce each other. By the end of the period, even middle-class Scottish opinion was outraged by the proposal to privatise Scottish water, the discontinuing of the London to Fort William railway sleeper and the high-handed way in which the structure of Scottish local government was drastically altered.[4]

These changes in underlying social cleavages were not reflected in party politics. The Labour Party had disdained co-operation with the SNP during the 1979 referendum and hostility between the two continued to be a feature of Scottish politics throughout the period. In part this was a product of the fact that they were competing for the same sorts of voters. Although the seats won by the SNP were mainly in the rural periphery of Scotland, party strategists realised that in order to make progress they would have to challenge Labour in the central belt. The SNP, therefore, moved consciously and decisively to the left in order to do just this. Labour and the SNP were (and still are) to a considerable extent fishing in the same pool for votes and this inhibited the extent to which they could come together on issues such as the poll tax, the decline of Scottish industry and, of course, devolution (see Brand *et al.,* 1994).

The idea that there should be another referendum in Scotland on the question of devolution originated, as we have seen, among opponents of constitutional change. It was taken up by the Labour Party for tactical reasons – it helped to deflect criticism during the general election campaign and also kept the focus on other areas where the Conservatives were vulnerable across Britain as a whole. When Labour won the election and moved quickly to organise a referendum some supporters of home rule may have felt some sense of trepidation, remembering what had happened in 1979. The context of the 1997 referendum was entirely different from that which had existed in 1979, however. In 1979 an unpopular government was coming to the end of its life; in 1997 a new, fresh government was on the crest of a wave of popularity. More importantly, however, the intervening 18 years had built up intense resentment in Scotland against the Conservatives and government from London. The stage was set for a referendum campaign and a referendum result that were to prove very different from what had happened in 1979.

NOTES

1. Some survey evidence from the 1960s shows that, at that time, Glasgow electors at least were more inclined to think that they had more in common with an English person of the same class than with a Scottish person of a different class (see Budge and Urwin, 1966: 118). By the 1997 election,

according to Scottish Election Study data, respondents with a preference opted for a Scottish person of a different class by a margin of two to one.
2. This was Iain Lawson who at the time was chairman of the panel of Scottish Conservative candidates.
3. On this basis three of the four authors of this book and the research assistant on the project – all Scots with a keen interest in the constitutional issue – were unable to vote in the referendum.
4. With reference to the latter, the *Scotsman* commented: 'Ministers' refusal to establish an independent commission to draw up the new boundaries was a piece of arrogance for which there was no respectable case to make, and none ever made.' (15 March 1995)

Figure 2.1: Schedule 1 to the Referendum (Scotland and Wales) Bill

REFERENDUM IN SCOTLAND
PART I
FORM OF FIRST BALLOT PAPER

Parliament has decided to consult people in Scotland on the Government's proposals for a Scottish Parliament:
Put a cross (X) in the appropriate box

I AGREE THAT THERE SHOULD BE A SCOTTISH PARLIAMENT	

OR

I DO NOT AGREE THAT THERE SHOULD BE A SCOTTISH PARLIAMENT	

PART II
FORM OF SECOND BALLOT PAPER

Parliament has decided to consult people in Scotland on the Government's proposals for a Scottish Parliament to have tax-varying powers:
Put a cross (X) in the appropriate box

I AGREE THAT A SCOTTISH PARLIAMENT SHOULD HAVE TAX-VARYING POWERS	

OR

I DO NOT AGREE THAT A SCOTTISH PARLIAMENT SHOULD HAVE TAX-VARYING POWERS	

3

The National Campaign[1]

Just 19 weeks elapsed between the general election in May 1997 and referendum day in September. During this period the necessary legislation to provide for a referendum was passed, the practical arrangements for the voting were organised, a white paper setting out the government's proposals was published, a referendum campaign was conducted and the vote itself took place. It was a tight timetable and, given that the House of Commons summer recess had also to be fitted in, it is difficult to imagine that the referendum could have been held any sooner. From the government's point of view, holding the referendum as soon as possible had obvious appeals. It would take place during Labour's honeymoon period, it provided clear evidence of the government's determination to implement its manifesto promises and supporters of devolution had been preparing for a referendum for some time. The Conservatives, the main anti-devolution force, were recovering from a humiliating election defeat and had more pressing concerns, including choosing a new leader whose election was to be ratified by the party as a whole.

The fact that supporters of devolution were much more thoroughly prepared for the referendum campaign than their opponents is itself important and so we begin this account of the campaign by examining the origins and development of 'Scotland Forward', the group which co-ordinated the Yes campaign.

THE EMERGENCE OF SCOTLAND FORWARD

Supporters of devolution had begun preparing in earnest for the campaign almost as soon as the Labour Party confirmed that there would be a referendum. One of the key figures involved in the early preparation was Nigel Smith, a businessman who had also been involved in the 'Business Says Yes' campaign in 1979. Before that, he had been active in arguing the case for devolution within the business community. While others debated whether a referendum was necessary, Smith took the view that if there was to be a referendum then there were lessons to be drawn from the experience of 1979. The main lessons were that preparations had to begin as early as possible and that co-operation between the parties which favoured devolution was essential. Although he was associated with the Constitutional Convention, Smith was seen as sufficiently independent to ensure that he would be trusted by the SNP as well as by the parties which played a part in the Convention.

Smith believed that research needed to be done to gain from the experience of referendums elsewhere and that money had to be raised to finance such research as well as the campaign itself. Money was sought from trade unions, the Rowntree Trust and individuals, and initial funding was forthcoming from the Scottish teachers' union (the Educational Institute of Scotland – EIS), Unison and some business people. In addition, advice was given by Peter Kellner, a well-known political analyst, who suggested that the evidence from referendums in other countries confirmed the necessity of a unified campaign. In October 1996, Smith was invited to a meeting of the Constitutional Convention at which he argued for a well-researched, well-funded campaign which could not be run by the Convention if the SNP was to be brought on board. There was resistance to this idea, however. Canon Kenyon Wright in particular was concerned that the Convention, of which he was chairman, should have a significant role. He also doubted the value of spending as much as £20,000 on research and employing a London-based expert. However, this view did not prevail. As early as September 1996, Smith had made contact with the SNP in order to prepare for that party's eventual involvement in the campaign.

Research was undertaken by Peter Kellner using System Three, a polling organisation with a long track record in Scotland. A major survey of the Scottish electorate was conducted in November 1996 and a key finding of this research was that, although 70 per cent of respondents indicated that they would vote for a Scottish Parliament and 59 per cent that they would vote for taxation powers, supporters of the two major political parties involved in the Constitutional Convention, Labour and the Liberal Democrats, would not on their own produce enough votes to ensure a Yes majority on either referendum question.

In order to explore voter attitudes towards devolution in more detail, survey respondents were asked to indicate whether they agreed or disagreed with a series of statements focusing on a mixture of positive and negative aspects of having a Scottish Parliament.[2] The results are shown in Table 3.1. In his report on the survey, Kellner, noted that the 'biggest single spontaneously-mentioned fear of a Scottish parliament is higher taxation' which was mentioned by 15

Table 3.1:
Scotland Forward research: responses to devolution-related statements

'Negative' statements	Agree %	Disagree %	Net
A Scottish Parliament within the United Kingdom would end up having rows with London the whole time.	62	26	+36
If Scotland has its own Parliament, the number of Scottish MPs at Westminster would be reduced and Scotland would have less influence on decisions relating to United Kingdom national issues.	47	33	+14
If a Scottish Parliament is set up, the British government in London is bound to reduce the public spending grant it allocates to Scotland, with the result that Scotland will be worse off.	48	35	+13
If a Scottish Parliament has the power to vary income tax, it would be certain to use that power to increase the amount of tax that most people pay.	41	31	+10
Whatever people may say, a Scottish Parliament is bound to lead in the end to the break-up of the United Kingdom.	45	40	+5
The current plans for a Scottish Parliament within the United Kingdom have not been properly thought out and it would not work effectively.	35	42	-7
'Positive' statements			
It's about time important decisions affecting Scotland were made by a Scottish Parliament, elected by Scottish people, rather than hundreds of miles away in England.	86	9	+77
Scotland needs to take more control of its own destiny and stop blaming other people for its problems.	80	11	+69
A Scottish Parliament would strengthen Scotland's pride in itself.	80	12	+68
Money for Scotland's public services such as schools and hospitals would be spent more wisely if the decisions about it were made by a Scottish Parliament.	80	12	+68
A Scottish Parliament would be able to do much more to boost jobs and investment in Scotland.	79	13	+66
A Scottish Parliament within the United Kingdom would be able to bring out the best of the talents of the Scottish people.	77	12	+65
It is vital for a Scottish Parliament to have the power to vary income tax up or down in order to make the right decisions about public spending in Scotland.	76	12	+64
Scotland's interests in Europe would be better represented if there was a Scottish Parliament.	77	13	+64
A Scottish Parliament would be able to make sure that the British government in London takes more notice of Scotland when deciding policies for Britain as a whole.	76	13	+63
A Scottish Parliament elected by a fair voting system would encourage politicians from different parties to work together for the good of Scotland as a whole.	67	20	+47
The plans to make sure that roughly equal numbers of men and women make up a Scottish Parliament would help it to make better decisions.	56	21	+35

Source: System Three (Scotland).

per cent of the sample (Kellner, 1996). Relative to some of the other issues covered in the survey, the data also showed that proportional representation and equal representation for women did not evoke great enthusiasm. Even so, they were endorsed by clear majorities of the voters.

Kellner's interpretation of the data was that 'economic issues drive the "double no" vote, while governance issues drive the "double yes" vote' (Kellner, 1996: 5). Anti-devolutionists believed that if devolution occurred taxes would go up, people would be worse off and the economy would be adversely affected. This governance–instrumentality dichotomy (or, as Kellner rather insensitively put it, 'thistle in your kilt, versus pound in your sporran' divide) led him to recommend that the best chances of maximising the 'Yes' vote was to

> stress the governance issues – Scottish pride, identity, the intrinsic virtues of taking its own decisions. If voters come to regard the central issue of the referendums to be Scotland's *right to assert its nationhood* and run its own affairs, then the evidence of this survey suggests that both referendum questions should yield a clear 'Yes' majority. On the other hand, if voters focus their minds mainly on the *amount of tax* they pay, then the 'yes' majority, especially regarding the second referendum question, must be regarded as being at risk. (Original emphasis, Kellner, 1996: 6)

This passage from the report was identified by those who had commissioned it as one of the most important findings and they resolved to base their campaign on this information. It would be important to set the agenda of debate so as to ensure that they had the advantage. Kellner informed Smith that the strategic task was to preserve the existing 'Yes' majorities and that there was little point in seeking to convert those who opposed the idea of a Scottish Parliament.

By November 1996, the press was reporting that discreet talks were taking place to build a single Yes campaign with Smith mentioned as the 'fixer' behind the embryonic organisation (*Scotsman*, 11 November; *Scotland on Sunday*, 17 November 1996). In the New Year, the executive of the Constitutional Convention formally accepted the 'blue water' principle, that if the campaign was to win the widest possible support then it had to be separate from the Convention. There was some reluctance to accept this principle among Convention members but the involvement of the SNP was thought to be essential in the campaign and this would require a new organisation. Between then and the general election, the organisation began to take shape, more money was raised and there were private discussions of tactics and strategy. By late February 1997 pledges of £120,000 had been made to the campaign. Partnership for a Parliament Ltd was incorporated as a company on 1 April 1997. Copies of forms registering Partnership for a Parliament, effectively Scotland Forward's embryonic executive, provide an insight into the type of people involved. Against 'nationality', seven had written 'British' and four had written 'Scottish'.[3] Sufficient money had been raised by the beginning of April to employ Esther Robertson, who had worked as full-time organiser for the Constitutional Convention, as an interim co-ordinator.

While Partnership for a Parliament was the working title for the organisation, a better name and slogan was sought. The public launch was planned for the week after the general election and it was only at a meeting in late April that the name Scotland Forward was agreed upon. At one stage it was suggested that the organisation should be 'politician free'. However, it had been Smith's intention all along to involve the parties, which he recognised would be the key players in the debate, but not to have any MPs on the board of the organisation. It was thought that MPs would be involved in some other capacity and that there were potential problems in having high profile MPs on the board. The initial intention had been to have 12 board members but in the event a larger board was created. It was also necessary to make clear from the outset that places would be kept available for the SNP, although it was recognised that the Nationalists would be unable to be associated with the campaign until after the election.

In addition to a board, a national forum and local campaign councils were planned. The trade unions played a significant part in preparing this part of the campaign. The Scottish Trades Union Congress (STUC) convened meetings of organisations which supported a Scottish Parliament in early 1997.[4] The forum was chaired by Campbell Christie, general secretary of the STUC and Alison Elliot, convenor of the Church and Nation Committee of the Church of Scotland, was vice-chair. In the event the forum had a limited role in the campaign, having only an advisory function. In the nature of modern campaigning, it proved more useful in giving the impression of consultation and allowing the campaign to appear broad-based rather than in feeding ideas into the campaign.

A draft of a campaign plan was written by Esther Robertson. In this it was acknowledged that the campaign had to be at 'arms length' from the Convention in order to allow SNP members, pro-devolution Conservatives and individuals associated with no party to participate.

Various names were suggested for the new organisation: Scotland Says Yes (rejected as it had been used in the ill-fated referendum in 1979); Scotland's Parliament Now (rejected because its abbreviation was too close to SNP) and Partnership for a Parliament. The last was chosen as the working title of the emerging body. The idea of having a short one word name was considered – 'Yes', 'Aye' and 'For' were discussed. Though there were concerns that 'Scotland Forward, with an emphasis on 'For' (Scotland FORward) might be too diffuse, this was thought to be the best name.

The 'phoney war' ended after the general election. The appointment of Donald Dewar as Secretary of State was welcome news for Scotland Forward. George Robertson, as Shadow Scottish Secretary, had seen no need for the formal involvement of the SNP in the campaign as he believed that SNP voters and supporters would rally to the cause anyway. From his point of view, gaining the support of SNP voters without the involvement of the SNP leadership would have been the best scenario. Dewar, on the other hand, accepted the arguments for a single unified campaign and direct SNP involvement. A week after the election, Scotland Forward was publicly launched at the Assembly Rooms in Edinburgh. Henry McLeish, Devolution Minister at the Scottish Office, addressed the meeting and gave every indication that a genuinely cross-party campaign was supported by the government. Though the SNP had no official presence, a number of members of the party attended. A few days later, Scotland Forward held a meeting with Alex Salmond, the SNP leader, and other senior members of the party. Although there had previously been private meetings at which the Nationalists had been briefed on Scotland Forward's activities, a press release was issued after this meeting acknowledging that it had taken place.

Prior to the election it had been thought that it would be advantageous if some Conservatives could be involved in the Yes campaign. The defeat of all Scottish Conservative MPs altered the situation, however, and attracting Conservatives on to the executive was no longer important. There was even some feeling that keeping the Conservatives out would be advantageous given the unpopularity of the party. Bill Spiers (deputy general secretary of the STUC) attended the Scottish Conservative conference in Perth after the election and spoke to some delegates thought to be sympathetic, but the issue of Conservative involvement in the organisation simply fell by the wayside.

One of the first tasks to be undertaken after the election was the appointment of full-time officers for Scotland Forward. Paolo Vestri was chosen as national organiser, his appointment being confirmed at a meeting of the Scotland Forward executive in late May. Vestri had been a Labour councillor in Edinburgh and was the director of the Scottish Local Government Information Unit. He was selected from 87 applicants including a former Lord Provost of Glasgow (who used a vice-chairman of the Scottish Conservatives as a referee), a former assistant general secretary of the Scottish Labour Party, a couple of Labour councillors, a pop star, a former convenor of the Scottish Liberal Democrats, Ron Brown (ex-Labour MP), a former assistant to ex-SNP MP Jim Sillars, an SNP candidate in the general election, a former vice-convenor of the SNP, a senior member of the Scottish Greens and a number of journalists. Further appointments were mad which took account of party membership so that the full-time staff included at least one member from each of the major pro-devolution parties.

THE LATE START OF THINK TWICE

At a meeting of the executive of Scotland Forward shortly after the general election, some frustration was voiced at the apparent absence of a No campaign organisation. Gaining television and radio exposure was proving difficult as the broadcasters felt the need to be balanced in their coverage of the issue. With the Conservatives in disarray after the election and no anti-devolution campaign organisation in existence, Scotland Forward found itself unable to get as much media coverage as it wanted.

Attempts by opponents of devolution to prepare for a referendum prior to the election had proved futile, as noted in Chapter 2. In October 1995, Michael Fry, a broadsheet journalist and Tory activist, had written an article critical of moves towards Quebec independence and he had subsequently been approached by a prominent businessman, seeking advice on what should be done to oppose Scottish devolution and also seeking access to senior Conservatives, but this 'feeler' came to nothing, as did contemporaneous efforts to establish a non-party movement against devolution. Just before the election, an attempt was made to gain the support of senior public and political figures not associated with the Conservatives. Lord Weir, who had played a significant role in campaigning against devolution in 1979, agreed to approach individuals, particularly senior trade unionists who were thought likely to support the anti-devolution cause. He had no luck, however, and when the election saw the return of a Labour government committed to a referendum anti-devolutionists were unprepared. Fry's view, expressed three weeks after the election, was that the Tories were devastated by the election result and unable to build a credible campaign, with only hard-liners willing to raise their heads above the parapets. Business, he suggested, had left it too late and was split on the issue, with many key figures in the business community taking a pragmatic line and being unwilling to challenge the new government.

Brian Monteith emerged to play a leading role in the No campaign. Monteith had led the Student Campaign Against the Devolution Act (SCADA) in 1979, which at least had added a dash of humour (of sorts) to a rather dreary campaign with slogans such as 'Nice girls say NO'. He was a partner in a public relations firm and had been closely associated with Michael Forsyth, Secretary of State for Scotland. Montieth identified two major handicaps for anti-devolutionists. Firstly, the absence of senior Scottish Conservatives would rob the campaign of well-known figures and secondly there had been insufficient preparation for a campaign. The 'generals had all been shot' as he put it. John Major's resignation as leader of the party meant that the energies of some of those later to be involved in the referendum campaign were immediately channelled into the contest for a new leader of the Conservative Party. Monteith himself was heavily involved in William Hague's leadership campaign.

Towards the end of May about ten of the 'usual suspects', as Monteith described them in a press report, met in Edinburgh to organise a campaign (*Herald*, 27 May 1997). An attempt to broaden the campaign failed as no significant non-Conservative politician was willing to join. The most likely Labour recruit, Tam Dalyell, chose to plough a lone furrow. Relations with the Conservative Party were not entirely easy. Although Monteith was an active party member, his relationship with the Scottish leadership had been difficult. Some elements in the party hierarchy feared that he would adopt the same style as had been used in his student days, when female strippers had been known to feature in campaigns that he had organised. However, the party had been slow in getting its act together and recognised the value of having a campaign that was not clearly identified as a Tory campaign. Their dilemma was that they wanted control over the campaign without it being seen as too close to the Conservatives. It was agreed that Lord Fraser, formerly Peter Fraser who had been a Scottish MP until his defeat in 1987 and was subsequently Lord Advocate, should act as campaign director. Fraser and Monteith had crossed swords in the past. In 1987, Monteith had attempted to gain the Conservative nomination for the Angus constituency, previously held by Fraser, in competition with Fraser's wife (neither was successful). A further concern of the Scottish Conservative hierarchy was the involvement in the campaign of Bill McMurdo, who had been invited to be a vice-chairman of Think Twice. McMurdo had links with the Orange Order and the party was intent on dispelling any impression that it had sectarian links.

The name 'Think Twice' was chosen. It was thought necessary, especially before the White Paper was published, not to launch a 'double No' campaign but to convey scepticism and fear. The most significant figure to join the campaign after the election was Donald Findlay QC. Findlay had been a prospective Conservative parliamentary candidate, was a leading criminal lawyer, a director of Glasgow Rangers Football Club and a well-known Unionist, of both Scottish and Ulster varieties. Sir Matthew Goodwin, a former treasurer of the Scottish Conservatives, acted as treasurer of Think Twice, providing an extremely valuable contact with the business community. The secretary was Mark Izatt who had been Conservative candidate in Clydesdale at the general election and who worked as a personal assistant to Jackson Carlaw, a senior figure in the Scottish Conservatives.

The Think Twice campaign was officially launched in late June in a function suite at Murrayfield Stadium in Edinburgh. Monteith had used this as a venue during William Hague's leadership campaign a few weeks before and it was thought to have powerful symbolic significance, being the stadium where Scottish international rugby matches are played. This was part of a conscious effort to dispel any suspicions that Think Twice was anti-Scottish. The launch was hosted by Donald Findlay, Brian Monteith and a three-man committee consisting of David McLetchie, former president of the Scottish Conservatives (and by 1998 leader of the party in Scotland), Oliver Thomson, managing director of an advertising agency who had been involved in the No campaign in 1979 and Richard Mowbray, formerly a Labour and SDP candidate who had been expelled from the Liberal Democrats and had urged voters to support the Conservatives in 1997. Mowbray was the nearest that Think Twice had to a non-Tory politician. Of the 13 vice-chairmen in place by early August, four were or had been Church of Scotland ministers. At its subsequent launch in Glasgow, Think Twice challenged Donald Dewar to a debate, the classic tactic of the underdog.

In a very short space of time Goodwin was able to raise a considerable sum of money for the organisation. In the event, the amount spent by Think Twice (£275,000) was slightly greater than that spent by Scotland Forward (£270,000). However, there were important differences. Much of the money raised by Think Twice came into its offices late in the campaign and, of course, only after the organisation was established. This impeded forward planning. There was also the matter of how it was spent. With almost no organisation on the ground and fewer active participants than Scotland Forward, Think Twice was forced to spend its money on newspaper advertising.

From the outset, the most likely outcome of the referendum was a Yes Yes vote. The next most likely outcome was a Yes No vote. Yet, no serious campaign was launched advocating a positive endorsement of devolution without tax-varying powers. Probably the least likely outcome was a No Yes vote but there was an unsuccessful effort to organise a campaign to promote this somewhat eccentric position by Struan Stevenson, a long-standing advocate of devolution within the Conservative Party. This won the support of Michael Fry and consequently gained some exposure in the *Herald* in mid May. The stated intention behind the move was to reject the government's proposals and demand a more powerful Scottish Parliament, with power over all government finances in Scotland and Scotland's share of United Kingdom services paid for from Scottish revenues. However, Stevenson failed to win either any wider backing for the campaign or any financial support. Little more was heard of the No Yes campaign although a columnist in the *Scottish Daily Express* advocated a No Yes vote in a fairly light-hearted piece at the start of the campaign proper (27 August 1997).

SNP INVOLVEMENT

Devolution has presented the SNP with problems throughout its history. Hard-line fundamentalists suspicious of devolution and opposed to working with others have had considerable influence in the party whereas its pragmatic wing has been willing to support devolution. Alex Salmond, elected leader of the SNP in 1990, is associated with the pragmatists and in the early 1980s was an active member of the Campaign for a Scottish Assembly. During his leadership, tension between the different strands of thinking in the party inevitably placed him in a difficult position. As the 1997 general election approached, hard-line pressure on Salmond to reject devolution was intense. At the same time, overtures were increasingly being made – by devolutionists outside the party, most notably in the trade unions, and pragmatists within it – not to rule out devolution.

By 1995, Salmond had successfully shifted the SNP towards a more pragmatic position. Devolution, he made clear, was his second choice after independence. In effect, he was distinguishing between devolution and the status quo, something which fundamentalists refused to do. This was a fairly comfortable position for him, both in terms of party management and electoral strategy, so long as the hard-liners accepted that he had no intention of playing down the importance of independence. He could reconcile the hard-liners by his advocacy of independence while refusing to rule out the possibility of devolution. One of the unintended consequences of the Labour Party's conversion to a two-question referendum, however, was to undermine this delicate balance. The SNP now had to explain what it would do in the event of a Labour victory and a subsequent referendum, which looked ever more likely. This new element on the agenda of Scottish politics caused the SNP leader some discomfort. Salmond did not want to have to acknowledge that his party would be unsuccessful in the forthcoming election. At the same time, he did not want to be seen to be unco-operative and recognised the very real dangers involved if the SNP either did nothing or, worse still from his viewpoint, joined with the Conservatives in opposition to devolution.

The SNP could not even be involved in the preparations for the referendum campaign, or at least be seen to be involved, until after the election. Labour's victory in May 1997, with a huge majority, clarified matters. A meeting between senior members of Scotland Forward and the SNP was held at the end of the month after which a joint press release was issued describing the meeting as 'extremely cordial and constructive', urging the government to publish a Scottish Parliament white paper and looking forward to 'developing our contacts in the weeks ahead' (*SNP News Release*, 29 May 1997). This was the first public acknowledgement from the SNP leadership of a willingness to be involved in the campaign. However, the leadership still required a mandate from the membership on the issue, which could not be given until after the White Paper was published. The Scotland Forward executive acknowledged the importance of avoiding making any statement which might prejudice the chances of the SNP becoming part of the campaign. At Bill Spiers' suggestion, some working arrangement with the SNP leadership was explored for the period before the publication of the government's White Paper. The campaign strategy was already in the process of being developed and it would be difficult to change the strategy at a later stage when the SNP came on board.

The government White Paper outlining its proposals for a Scottish Parliament and the referendum was published on 24 July. Some attempt to meet SNP concerns was evident in it. The SNP's main concern had been that a 'glass ceiling' would be written into the proposals – some statement and mechanism obstructing further devolution of power – but the White Paper satisfied the SNP leadership. The party's national executive unanimously approved a motion recommending a Yes Yes vote in the referendum which was put to the party's national council, the main decision-making body between annual conferences, in early August. It was passed overwhelmingly with only a tiny handful of dissidents led by Gordon Wilson, Salmond's predecessor as leader. The motion read:

> National Council re-iterates standing policy that gives primacy to the independence campaign, but which does not seek to obstruct devolution. In that context, National Council resolves that the Scottish National Party will campaign for a 'Yes, Yes' vote in the referendum on September 11th and instructs the NEC to organise and run a distinctive SNP campaign designed to mobilise the support of the more than 620,000 people who voted SNP on May 1st and the many others who believe in independence. Council further instructs the NEC to co-operate with 'Scotland Forward' in order to strengthen the positive turnout for the referendum.

As one leading anti-devolutionist remarked later, the result of the referendum was sealed with this decision. The combination of Labour, Liberal Democrats and the SNP, who between them had won over 80 per cent of Scottish votes in the general election, was formidable.

The SNP joined Scotland Forward and three members of the party's executive took places on the latter's executive. The three came from different wings of the party. George Reid was a confirmed pragmatist and close to Alex Salmond. Alex Neil was a hard-liner who had frequently been at odds with the leadership and Kay Ullrich's position lay somewhere between these two. In the event, Reid played the most active and prominent part in Scotland Forward and in the campaign generally. Reid and Ullrich attended their first meeting with Scotland Forward in early August.

Some guiding principles were set down by the participants in Scotland Forward to ensure the smooth running of the campaign. The parties agreed that each would have separate days for major press conferences and events during the campaign and that, though details may be kept secret, there should be 'no major surprises'. Each party would inform Scotland Forward of media events by 15 August and inform each other during the campaign. Scotland Forward would act as the 'clearing house' and try to avoid clashes. It was also agreed that each party would concentrate on getting its own known support out to vote on referendum day. The Scotland Forward campaign launch was set for 19 August, to be followed the next day by Labour's, with the Liberal Democrat and SNP launches following on 21 and 22 August.

FURTHER CAMPAIGN RESEARCH

As already noted (see p.52), Scotland Forward had commissioned survey research at the end of 1996 which it used to persuade the parties of the need for a co-ordinated and well-funded campaign. In May 1997, further qualitative research was commissioned. The purpose of this was to provide:

- an understanding of the beliefs and attitudes relating to a Scottish Parliament;
- insight into the ability to interpret new information concerning the proposed Scottish Parliament;
- guidance on the development of persuasive communications which would be designed to maximise the Yes vote. (System Three, 1997: 1)

Six focus group discussions were conducted with members of the public not fully committed to voting either Yes or No. The participants were selected so that they included men and women, people of various ages and occupational classes and voters for each of the parties. This research concluded that the main motivating factor for supporting a Scottish Parliament was the perceived need to be able to limit some of the actions taken by a centralised and centralising Conservative government. There was, however, evidence that the need for a Scottish Parliament was no longer seen as being as urgent as in the past, although there was some concern that New Labour was too concerned with pleasing the electorate in the south-east of England.[5] The research suggested that voters were not very clear about what would be the benefits of having a Parliament and that they perceived some risks. There was some evidence of confusion between devolution and independence and there were concerns about the cost of setting up a Parliament, as well as about the prospect of higher taxes. The research also showed that the potential dominance of the central belt, a campaign theme during the 1979 referendum, had been effectively countered by the proposed use of proportional representation to elect the Parliament. In fact, the proposed voting scheme would leave the relative balance of representation between the central belt and the rest of Scotland virtually unchanged. At the 1997 general election, 53 per cent of

Scottish MPs were elected from seats in the central belt. Under the system adopted for the Scottish Parliament, this proportion would drop for Members of the Scottish Parliament (MSPs), but only to 51 per cent – and half of the decline is accounted for by splitting Orkney and Shetland into two constituencies for the Edinburgh Parliament.

One firm conclusion of this research was that there was a need for more public information. Some people thought that the Scottish Parliament would consist of Westminster MPs elected at the recent general election and there was a generally tendency for respondents to refer to tax-*raising* rather than tax-*varying* powers. This was seen as a potential threat, especially as these powers were also thought to be essential to a meaningful Parliament. The Parliament and taxes were very much linked in the public's mind. The negative conclusion, from Scotland Forward's viewpoint, was that opposition to increased taxes might even deflate support for the first referendum question. On the other hand, strong support for the Parliament might bolster support on the second question.

Further qualitative research was conducted in late June. This was again completed by System Three but on this occasion involved six focus group discussions with supporters and opponents of devolution, as well as those who remained undecided, in three locations in Scotland (Paisley, Aberdeen and Edinburgh). A report on the findings was presented to Scotland Forward at the end of July. Certain phrases were found to resonate well with respondents: 'taking control' and 'having a real voice' were found to be successful but though the idea of 'Scottish solutions' was found to have positive connotations it did not resonate as well as the others. The poll tax remained an emotive issue, and health and education were found to be high priorities. It was suggested that these issues would not have a major impact on the referendum, however, as there were high expectations that the new Labour government would 'deliver' on these across the United Kingdom. Moreover, the link between establishing a Scottish Parliament and improvements in health and education was not clear to participants. There was considerable confusion over the terms 'devolution' and 'Parliament' which were thought to be synonymous with 'independence' while references to relations with Westminster merely added to the confusion.

This research also suggested, however, that there was a strong desire among the electorate for more information about devolution. Moreover, the more informed people were, the more likely they were to support devolution.[6] This prompted Nigel Smith to urge Donald Dewar to launch a government-sponsored public information campaign on the issue. He referred to the New Zealand government's establishment of an Electoral Commission to fund information campaigns prior to its referendum on proportional representation and noted the levels of expenditure by previous Conservative ministers at the Scottish Office on publicising controversial policies such as nursery vouchers, school boards, the poll tax and testing in primary schools. Dewar refused to accede to this demand, however.

A major conclusion drawn from the second round of focus group research was that countering criticisms of devolution would be 'almost impossible'. Fears related to the cost of a Parliament, the possibility of higher taxes or the argument that it might be the first step to independence were simply unlikely to be allayed by any campaign.

The results of their research were used by Scotland Forward in devising its campaign strategy and were also made available to the three participating parties to use as they saw fit. Think Twice, on the other hand, had neither the time nor initially the money to engage in this kind of research. Nonetheless, its campaign followed the lessons drawn from Scotland Forward's work, concentrating on 'the pound in your sporran' issues, to use Kellner's phrase, and attempting to play upon misgivings about the taxation powers.

THE CAMPAIGN PROPER

A remarkable press conference in mid August officially launched Scotland Forward's 'short' campaign. It was chaired by Vestri and attended by Donald Dewar, Alex Salmond, Menzies Campbell (for the Liberal Democrats) and a range of other figures who had been involved in the home rule movement. Questions from journalists focused almost exclusively on events in Paisley. Gordon McMaster, Labour MP for Paisley South, had committed suicide, leaving a note accusing neighbouring Labour MP, Tommy Graham, of spreading malicious rumours about his private life. This took place against a background of allegations of corruption in local Labour politics and investigations into alleged electoral malpractice by Mohammad Sarwar, the newly elected Labour MP for Glasgow Govan. Labour sleaze was becoming an issue, to the embarrassment of the party leadership. It was almost universally agreed by participants that the press conference was badly managed and got the campaign off to a bad start. There were fears that 'Paisley' would dominate the campaign and that anti-devolutionists would be able to take advantage of Labour's troubles. Within days, massive advertising hoardings and newspaper advertisements appeared asking, 'Can you really face a Scottish Parliament?' with the answer 'NO NO' and pictures of Graham and Sarwar in the 'O's. The most remarkable feature of the press conference was Alex Salmond's support for Donald Dewar, following years of bitter rivalry between Labour and the SNP, when Dewar was under attack. Labour's problems were not over, however. At the launch of Labour's own campaign on the following day, the accompanying news release confronted the issue of sleaze head on. Dewar conceded that the previous 100 hours had been difficult for Labour in Scotland and announced that an internal party enquiry was being held before launching the case for devolution.

Tommy Graham presented Labour with further problems. Reports that he might speak out and give his version of events in Renfrewshire raised the possibility of a damaging issue dominating the news agenda. It was made clear to Graham that this would not be helpful and he disappeared from the limelight for the duration of the campaign but not before issuing a statement supporting the double Yes campaign, to which Brian Monteith responded, 'I think we will let this speak for itself' (*Courier*, 26 August 1997). Opponents attempted to associate devolution with sleaze and raised the prospect of the Parliament being dominated by corrupt and venal politicians. This was the equivalent of the 'central belt domination' argument which had proved effective in 1979. Michael Ancram, Conservative spokesman on constitutional affairs and a former Scottish MP now representing an English constituency, warned in a speech in Aberdeen that central belt dominance would be 'Paisley writ large' (*Scotsman*, 28 August 1997). Supporters of devolution feared that sleaze would fester away, undermining their campaign in much the same way as it had for the Conservatives during the general election. A twist to the sleaze issue was provided by the Orange Order with the Scottish Grand Master telling members that they must fight the 'tide of green corruption' if devolution came about. Labour, he warned, was the 'child of Roman Catholicism in the West of Scotland' and would dominate the Parliament (*Daily Record*, 28 August 1997). Fortunately for the Yes campaign, sleaze was removed from the news agenda – not due to tactical or strategic planning but rather to events in Paris in the early hours of Sunday, 31 August.

BUSINESS AND DEVOLUTION

In the 1979 referendum the leaders of Scottish industry and business had been generally hostile to devolution and prominent businessmen were actively involved in the Scotland Says No campaign. In the early

1990s, polls of business opinion suggested that there was still little enthusiasm for change.[7] Nonetheless, the Federation of Self-Employed and Small Businesses in Scotland participated in the Constitutional Convention and other business groups took observer status. Shortly after the 1997 election, Henry McLeish met representatives of the Federation, the CBI in Scotland and the Scottish Chambers of Commerce to reassure them that devolution would not damage business (*Scotland on Sunday*, 1 June 1997).

Despite this, at the start of the referendum campaign, on 21 August, a statement was issued by Sir Bruce Patullo, chairman of the Bank of Scotland and one of the most respected figures in Scottish business, opposing the tax-varying powers of the Parliament. In the *Scotsman*'s words, Patullo broke 'the silence of the country's devolution-sceptic business community with a calculated assault on the government's home rule proposals' and in this he had the support of the Bank's board, which included many other leading figures in Scottish business (*Scotsman*, 22 August 1997). In fact, Patullo was careful to emphasise that his concern was only with taxation powers which, he suggested, could damage jobs and discourage investment and he commented that 'Scottish business can live with a Yes, No' (*ibid.*). The response was swift and uncompromising. Patullo's claim that the Parliament would cost each taxpayer an additional £300 per year was dismissed by Alex Salmond, who produced detailed figures to undermine the argument, and by Deputy Prime Minister John Prescott, who was one of the first senior London politicians to travel north for the campaign. A few days later, Patullo appeared on the defensive, distancing himself from the Think Twice campaign, and the Bank's public relations director issued a statement denying that the Bank and its chairman had helped Think Twice. By the end of the week, Nigel Smith argued in the executive of Scotland Forward that Patullo's intervention had actually helped the Yes campaign since it had dislodged sleaze from the front pages. The momentum had been regained. Evidently Yes campaigners believed that the taxation issue was less damaging to their prospects than sleaze.

According to one account, Labour's strategy at this stage was deliberately designed to 'play rough' with Patullo in order to discourage him and others from speaking out again (Jones, 1997: 11). If this was the intention it appears to have worked. Few figures in the business community entered the referendum debate except for a number of co-ordinated interventions by supporters of devolution. One exception on the No side was Sir Alistair Grant, chairman of Scottish and Newcastle Breweries. What was curious about Grant's intervention was that he had previously stated his support for devolution. In December 1995, Nigel Smith had sent Grant a letter congratulating him for speaking out in favour of constitutional reform and urging a calmer response from business on the issue of devolution. During the campaign, however, Grant warned that the Parliament might become an 'elephant's graveyard for failed politicians' and repeated criticisms of the taxation powers which he had recently made in his company's annual report (*Scottish Daily Express*, 29 August 1997).

During the campaign, the Secretary of State made changes in the composition of the Scottish Economic Council (the body initially set up by the Attlee government and revived by Michael Forsyth – see pp.5, 40). Some prominent business people opposed to devolution and two involved with Think Twice were dismissed. Sir Matthew Goodwin, Think Twice treasurer, was removed and accused the government of stifling debate, suggesting that his dismissal was a warning to other people in public positions about speaking out against devolution (*Scottish Daily Mail*, 29 August 1997). Vera Weisfeld, a vice-chairman of Think Twice and founder of 'What Everyone Wants' department stores, was also removed from the Council as was Rodger Young, a member of the board of the Bank of Scotland, headed by Sir Bruce Patullo.

On the other hand, there was evidence of significant support among business and industry for the devolution proposals. James Scott, who had formerly headed the Industry Department for Scotland in the Scottish Office and also Scottish Financial Enterprise, the body which represents Scottish financial institutions, publicly endorsed the Yes Yes campaign and announced that he would seek to stand for the Parliament as an SNP candidate. Later in the campaign, the SNP introduced a number of other prominent business supporters who advocated a Yes Yes vote including Brian Soutar, founder of a multi-national transport company and reputedly the richest person in Scotland. Sir Lewis Robertson, former head of the Scottish Development Agency, also came forward to support the Yes Yes campaign. The Scottish Council Foundation, a recently established think tank associated with the respected Scottish Council (Development and Industry), produced a *Business Guide to Devolution* which was written to assuage fears in the business community (Scottish Council Foundation, 1997). The *Daily Record*, which was enthusiastically pro-devolution, produced a list of ten prominent pro-devolution businessmen (*Daily Record*, 27 August 1997).

The relatively low profile adopted by business opponents of devolution during the referendum campaign is explained by the fact that they had largely been neutralised before the campaign got going.

The CBI (Scotland) had concluded after the general election that devolution would happen anyway and that there was little to be gained, and potentially much to be lost, by attacking a popular policy deriving from a government with a huge electoral mandate. As compared with 1979, business appeared less hostile to devolution. Yes campaigners made good use of business supporters, priming key figures to speak out, and managed to neutralise the considerable opposition which remained.

CONSERVATIVE DILEMMAS

The referendum presented the Conservatives with a number of problems. The prospect of another humiliating defeat made getting involved in the campaign an unattractive proposition but, having been the main opponents of devolution over the previous 18 years, they clearly had to play some sort of role in the campaign. Many activists had no stomach for another battle, however. William Hague, the new leader, had no Scottish MPs and the Scottish party chairman had been forced to resign at the outset of the general election campaign over accusations relating to his private life. There were a number of prominent Scots representing English constituencies. Michael Ancram had been defeated as Tory MP for Edinburgh South in 1987 but had been elected for Devizes in 1992 and again in 1997. He became the Conservatives' Constitutional Affairs spokesman after the election, but his background as the Scottish Minister responsible for the introduction of the poll tax proved a hindrance. This was frequently referred to during the campaign by supporters of devolution, putting to good use System Three's research finding that the poll tax still had potent symbolism.

The Conservative preference was to control Think Twice without being seen to do so. Party members were urged to channel their energies through the organisation. However, it was inevitable that some prominent Conservatives would be forced to play an active part in the campaign as representatives of the party. The leadership of Think Twice urged party headquarters in London to limit the number of senior Conservatives sent north for the campaign. It was acknowledged that William Hague, as Leader of the Opposition and former Secretary of State for Wales, should have a role as, indeed, should Peter Lilley as Shadow Chancellor, given the central importance of tax for the anti-devolutionists, but other senior Conservatives should stay away. For the most part this advice was heeded. Ancram was the only other prominent Conservative representing an English seat to have a major role in the campaign. Peter Fraser's part in the campaign was performed under the aegis of Think Twice rather than the Conservative Party, though his role included maintaining a watching brief on Monteith's activities. The part to be played by Michael Forsyth, former Secretary of State for Scotland, was discussed and it was agreed in Think Twice that should Forsyth wish to be involved then he would be welcomed but that he would not be approached. In the event, the man who popularised the term 'tartan tax' made no public statement during the campaign.

The pro-devolution forces also had problems (if far less important) with regard to what to do about Conservatives. Polls showed that a substantial minority of Conservative voters supported devolution and some pro-devolutionists wanted to provide some means of encouraging these people to vote Yes Yes in the referendum. Others, on the other hand, preferred to equate anti-devolutionists with the Conservatives, hoping to capitalise on the party's unpopularity in Scotland. In the event, this proved a less important problem than had been anticipated before the election. Little effort was made to attract Conservatives to Scotland Forward. No Conservatives were active in the organisation at national level and very few were involved on the ground (see Chapter 5).

One unforeseen campaign contribution from a prominent Conservative was completely unplanned. Margaret Thatcher, the *bête noir* of Scottish politics, had an engagement to address a conference of American travel agents in Glasgow during the last week of the campaign. This was a private engagement but its venue made it impossible to escape media attention and Mrs Thatcher issued a statement opposing devolution. This visit was a godsend to Yes campaigners (and cartoonists). The *Daily Record* professed itself to be:

> DELIGHTED she is here. Why? Because she's the best possible reason yet why Scots should vote YES YES on Thursday. Thatcher ruled Scotland from London for more than a decade and caused untold misery. We didn't vote for her. Again and again the Scottish voters rejected her cynical brand of greed and callousness. But we could not escape her malign influence ... VOTE YES, YES – FOR NO MORE MAGGIES. (*Daily Record*, 9 September 1997)

The general view amongst anti-devolutionists was that paying her the equivalent fee she received for the speech in order to stay away would have been good use of the money that they had raised.

DIANA'S DEATH

In the 1970s, the monarchy had made its doubts about devolution known but the royal family had other problems to contend with in 1997. The death of Diana, Princess of Wales, had a devastating effect on the campaign. The media immediately turned its focus away from devolution. Mrs Frances Shand-Kydd, Diana's mother and a Scottish resident, had entered the debate in the early stages of the campaign with a plea for a strong turnout to provide a clear indication of support for or opposition to a Scottish Parliament. She informed the press that she had made up her mind on the first question but had yet to decide on the second, which was taken to mean that she intended to vote either Yes Yes or Yes No.

With the death of Diana, however, campaigning was officially suspended until after the funeral on Saturday 6 September, although in some localities there was still a little activity. There was some media comment on the possibility of postponing the date of the referendum and much speculation on the likely impact of her death on the campaign. As a British institution with strong Unionist symbolism, the overwhelming focus on the monarchy on the part of the media might have resulted in an increase in opposition to devolution since it was bound to remind voters of their Britishness. However, Diana's ambiguous status – divorced from the Prince of Wales and, strictly speaking, no longer part of the royal family – made her simultaneously part of the establishment and anti-establishment. This ambiguity came to the fore during the week leading up to the funeral when the Queen was criticised by normally loyal newspapers for failing to appear in public or to allow flags at Royal residences to fly at half-mast.

The plans of campaigners and the media were thrown into confusion. Special television programmes had to be postponed or abandoned. Before Diana's death the campaign was generally described by commentators as being 'low key'. In later interviews, key participants suggested that the campaign was just about to 'take off'. Indeed, one journalist commented that the bitterness which was largely absent from the campaign and the relative absence of complaints to the broadcast media, at least as compared with a general election, was a result of two factors: the expectation that the result was a foregone conclusion and the removal of a week of campaigning at a crucial stage due to Diana's death. During the first part of the week leading up to the funeral, within both Scotland Forward and Think Twice the general impression was that the death had helped the anti-devolution cause. Scotland Forward's feeling was based on the belief that it was better prepared than Think Twice and would therefore suffer more disruption. A special event planned by the *Daily Record* in support of Scotland Forward's campaign on the Sunday prior to polling day had to be postponed and the paper altered its plans in order to issue special commemorative material on Diana. Think Twice leaders believed that they would benefit from the monarchy's status as an important British institution. Not all shared these views, however. George Reid of the SNP informed a meeting of the executive of Scotland Forward in the week before the funeral that his experience had been that there was an anti-establishment mood among the voters. The minutes of the executive meeting held on 2 September also note that the 'lack of mention of tax, tax-varying powers and the second question, since the death of Diana, Princess of Wales might, actually, be positive'. After the campaign was over, this interpretation was more widely shared by supporters and opponents of devolution alike. Some Scotland Forward press conferences before the death had become quite heated but the campaign break ensured that potential bad publicity arising from this never appeared.

Think Twice effectively closed down for the purposes of public campaigning during the week leading up to the funeral although much preparatory work went on in private. This was not quite the case amongst supporters of devolution. There was much confusion among local campaigners about what to do and the Scotland Forward campaigns organiser reported to the executive that a lot of time was being spent giving advice on the level and type of campaigning which was permissible. Each of the three parties campaigning for a Yes Yes vote agreed that leafleting could go ahead, but not canvassing. Jack McConnell of the Labour Party reported, however, that Labour activists had encountered some opposition to leafleting. Many activities which had been planned were re-scheduled and squeezed into the final few days of the campaign but others were abandoned altogether. A planned photo-opportunity involving supporters of devolution on Seil Island, 'crossing the bridge over the Atlantic' to vote, was cancelled as Diana's mother lived on the island.

It is difficult to assess the impact of Diana's death on the outcome of the referendum. The campaign was certainly severely disrupted. One of the key findings of research carried out by Scotland Forward in late 1996 was that pro-change forces tend to lose support during referendum campaigns. The advice offered by Peter Kellner had been that the pro-devolution forces should seek to protect their advantage among the electorate and not expect to make gains. If these assessments were correct, and assuming *ceteris paribus*, then the disruption in the campaign was probably to the advantage of supporters of devolution. However, not all else was equal and it is difficult to assess the impact of the focus shifting to a very British dimension, especially to such a symbolically significant institution as the monarchy, or the significance of the sympathy for Diana as an anti-establishment figure.

THE LAST 100 HOURS

Campaigning resumed on Sunday 7 September, the day after Diana's funeral. Scotland Forward's condensed campaign in the final four days before polling began with Sean Connery, who had given public support to the SNP for many years, quoting the Declaration of Arbroath (1320) – 'It is not for glory, it is not for riches, neither is it for honour, but it is for liberty alone that we fight' – alongside Chancellor Gordon Brown claiming, more prosaically, that the Scottish Parliament would work with business to create new jobs. Connery had given his backing to the Yes campaign at the outset ('Yesh! Yesh!' was the headline in the *Daily Record*, 25 August 1997) and on the eve of poll the *Sun's* front-page headline was 'Stand Up for Scotland Says Sean Connery'. During the campaign he appears to have persuaded the actor Michael Caine to endorse devolution when appearing at the Edinburgh Film Festival, although the latter had no apparent association with Scotland.

Opponents concentrated on sleaze, the tartan tax and an uncertain future. Think Twice demanded that Labour publish an enquiry into Glasgow City Council. Tam Dalyell warned that the 'tartan tax' would lead to a 'brain drain' and that devolution would inevitably lead to independence. The *Press and Journal* reported Keith Schellenberg, a controversial Highland landowner, arguing against a Scottish Parliament and 'any illogical counter-productive ideology like land reform in the Highlands' (*Press and Journal*, 8 September 1997) which gave heart to devolutionists, many of whom hoped for exactly what Schellenberg warned against. A change of emphasis emerged amongst anti-devolutionists in the closing stages, as it became clear that there was no shift in public opinion. Michael Ancram warned that a low turnout would raise doubts about the legitimacy of the result. This had become the last hope of the anti-devolutionists.

Jim Sillars, former deputy leader of the SNP, used his column in the *Sun* two days before polling to urge voters to abstain, although he conceded that the result was a foregone conclusion. Sillars had joined the SNP in 1981 as a pragmatist who supported devolution but he had become more hard-line during his time as an SNP MP between 1988 and 1992. Devolution, he believed, would stall Scotland's move towards independence. In this respect he disagreed fundamentally with Tam Dalyell, with whom he had travelled around Scotland debating devolution in 1979, although Sillars' recommendation in 1997 differed sharply from that which he had made 18 years before. Peter Mandelson appeared to endorse Sillars' position when he reportedly urged Nationalists not to vote for the Scottish Parliament as to do so was to vote for a 'Scotland that is an integral part of the United Kingdom' (*Scottish Daily Mail*, 10 September 1997). This was either a Machiavellian ploy designed to allay the fears of Unionist-inclined voters and help Labour lay claim to full credit for devolution after the result, or an unusual example of a blunder by New Labour's renowned strategist. What was not in doubt was that it contradicted agreements reached between the parties within Scotland Forward and left an impression of metropolitan meddling.

Both the Prime Minister and the Conservative leader were in Scotland during the last week of the campaign. Tony Blair received extensive coverage. He featured on the front pages of both the *Record* (8 and 9 September) and the *Sun* (9 September) and had lengthy interviews reported in the *Herald* and the *Record*. All the main papers published photographs of the Prime Minister and his wife being 'mobbed' by enthusiastic crowds in Glasgow and Edinburgh. 'The Blairs were treated like heroes', said the *Scotsman*, 'the Special Branch officers could have gone to the pictures'. Reporting of William Hague's campaigning was more muted. He addressed pupils at Edinburgh Royal High School but they promptly voted to support a Parliament. On the eve of poll, most of the press carried a picture of a lonely looking Hague with Loch Lomond in the background. This seemed to symbolise the Conservative predicament in Scotland. Hague argued that Scottish tourism would be damaged if a Scottish Parliament imposed a 'tourism tax' and that devolution threatened the existence of the United Kingdom. However, his speech was overshadowed by Margaret Thatcher's visit to Glasgow. Although Hague indicated that he would accept the will of the Scottish people, Mrs Thatcher argued that a majority support for devolution did not make it right. This was further evidence of Conservative disarray.

As the campaign drew to a close there was much that devolutionists could be pleased with. As discussed in Chapter 2, Scottish antipathy to Margaret Thatcher's personality and policies had contributed significantly to the developing consensus amongst non-Conservatives in favour of constitutional change during the 1980s. Her presence in Scotland just before the referendum and that of William Hague, a leader with no Scottish MPs, was perceived by opponents and supporters of devolution alike as a boost to the devolution cause. Indeed, the clear identification of the Conservatives with opposition to change played into the hands of supporters of constitutional change. Economic arguments were made on all sides but the emphasis, especially from supporters of change, was on emotional messages. In conformity with guidance from Scotland Forward's research, heroic images from Scotland's distant past – William Wallace, 'Braveheart' and the Declaration of Arbroath – jostled with more recent emotive imagery and messages, including pictures of the daughters of the late Labour leader, John Smith, urging a Yes Yes vote in honour of their father (*Daily Record*, 10 September) and the claim that 'Barnsley get more money (from Sky Television) than (the) whole of Scottish football' (*Sun*, 9 September). There was little that opponents could offer to combat these sorts of appeals to emotion.

CONCLUSION

At a superficial level the conduct of the national campaign in the referendum was similar to what happens at a general election. There were visits to different parts of the country by party bigwigs, advertising hoardings urged people to vote one way or another, press conferences were called and press releases issued and politicians debated on television. On the other hand, in the Scottish context, election campaigns also involve complex interactions between four distinct party campaigns, a series of televised party election broadcasts and discussion of a wide range of issues. Their purpose is to elect Members of Parliament in 72 different constituencies, across which their prospects vary widely, and three of the parties have to integrate their strategy and tactics with the wider United Kingdom campaign. None of these applied in the referendum. There was only one central issue (albeit two questions) and two opposing campaigns; there were no partisan broadcasts and in terms of the result, constituencies were irrelevant.

In evaluating the 1997 campaign a more fruitful comparison is with the 1979 Scottish referendum campaign. In both cases the issue was devolution, cross-party campaigns were established and the familiar campaign methods were employed. The differences are more striking, however. Firstly, as compared with 1979 the Yes campaign in 1997 was much more unified. The three major pro-devolution parties worked together, whereas Labour had stood aloof in 1979. Secondly, and critically, the Labour Party itself was almost 100 per cent behind devolution, having been seriously divided in the previous referendum. Thirdly, on the Yes side, as we have seen, much more effort went into preparing for the campaign. Between 1979 and 1997 political campaigning became more professional and sophisticated and in line with this trend the Yes supporters commissioned serious research to guide their campaign strategy. Fourthly, the No campaign was undeniably weaker than in 1979. Business did not provide the support that it previously had and neither did prominent Labour dissidents or non-partisan celebrities. The burden of campaigning for a No vote had to be borne almost entirely by a thoroughly demoralised Conservative Party. Finally, due to the chance (or mischance) of Diana's death the campaign ended in a frenzy of activity and we have suggested that this aroused the interest of the voters and probably worked to the benefit of the pro-devolution forces.

One other important difference between between 1979 and 1997 is that in the latter case the Scottish press, and especially the most widely read papers, were more enthusiastically in favour of a Parliament for Scotland. The mass media are participants in, as well as reporters of, general election campaigns and this was no less true of the referendum. The role of the media is considered in Chapter 4.

NOTES

1. Much of the material in this chapter derives from interviews with participants, reports in the media and information supplied by the various organisations active in the referendum campaign. We were particularly fortunate in having access to the files of Scotland Forward. The political parties were, understandably, more reluctant to provide access to information since future campaigns may be based on previously gathered intelligence. Think Twice was not established until shortly before the referendum and had neither the time nor the resources to engage in the kind of pre-campaign research which Scotland Forward undertook.
2. The sample was split into two groups each comprising 750 respondents. The first group were presented with the positive statements first while the negative statements were presented first to the second group. The purpose of this procedure was to discover whether an initial focus on 'fears' associated with devolution would produce a less favourable response. In fact there were no significant differences between the two groups.
3. Those who listed themselves as 'British' were Yvonne Strachan (of the Transport and General Workers Union), Matthew Smith (of UNISON), Kevin Dunion (Director of Friends of the Earth), Morag Alexander (Director of the Equal Opportunities Commission in Scotland), Margaret Anne Ford (Managing Director of Eglinton Management Centre), Stefan Kay (Liberal Democrat and Chief Executive of Inveresk Group) and Margaret Smith (Leader of Aberdeen City Council). Those who listed themselves as 'Scottish' were Esther Robertson (of the Scottish Constitutional Convention), Bill Spiers

(Deputy General Secretary of the STUC), Joan Mitchell (Liberal Democrat Councillor in Dumfries and Galloway) and Malcolm McLeod (of Labour Campaign for a Scottish Parliament). There were no papers for Ian McKay (Assistant Secretary of the Educational Institute of Scotland) and Nigel Smith, chairman of Scotland Forward (Managing Director of David Auld Valves Ltd).

4. An address list of representatives of the following organisations was amongst the Scotland Forward papers:

   Campaign for a Scottish Parliament, the Church of Scotland, the Church of Scotland Women's Guild, PTC, Democratic Left Scotland, the Iona Community, Partnership for a Parliament, Scottish Council for Voluntary Organisations, the AEEU, the Scottish Joint Action Group, Common Cause, CPSA, Professor Alice Brown of the Politics Department in Edinburgh University, NUS Scotland, Church and Nation Committee of Church of Scotland, the Scottish Constitutional Convention, ACTS, Charter 88, Democracy for Scotland, Campaign for a Scottish Parliament, Coalition for Scottish Democracy, UNISON, TGWU, Glasgow TUC, MSF, Women's Forum Scotland, AUT (Scotland), Labour Campaign for a Scottish Parliament, STUC, Scottish Civic Assembly, Edinburgh University Campaign for a Scottish Parliament, the Communist Party of Scotland, Scottish Labour Action, Co-operative Party.

5. Labour's own research in Scotland, before the general election, found the same concern. This was leaked to the press.

6. An alternative interpretation of the relationship between information and opinion on devolution is, of course, that opponents were likely to be less interested in the subject than supporters.

7. In August 1991, for example, a poll of members of the Scottish Chambers of Commerce found that 67 per cent favoured the constitutional status quo.

4

The Scottish Media and
the Referendum

The distinctiveness of Scotland within the United Kingdom is both reflected in and bolstered by the fact that there are specifically Scottish mass media (see MacInnes, 1992, 1993). This is especially the case with respect to the press. Three types of papers selling in Scotland can be differentiated – the 'purely Scottish' which are entirely produced in Scotland, Scottish editions of national (United Kingdom) papers and 'English' papers. The circulation figures for daily papers (Table 4.1) show that the tabloid end of the market is dominated by the 'purely Scottish' *Daily Record* which sells almost as many copies as all other tabloid titles combined. Although the *Record* is a stable-mate of the *Daily Mirror*, it is separately edited and produced in Glasgow and focuses very strongly on 'internal' Scottish affairs. The other tabloids are Scottish versions of national papers and they also, to a greater or lesser degree, provide coverage of matters of interest to a Scottish audience. Among the broadsheets, the four purely Scottish papers easily outsell the others. The *Herald* and the *Scotsman*, emanating from Glasgow and Edinburgh respectively, see themselves as Scottish national newspapers while the *Press and Journal* (Aberdeen) and the *Courier* (Dundee) are regional papers with large circulations in their respective areas. Although all four broadsheets carry United Kingdom and international news, they are distinctively Scottish, giving a high profile to Scottish news. Overall, the readership of 'English' daily newspapers in Scotland – whether tabloid or broadsheet – is very small. On Sundays the picture is similar. The *Sunday Mail* (from the same stable as the *Record*) and the indefatigable and eccentric *Sunday Post* have by far the largest circulations, with *Scotland on Sunday* (sister paper of the *Scotsman* and produced, as the title suggests, specifically for Scottish readers) and the *Sunday Times* (which includes a special Scottish supplement) leading among the quality press.

Television in Scotland is less distinctive than the press in that most output derives from the United Kingdom networks. Nonetheless, BBC Scotland, based in Glasgow, has some autonomy and broadcasts daily

Table 4.1: Newspaper circulation in Scotland

Dailies Tabloids		Broadsheets	
Daily Record	696,332a	Press & Journal (Aberdeen)	105,176a
The Sun	392,502c	The Herald	102,682a
Scottish Daily Express	122,089c	Courier (Dundee)	97,727a
Scottish Daily Mail	116,607c	The Scotsman	81,727a
Scottish Daily Star	41,121c	The Times	28,823c
Scottish Mirror	38,000c	Daily Telegraph	27,290b
		The Guardian	17,880b
		The Independent	13,097b
Sundays Tabloids		Broadsheets	
Sunday Mail	818,081a	Scotland on Sunday	113,516a
Sunday Post	791,400a	Sunday Times	88,344d
News of the World	383,742d	Observer	not available
Sunday Express	123,000d	Sunday Telegraph	30,000d
Mail on Sunday	106,083d	Independent on Sunday	14,500d
The People	65,000d		

Notes: a = Audit Bureau of Circulations (ABC) figure (July–December 1997); b = estimated ABC figures as supplied by 'The Media Shop', Glasgow; c = trade estimates for sales in Scotland, provided by 'John Menzies' (as printed in the *Drum*, September 1997); d = sales in September 1997 as reported by newspapers concerned.

television news programmes as well as regular current affairs programmes catering for the Scottish audience. The same is true of the three independent television companies – Scottish Television (STV, which covers central Scotland), Grampian (covering the Highlands, Islands and the north-east) and Border (which rather uncomfortably straddles the Scottish–English border). As elsewhere in the United Kingdom, most radio stations – local and national, BBC or independent – concentrate on music, but BBC Radio Scotland is a national station with a large news and current affairs content. The difference between Scotland and other 'regions' of the United Kingdom in respect of news broadcasting is highlighted by Denver and Hands in their study of campaigning in the 1992 election (1997a: ch. 6). They report that television in Scotland gives far more attention to 'regional' matters than regional media in England, and coverage of elections in particular is very distinctive. Separate party election broadcasts are made for Scotland and in 1992 BBC Scotland ran a series of 'Scottish Hustings' on television while STV had a 'Scottish 500' series in which Scottish politicians were questioned by 500 representative Scottish voters. In 1997 the 'Scottish 500' was repeated and the BBC broadcast 12 editions of 'Campaign Scotland' and three of 'Words with

Wark' (Kirsty Wark being a well-known Scottish television presenter) in which audiences questioned Scottish politicians.

In this context, then, we would expect the Scottish media to provide massive coverage of the referendum campaign and of the issues involved since the referendum was clearly a very big Scottish story. What sets Scotland apart from English regions so far as political coverage by the media is concerned – it has an extra political dimension with specifically Scottish issues and personalities – was encapsulated in the referendum itself.

BROADCASTING[1]

The rules of the game
Broadcast coverage of election campaigns (and of politics more generally) is guided by a legal framework and a set of standard operating procedures based on the networks' interpretations of the rules, their own experience and a number of judicial decisions. The legal framework governing political broadcasting derives from the BBC's Licence and Agreement with the government, the Broadcasting Act of 1990 and relevant provisions of the Representation of the People Act of 1983. The general requirement is that broadcasters must show 'due impartiality' in their coverage of politics, but the regulations do not spell out in any detail what this means. In practice, during general elections impartiality is interpreted to mean that coverage must be balanced in terms of time. This does not mean equality for all points of view. Rather the broadcasters and the parties agree ratios for allocating time to each party and programme makers then 'stopwatch' political coverage and keep meticulous records to ensure that they stick to the agreed allocation.

Covering a referendum poses problems, however. The requirement for impartiality remains but broadcasters lack experience of referendums and there is no widely acknowledged set of ground rules to guide them. The main difficulty revolves around the question of balanced coverage. Is 'balance' to be interpreted as balance between the political parties or between the opposing sides on the referendum issue? In the 1975 United Kingdom referendum on membership of the European Community, the government allowed the broadcasters to use their discretion. The BBC decided that there should be a 50:50 time split between coverage of the pro- and anti-forces in campaign news coverage. The Independent Broadcasting Authority (IBA), which regulated commercial television, did not make a rigid rule about time balance, however. As far as 'party political' broadcasting was concerned, it was agreed, at the prompting of the government, that there should be 'referendum broadcasts' analogous to party election broadcasts but that they would be allocated to and under the control of the 'umbrella' groups campaigning on each side. Eight such broadcasts were made – four for each side (for details see Smith, 1976).

In the Scottish referendum of 1979 things did not go so smoothly (see Fowler, 1981). The government proposed that party political broadcasts which were scheduled during the campaign should go ahead. This would have meant a 3:1 split in favour of the devolution proposals (Labour, the Liberals and the SNP for, the Conservatives against) and was a clear reversal of the approach taken in 1975. Some Labour anti-devolutionists, including Brian Wilson (who by 1997 was a junior minister at the Scottish Office and supported government policy by advocating a Yes Yes vote), issued a writ in the Court of Session to prevent the IBA going ahead with the broadcasts on the grounds that they breached the requirement for balance. The judge agreed and prohibited the broadcasts (see Chapter 1). The BBC fell into line and attempts by the politicians to reach a compromise failed. As a result, there were no referendum broadcasts of the kind that had been produced in 1975. There was, of course, considerable coverage of the referendum on television, with the BBC setting up an autonomous referendum unit to plan and monitor coverage, and both channels sought to maintain impartiality through a 50:50 balance of time between the Yes and No sides.

Despite broadcasters' pleas for more government guidance on coverage of future referendums, nothing had happened by 1997. The Conservatives had little interest in referendums and once Labour decided to have one there was little time to think about broadcasting rules. As a result, the difficulties experienced in 1979 reappeared. As in the first referendum, three of Scotland's main parties supported devolution while only the Conservatives, now without any Scottish MPs following the May election, were opposed to it. Mindful of the court case in 1979, broadcasters decided at an early stage that there would be no campaign broadcasts by the parties or *ad hoc* groups. Nonetheless, in a series of briefings between broadcasters and interested parties held shortly after the general election, supporters of devolution rehearsed the familiar refrain that 'fairness' required that the disparity in the line up of the parties should be taken into account in other television and radio coverage. There was also a new problem in 1997 – the possibility of a Yes No vote meant that Scottish opinion could not be neatly divided into two camps with each being given equal coverage.

The response of the BBC was once again to set up a special referendum unit to oversee coverage of both the Scottish and Welsh referendums. A set of guidelines was drawn up in London and sent to BBC Scotland but these were not published, nor made available to the parties and other campaigners. The guidelines conceded that account had to be taken of the party imbalance but also suggested that, since this might not reflect public opinion on devolution, an approach was required which somehow took account both of the 3:1 party split on the issue and the desirability of a 50:50 split for 'non-party' campaigners. Thus the BBC in Scotland based its approach to referendum campaign coverage on a fairly loose and vague set of guidelines; coverage was intended to be flexible and, in some vague way, fair. Whether some approximation to fairness was actually achieved in television coverage is a largely subjective matter. During and after the campaign Scotland Forward supporters complained that the BBC had not fulfilled its statutory obligation to provide public information on the issues involved and relations between the BBC and Scotland Forward and the SNP were strained. In particular, officials of Scotland Forward and the SNP suggested that decision-making by BBC staff in London demonstrated an ignorance of the political situation in Scotland.[2] For their part, BBC staff in London saw an ulterior motive behind these sorts of complaints, namely a desire to extend the devolution debate to include devolution from the BBC nationally to BBC Scotland. On the other hand, a report written by independent assessors for the Broadcasting Council for Scotland some months after the referendum concluded that there had been bias in some BBC news coverage *in favour* of supporters of devolution (BBC, 1997).

Campaign coverage

The coverage of general election campaigns by television in Scotland (and in English regions) follows well-worn paths. Daily news magazine programmes – Reporting Scotland (BBC), Scotland Today (STV) and North Tonight (Grampian) – follow the national news in the early evening. They provide a familiar mix – reports of campaigning and press conferences by leading Scottish politicians and of visits to Scotland by national leaders; discussion of issues of special relevance to Scotland (especially, in the last two elections, the question of constitutional change); profiles of individual constituencies; analysis of opinion poll results; interviews with party spokespersons and occasional items of trivia designed to add a humorous touch.

With two exceptions these also formed the staple of referendum reporting. For obvious reasons there were no constituency profiles and there was only one issue to discuss (although it had, of course, many ramifications). During the first week of the campaign (25–29 August) there was a steady stream of campaign reporting in the magazine programmes. In the following week, however, the referendum was clearly overshadowed by the events surrounding the death and funeral of the Princess of Wales. Since campaigning was suspended there was nothing very much for television to report in any case. In the last few days, however, from 8–11 September it would be fair to say that the referendum dominated television news in Scotland. Television is the electorate's most important source of political information and the early evening news magazines command substantial audiences. During the three weeks of the campaign the average audience for Reporting Scotland was 578,000 while Scotland Today was viewed by an average of 423,000 people and North Tonight by 139,000.[3]

In addition to the regular daily news programmes, both the BBC and the independent companies mounted special referendum programmes. Three editions of BBC1's 'Cross Examination' discussion programme (shown on Tuesday 26 August and on the Monday and Tuesday before polling day with an average audience of 155,000) were devoted to devolution, the last of them featuring Donald Dewar facing a panel of sceptics. In addition, on the Tuesday before voting BBC2 screened 'Catalonia to Caledonia' which explored the effects of devolution in Spain. The BBC's main contribution to the referendum debate, however, was an hour-long 'Panorama Special', broadcast on the eve of the poll from the old Edinburgh Royal High School (which had been intended to be the home of the Scottish Assembly in 1979). This was a live debate and involved politicians, celebrities and others who were supporting each side being cross-examined by two leading Scottish advocates, Donald Findlay of Think Twice and Des Browne, Labour MP for Kilmarnock. An invited audience also participated and the BBC had aimed for 50:50 representation of supporters and opponents among the audience. The plans for this programme led to considerable controversy about the format of the programme, the choice of who would be cross-examined and the composition of the audience (see Brogan and Campbell, 1997). The three pro-devolution parties objected that the programme was 'inherently biased' and 'ill-conceived' and that the BBC was manufacturing or exaggerating the extent of opposition to devolution. At one stage there was talk of some parties boycotting the programme. It was also rumoured that a number of young Conservative supporters had to be brought from Manchester to boost the anti-devolution numbers in the audience but that, in the event, they were not allowed to participate as they had over-indulged in alcohol en route. The programme, which attracted 239,000 viewers in Scotland, might have been livelier had they taken part.

STV and Border screened a half-hour referendum special on Thursday 28 August in which Donald Findlay put the case for a No No vote, followed by a studio debate. This attracted 158,000 viewers in the STV area. On the same evening Grampian broadcast 'Scotland's Parliament', which offered an informative guide to the devolution proposals and was viewed by 61,000. On the last Monday of the campaign all three independent channels offered 'Scotland Debates', which followed the familiar 'Question Time' format. This was screened at prime viewing time (8.30pm) by STV and Grampian (but at 10.40pm by Border), lasted for 90 minutes and had an audience of 300,000 in the Grampian and STV areas. The programme was produced by STV and in selecting the audience the intention was to have a representative cross-section of the Scottish public. As a consequence, the audience was clearly and noisily pro-devolution, much to the satisfaction of the Yes campaigners.

A lighter side to television coverage of the referendum was introduced by Channel 4. On each evening during the last week of the campaign a short (ten-minute) programme was shown, starring the impressionists and comedians Alistair McGowan and Jonathan Watson, in which they humorously portrayed Scottish sporting celebrities discussing how they would vote.

On the night of the referendum both BBC and independent television (as well as numerous radio stations) mounted full-scale results programmes ('Scotland Decides'), with the usual array of studio pundits and politicians, outside broadcasts from the counts and computer graphics. The BBC programme was broadcast across the entire United Kingdom and continued until around six o'clock in the morning. Since there were only 32 counts to report and the overall outcome quickly became clear, there was inevitably some repetition and inconsequential time-filling in these programmes but they nonetheless provided a comprehensive service for viewers interested enough to stay up late.

Conclusion

It is clear that broadcasting during the referendum once again raised difficulties. The basic problem was that there were no clear guidelines for the broadcasters. The rules of the game had to be determined by those who would have to implement them rather than some independent body and this led to some acrimony, especially between the BBC and campaigners on the Yes side. A possible way out of these difficulties was proposed in 1996 by an independent Commission on the Conduct of Referendums, chaired by Sir Patrick Nairne, which was established jointly by the Constitution Unit, an academic think tank in University College London, and the Electoral Reform Society. The report of the Commission recommended that a balance should be maintained between the competing viewpoints in a referendum rather than between the different parties. It also recommended that a limited amount of air time should be set aside for broadcasts which would be the responsibility of recognised umbrella campaign organisations (Constitution Unit, 1996). Similarly, in its report on the funding of political parties (Committee on Standards in Public Life, 1998) the Neill Committee proposed that free air time should be granted to the two sides in referendum campaigns. Unfortunately these suggestions raise as many problems as they solve, particularly in relation to umbrella organisations – what if there are many of these, or none? Also, the kinds of complaints, which we have referred to, mostly made by the Yes side in the Scottish referendum would persist. Nonetheless, the 1997 Scottish referendum highlighted the fact that in the absence of clear guidelines, or a statutory body with the authority to provide guidelines, broadcasters are placed in an invidious position of having to devise their own rules which results in complaints being directed at them, especially when competing broadcasters interpret vague notions of 'fairness' in different ways.

It should be said, however, that these problems and debates were and are of interest only to political 'insiders' and broadcasters themselves. During the referendum they passed without very much public comment and few Scottish voters would have been aware of the negotiations and arguments that took place. The average voter, sitting at home watching television, would have been aware that the referendum was taking place, been able to follow the main events of the campaign through news programmes, had the chance to hear the issues debated in more detail and, finally, to watch the results being announced, analysed and discussed at length.

THE SCOTTISH MORNING PRESS

Positions taken
Unlike radio and television, political coverage in newspapers is uninhibited by legal regulation and most Scottish papers took a clear stand on the referendum issue. Table 4.2 compares (where appropriate) the papers' positions in 1997 with their views at the time of the 1979 referendum. Our description of the *Daily Record* and

Sunday Mail as 'strongly pro' on both occasions is unsurprising as both are strongly Labour-supporting papers. In 1997 the *Record* was virtually a mouthpiece for Scotland Forward. In the first week of the campaign (25–30 August) it headlined Sean Connery's backing for devolution (*Yesh! Yesh!*), ridiculed the proposed visit to Scotland of Margaret Thatcher and published a list of pro-devolution business-men to counter claims that business was opposed to home rule. In the final three days of the campaign front-page headlines included 'YES! Vote for bright new Scotland', 'Devo: do it for dad!' (accompanied by a picture of John Smith's daughters) and other pieces included 'Two reasons for voting Yes! Yes!' (over pictures of Margaret Thatcher and William Hague). On voting day itself the front page comprised appeals for a double Yes vote. There was also a centre page spread titled 'Scotland, We Love You', featuring members of the public saying why they love Scotland, and even the sports pages carried pictures of sports stars all advocating a Yes vote.

Table 4.2: Newspapers' attitudes to devolution, 1979 and 1997

	1979	1997
Daily Record	Strongly Pro	Strongly Pro
The Sun	n/a	Strongly Pro
Scottish Daily Express	Strongly Anti	Strongly Pro (at end)
Scottish Daily Mail	n/a	Strongly Anti
Press & Journal	No commitment	No commitment
The (Glasgow) Herald	Pro	Strongly Pro
Courier	Strongly Anti	Strongly Anti
The Scotsman	Strongly Pro	Pro
Sunday Mail	Strongly Pro	Strongly Pro
Sunday Post	Sceptical	Anti
Scotland on Sunday	n/a	Pro

Note: The table is confined to what might be defined as 'Scottish' papers.

In 1979 there was no separate Scottish edition of the *Sun* and at that time – and throughout the 1980s and early 1990s – the paper strongly and stridently supported the Conservatives. In the 1992 election, however, the Scottish *Sun*, while still anti-Labour, caused something of a sensation by coming out in favour of the SNP. In the 1997 election there was another change of tack. Following the line laid down in London, the Scottish version of the *Sun* backed Tony Blair and Labour, although it continued to give the SNP a favourable press. There was little doubt, then, that the *Sun* would back devolution in the referendum and so it proved. Although there was relatively little coverage of the referendum until the final week, the message was clear, with headlines such as 'Stand up for Scotland, says Sean Connery' and 'X marks the Scot: Yes Yes Vote will reshape Your Future'.

The *Express* had been strongly against devolution in 1979 but at first during the 1997 campaign its position was more ambiguous. In the first week Tam Dalyell's opposition to home rule was headlined and the concerns expressed by leading businessmen prominently featured but there was also more neutral reporting of the Yes campaign. Even as late as two days before the vote the editorial line continued to be less than enthusiastic, with the 'Express Opinion' column asking only for a clear decision and a high turnout, but the paper carried an article by the Prime Minister calling for Yes votes. On the eve of poll, however, although the letters page was dominated by opponents, the paper finally came out emphatically in favour of a Yes Yes vote with the front-page headline reading 'Your Chance to Shape OUR DESTINY: YES YES'.

The *Daily Mail*, on the other hand, remained firmly opposed to devolution. In the first week the paper focused heavily on the question of tax-varying powers ('Dewar Admits "Fearsome" Tax'; 'Bosses Reject Tartan Tax Deal'). In the last week the paper featured comment on opinion poll results that apparently showed a narrowing of the gap on the second referendum question, argued in a full-page spread that devolution would 'tear apart the union we value so much' and, on polling day, strongly advocated a No No vote with a front-page headline proclaiming '£280 million bill for Scottish parliament'.

Among the daily broadsheets the *Press and Journal* retained its traditional political stance – sitting resolutely on the fence. The *Courier* also maintained the same stance as before, in opposition to change, with editorials raising concerns over tax worries, increased business rates and claims that home rule would result in an exodus of talent from Scotland. On the eve of poll, the Courier's headline was 'Cash warning for Scots Parliament' and the editorial argued that as far as the devolution plans were concerned, 'there is a great deal to be negative about'.

On the other hand the *Herald* (in 1979 the *Glasgow Herald*) was much more enthusiastically in favour of devolution than it had been before. It started a daily feature called '20 reasons to vote Yes Yes' on 20 August and actively led the counterattack on claims about business opposition with headlines such as 'Industry big guns side with Dewar', and 'Firms reject CBI director's stance on Home Rule'. On the day before polling, the editorial comment was shifted to the front page and under the heading 'The Decision Belongs to Us' argued 'It is Scotland's chance to join the modern world. We should seize it gratefully with both hands.'

In 1979 the *Scotsman* had been the most strongly pro-devolution of the broadsheet newspapers. In 1996, however, Andrew Neil, an abrasive Unionist who had previously been dismissive of Scottish demands for home rule, became editor-in-chief of the paper. This probably explains why in 1997 the *Scotsman* gave only lukewarm support to the Yes Yes campaign. As with hostile papers, reports early in the campaign emphasised the alleged concerns of the business community ('Patullo's tax bombshell') and allegations of Labour sleaze, and throughout the campaign the weakness of the No No campaign was bemoaned. Regular columnists Alan Cochrane and Alan Massie consistently sounded a sceptical note. On referendum day, although a very long editorial, entitled 'The rebirth of a nation' and written with great rhetorical flourish, argued passionately (indeed emotionally) for a Yes Yes vote, Neil himself wrote a column which began, 'I would prefer, of course, not to be starting from here. For a long time I saw no pressing need to tamper with a status quo which has stood Scotland in mighty good stead in the past. Why tinker with it?' Neil nonetheless went on to concede that the argument had been lost and that 'the home rule tide is unstoppable'.

As far as Sunday papers are concerned, we have already noted that the *Sunday Mail* was strongly in favour of devolution (its 'Thought for the week' on 7 September was 'Yes, Yes ... nothing less! For Scotland's sake use your vote on Thursday'). Its rival, the *Sunday Post* began its 'As We See It' column with a quotation from the Bible and after reviewing the arguments concluded that, although the paper 'is as Scottish as the hills and the heather' a No No vote would be the right one. *Scotland on Sunday*, on the other hand, despite highlighting the fears of business, clearly advocated a Yes Yes vote to achieve the 'glittering prize of devolution'.

As the foregoing has made clear, the Scottish press was over-whelmingly in favour of a Yes Yes vote in the referendum and generally made its position very clear. Support was even stronger than it had been in 1979 and was expressed with more vigour in the tabloid press. This did not guarantee success for the Yes Yes camp, of course – the support of most of the press had been unavailing in 1979, after all – but it certainly created an impression of very widespread and enthusiastic support for a Scottish Parliament.

The style and extent of press coverage
Like other aspects of the referendum, press coverage was dramatically affected by the death of the Princess of Wales over the weekend of

30/31 August and subsequent events culminating in her funeral on 6 September. During that week the referendum all but disappeared from the tabloids, with both the *Record* and the *Sun* calling for polling to be deferred to a later date. Referendum reporting was also thin in the *Scotsman* and, such as there was, was mostly confined to inside pages. Only the *Herald* continued to feature the referendum prominently, justifying its decision to do so by arguing on Tuesday 2 September that 'a quiet week in Scottish politics has the potential to become a harmful hiatus'.

It could be argued, however, that the 'hiatus' was a blessing in disguise for those who hoped for a high turnout and a large Yes majority. The absence of referendum coverage in most papers reduced the likelihood of readers becoming bored with the issue and when the newspapers returned to it, on Monday 8 September, they did so with a vengeance. During the last week of the campaign the referendum was never off the front pages of all the papers. The *Record*, in particular, pulled out all the stops. On the day before polling, it had a 16-page devolution supplement in full colour including articles by Donald Dewar, Alex Salmond and Jim Wallace, a full-page picture of a child wrapped in Scottish flags ('my future is in your hands') and a 'Vote Yes Yes' poster to 'cut out and keep'. On polling day almost the entire paper was devoted to urging a Yes vote in the referendum. Articles included 'Seize the Moment'; 'Don't fall for the Tories' lies on tax'; 'Every vote counts. Go out there and do the business'; 'How to Create History'; 'Betrayed by 18 years of Tory misrule'; 'Get up there and Win it for me, Lads' (Alex Ferguson); 'Our nation can be top drawer'; 'Some like it Scot' (Scottish actors and actresses); 'The Jock 'n' Roll Years' (Scottish pop stars); 'Made in Scotland' (Irn Bru, Baxter's soups, Tunnock's Tea Cakes etc.); 'Scots Who Shook the World'; 'Win a Super Braveheart Break'; 'John will be looking down and willing us to vote Yes Yes' (John Smith's widow); 'I will make my second million in a new Scotland' (business tycoon); 'Patriot Games' (Scottish sports heroes) and 'Scotland We Love You'. Coverage in the *Sun* in the last few days of the campaign was similar although on a slightly less epic scale (the 'devolution special' supplement ran to only eight pages). In these two top-selling tabloids there was no attempt to provide balanced coverage or to analyse the issues involved in devolution. Rather they used patriotic imagery and celebrities to do everything that they could to ensure a Yes victory.

As we have seen, the *Daily Express* only came out for home rule at the very end of the campaign. Up to that point its coverage was restrained and a fair airing was given to both sides of the devolution argument. Indeed, unlike the *Record* and the *Sun*, the *Express*'s special (eight-page) supplement on Wednesday 10 September ('Scotland at the Crossroads') set out arguments against devolution as well as those for. The only anti-devolution tabloid, the *Mail*, did not feature the issue prominently – it shared the front page on both Wednesday 10 (with a picture and story related to Princess Diana) and Thursday 11 (with a picture and story concerning the 'MP who has come out as a lesbian'). Coverage in the inside pages was unsensational and in the last week of the campaign only 14 pages (of 312) were devoted to the referendum, compared with 39 to the funeral of the Princess and its aftermath.

As might be expected, referendum coverage in the *Scotsman* and the *Herald* was more detailed and analytical than in the tabloids. From 25 August to polling day there were only two occasions when the issue was not featured on the *Herald*'s front page – on the Monday after Diana's death and on the following Wednesday. The *Scotsman* had front-page referendum stories on all but four days – three of them in the week after Diana's death. In both papers coverage was extensive and heavyweight, with assiduous reporting of the campaign and careful examination of the issues. In both cases too – but especially in the *Scotsman* – ample space was afforded to columnists who took a different line on devolution from that of the paper itself. If anything, the *Herald* gave the referendum more prominence and also provided livelier coverage. We have noted the '20 reasons to vote Yes Yes' feature and in addition there was a special 'Letters on Devolution' page from 2 September and a referendum day poetry competition.[4]

There is no doubt that the referendum was a very big story for the Scottish press. The fact that it had to compete with a truly sensational story for a week in the middle of the campaign meant that, especially in the tabloids, coverage of the referendum was crammed into the final four days. The result was, more or less, blanket coverage, mostly strongly advocating a Yes Yes vote. Rarely can the Scottish press have given such prominence to a political event and also been so close to being uniformly partisan on a political issue. On the day following the referendum the pro-devolution press was euphoric. The *Scotsman* headline was 'A nation again' while the *Herald* had simply 'YES YES'. The front pages of the tabloids featured full colour pictures containing patriotic images and headlines such as 'A NEW DAWN' (*Record*), 'YES YES' (*Sun*) and 'AT LAST: Today a new chapter begins in our nation's history' (*Express*).

THE LOCAL WEEKLY PRESS

Like other parts of the United Kingdom, Scotland has a network of local weekly (or in some cases twice-weekly) newspapers covering the country outside the four main cities. There are just over 100 local papers with a combined circulation approaching 1 million (not counting 'freesheets') and they are a potentially important medium of political communication. Franklin and Murphy (1991) and Franklin (1994) have studied the role that the local press in West Yorkshire plays in general elections and argue that it is a significant one. Franklin suggests that 'parties increasingly subscribe to the view that their political messages are best communicated ... not in poorly attended meetings, or in acrimonious doorstep encounters, but most subtly and persuasively in the columns of the local "rag"' (1994: 184). In the 1979 Scottish referendum Bochel and Denver (1981) found that, although they generally avoided expressing an editorial opinion, local newspapers made their own contribution to the referendum by extensively reporting local campaign news, being used for political advertising by the participants and publishing letters on the issue. In 1997 we examined the content of 84 local newspapers during the four weeks preceding the referendum.[5]

As in the previous referendum, local newspapers were far less likely than national dailies to make editorial comments about the event and, when they did, they were far more likely to take a neutral stand than the nationals. Of the 84 local weekly papers studied, only 23 (27 per cent) had editorials on the referendum, compared with 39.5 per cent in 1979, and 15 (65 per cent) of these were neutral on the issue or confined themselves to an exhortation to vote. Six advocated a Yes vote and two a No vote.

Letters to the editor used to be an important feature of local papers and on political issues they were an easy way to get propaganda across in default of, or in addition to, other activities. The provision made for letters from readers has declined sharply over the last two decades, however, with fewer papers having correspondence columns and far fewer letters being printed. As a consequence, the number of letters connected with the referendum which were published in 1997 was drastically reduced as compared with 1979. In 1979 only 7 per cent of local papers did not have letters about the referendum and 1,536, from protagonists on both sides, were published; in 1997 there were only 440 referendum letters and 40 per cent of papers had none at all. Of those that were published, 56 per cent favoured a Yes vote while 44 per cent were from No supporters. In 1979 a significant proportion of the letters printed were the result of orchestrated letter writing campaigns by both sides but in 1997 there was no evidence of such activity.

Coverage of campaign news in the local press during elections is dominated by reports of meetings held locally and the same was true of the 1979 referendum. In 1997, however, there were many fewer meetings or public debates and news coverage was considerably reduced, largely comprising reports of speeches and statements together with occasional interviews with protagonists. The bulk of this coverage (80 per cent of the space) was focused on the Yes campaign. The same was true of special features (of which there were 47). In these, which frequently outlined the background to the referendum and/or considered arguments for and against devolution, 71 per cent of the space favoured the Yes side.

In the 1979 referendum both sides used the local press extensively for advertising – there were 366 advertisements for local meetings and 403 propaganda advertisements. In 1997 there were only 19 advertisements for public meetings and 17 others. This very dramatic reduction highlights the change in referendum coverage in local papers between the two referendums. While they have the potential to communicate political messages to a large number of readers this was not fulfilled during the referendum. In part this is because many editors eschew reporting of national political events altogether but it is also the case that the campaign was not very newsworthy from a local perspective. The unity within the Yes camp and the demoralisation of the Conservatives made for an uncontroversial campaign; the dearth of public meetings meant that there were few local pegs on which to hang a referendum story. In addition, over the past 20 years Scottish local newspapers have increasingly become tabloid in style and political coverage in general has declined.

THE MEDIA AND THE PUBLIC

Television

Having described and discussed the content of the mass media's coverage of the election we turn now to consider the impact that it had on the electorate. For this purpose we make use of data from the survey of Scottish electors that we conducted immediately after the referendum (see Appendix 2). With reference to television, we asked our respondents two questions – how much attention they paid to television news reports about the issue of a Scottish Parliament and whether they watched any other programmes that dealt with the referendum. Table 4.3 shows responses to the first and, for comparison, the attention paid to television news about politics by Scottish voters at the time of the 1997 general election. The two survey questions involved are very similar[6] and the data suggest that Scots were more attentive during the referendum – only 19 per cent reported that they paid little or no attention during the referendum campaign compared with 39 per cent saying the same at the time of the election. In addition, 56 per cent of our sample claimed to have watched other programmes dealing with devolution and, although we have no comparative data, this seems to us a substantial figure. Not unexpectedly, those who viewed special devolution programmes were also more likely to pay attention to the news – 67 per cent of them (N=1,286) paid a great deal or quite a bit of attention to the news compared with 20 per cent (N=1,004) of those who did not.

Table 4.3: Attention to television news coverage of the referendum and the general election

	Referendum %	*General election 1997* %
Great deal	16	8
Quite a bit	30	24
Some	35	29
A little	13	24
None	6	15
(N)	(2,313)	(851)

Source: Data for the general election are from the 1997 Scottish Election Study survey.

There was a clear relationship between voting in the referendum and attention paid to reporting the issue on television (see Table 4.4). First of all, turnout was much higher among those who paid a good deal of attention and much lower among those who paid little or none. This does not mean that there is a causal connection between the two – a likelier explanation is that both voting and following the referendum on television are products of general political interest or a particular interest in devolution. Secondly, those who paid most attention to television coverage were also more likely to vote Yes Yes (71 per cent) while the Yes Yes vote was lowest (54 per cent) among those who paid least attention. Again we would hesitate to interpret these data as showing that watching television affected how people voted. Apart from anything else, television news reporting did not clearly favour the Yes side. A more plausible interpretation is that cause and effect go in the opposite direction. The keener respondents were on constitutional change, the more likely they were to follow television coverage of the issue closely: it was their constitutional preference which led to their viewing habits, not *vice versa*. Support for this interpretation is given by the data showing the relationship between attention paid to television news about the proposed Scottish Parliament, and respondents' attitudes towards it. As the table shows, the proportion strongly in favour declines from 56 per cent of those who paid a lot of attention to 34 per cent of those who paid some and to 26 per cent among those who paid little. Put another way, 61 per cent of those who strongly favoured a Parliament paid at least quite a bit of attention to news reporting compared with 36 per cent of all others. Holding strong views in favour of a Parliament seems to have predisposed respondents to pay close attention to the news. Even strong views against a Parliament did not. This almost certainly reflects the widely held expectation of a strong Yes vote prior to the referendum: opponents of devolution must have anticipated defeat and, in these circumstances, paying little attention to media reporting of the campaign would have been a rational reaction on their part.

Table 4.4: Attention to television news and referendum voting/attitude to Scottish Parliament

	Great deal/Quite a bit	Some	A little/None
	%	%	%
Voted	73	59	40
(N)	(958)	(798)	(532)
Voted Yes Yes	71	63	54
Voted Yes No	9	15	13
Voted No No	21	23	33
(N)	(918)	(613)	(271)
Scottish Parliament			
Strongly favour	56	34	26
Favour	23	41	34
Neither	2	6	12
Against	10	12	19
Strongly against	9	7	9
(N)	(967)	(726)	(389)

Note: Turnout data are weighted (see Chapter 7).

The press

As we have seen, the Scottish press covered the referendum extensively and prominently, especially in the last week of the campaign and, unlike television, most papers took a strong stand on the issue. The readership of daily newspapers by our respondents is shown in Table 4.5. Only 8 per cent did not read a newspaper so the press is clearly an important channel of political communication reaching almost all of the Scottish electorate. In line with circulation figures (although it is worth noting that readership is not the same as sales, since one newspaper may be read by several people) the *Daily Record* is by far the most widely read paper. The combined readership of the tabloids (64 per cent of respondents) far outweighs that of broadsheets (27 per cent). It is also worth re-emphasising the heavy predominance of Scottish titles – around two-thirds of our sample read papers entirely edited and produced in Scotland. Among broadsheet readers the figure is 83 per cent. The fact that coverage of the referendum in the British press was low-key was irrelevant to the great majority of Scots. Moreover, the great majority (73 per cent) of our respondents read a newspaper which was in favour of devolution.

Table 4.5: Readership of morning newspapers

	%		%
None	8	*Herald*	9
Daily Record	42	*Scotsman*	7
Sun	9	*Press & Journal*	5
Daily Mail	7	*Courier*	3
Daily Express	6	*Telegraph/Times*	3
		Other	3
		(N)	(2,318)

Most newspapers took a clear stand on the referendum issue, but it is not always the case that readers recognise the message which newspapers attempt to put across. During the 1987 election campaign, for example, when the *Sun* was at its most virulent in supporting Margaret Thatcher, only 63 per cent of the paper's readers thought that it supported the Conservatives and 12 per cent believed that it supported Labour (Butler and Kavanagh, 1988: 187). To test readers' perceptions of papers' stances on devolution we asked our respondents to indicate whether they thought that on the question of setting up a Scottish Parliament their paper was generally in favour, generally against or had no clear position. Responses are shown in Table 4.6.

Among the tabloids, the pro-devolution stances of the *Record* and the *Sun* were clearly recognised by vast majorities of readers. This is

Table 4.6: Readers' perceptions of newspapers' position on Scottish Parliament (row percentages)

	For	Against	Unclear	Don't know	N
Daily Record	93	1	1	5	(969)
Sun	82	1	4	13	(194)
Daily Mail	18	33	24	25	(154)
Daily Express	65	9	9	17	(132)
Herald	83	4	3	11	(202)
Scotsman	87	1	4	8	(155)
Courier	26	19	25	31	(65)
Press & Journal	44	9	7	40	(113)
Telegraph/Times	15	37	22	26	(54)
Other	66	5	9	20	(56)
All	76	6	6	13	(2,094)

not surprising given the nature of their coverage; what is perplexing is that 7 per cent and 18 per cent of readers respectively were not certain that the two papers were strongly in favour. The more equivocal stance of the *Express* (until the last few days) is reflected in the fact that there was much less unanimity among readers as to its position – 65 per cent thought that it favoured devolution. In marked contrast, the *Daily Mail* signally failed to get its anti-devolution message across. Readers knew what the paper did not favour – only 18 per cent thought that the paper was pro-devolution – but not what it did support. Only 33 per cent of *Mail* readers thought that it opposed devolution, while almost half thought that the paper was undecided or were unsure of where it stood. These patterns are repeated for the broadsheet papers. Readers of the *Herald*, and the *Scotsman* were in little doubt concerning their title's support for a Scottish Parliament while there was little consensus among readers of other papers, which were either hostile or equivocal, over the positions being advocated on the issue. These data suggest that papers which did not support devolution were not as good at getting their message across to their readers as the others. On the other hand, there was a strong pro-devolution tide running in Scotland and newspaper readers were not particularly on the lookout for anti-devolution signals. There is a well-established theory that in using the mass media, voters seek re-inforcement for their pre-existing opinions rather than challenges to it (see, for example, Harrop, 1987). Given that a large majority of Scottish voters were in favour of devolution, opinions expressed in the press which argued a different position tended to pass them by.[7]

Table 4.7 shows how the readers of the various newspapers voted
in the referendum. Readers of the *Daily Record* produced the largest
Yes Yes vote (79 per cent) and only 10 per cent of them voted No No.
Sun readers were less keen, however, and voted in much the same
way as the electorate as a whole. The late conversion of the *Daily
Express* to a Yes Yes appeal does not seem to have had much impact on
its readers – a plurality (47 per cent) voted No No and the general
pattern of voting is not very different from that among readers of the
avowedly and consistently anti-devolution *Daily Mail*, a majority (52
per cent) of the latter's readers voting No No. We have suggested that
the *Herald* was more enthusiastically in favour of a Scottish Parliament
than the *Scotsman* but this is not reflected in the voting figures which
are very similar, with around two-thirds of readers voting Yes Yes. The
largest No No vote was among (the small number of) readers of *The
Times* and the *Daily Telegraph*, which are regarded in Scotland as
English papers.

Table 4.7: Morning newspaper read by respondent's vote in referendum
(row percentages)

	Yes Yes	Yes No	No No	N
None	61	13	26	144
Daily Record	79	11	10	754
Sun	63	14	23	128
Daily Mail	37	10	52	126
Daily Express	38	15	47	113
Herald	66	11	23	184
Scotsman	67	8	24	131
Courier	52	12	37	52
Press & Journal	57	19	24	86
Telegraph/Times	29	4	67	45
Other	72	6	21	47
All	66	11	23	1,810

On the whole, then, newspaper readers had a reasonable idea of
where their papers stood on devolution and tended to vote roughly in
line with the papers' recommendations. This does not mean, however,
that there is necessarily any causal connection involved. The problem
is a general one when trying to untangle the impact of the media on
political attitudes (see, for example, Curtice and Semetko, 1994). Do
people think the way they do because of the paper they read (a media
effect), or do they read their paper because it matches what they
already think? Thus the fact that the *Daily Record* was strongly in
favour of devolution during the referendum campaign may not be
significant if its readers were already strongly in favour. It might even

be suggested that the *Daily Express* (at the end) and the *Scotsman* (rather grudgingly throughout) came down in favour of Yes votes because their editors could see the writing on the wall, as it were, and could not afford to antagonise their pro-devolution readers.

The problem is illustrated by the fact that readers of the consistently pro-devolution papers (*Record, Sun, Herald* and *Scotsman*) had a stronger sense of Scottish identity than readers of other papers. Among the former, 70 per cent (N= 1,525) felt themselves to be either Scottish or more Scottish than British compared with 48 per cent (N=585) of the latter. As we shall see in Chapter 7, sense of national identity was an important influence on voting in the referendum and on attitudes towards constitutional change in general, and there can be little doubt that voters' national identities were developed well in advance of the referendum. If anything, then, the pro-devolution press as largely reinforcing a predisposition among its readers to vote for change.

There are other difficulties in trying to assess the effect of the press on voting behaviour – most notably the multiplicity of other influences to which voters are exposed – and we shall not enter that particular minefield here. Suffice it to say that the great majority of Scots read pro-devolution papers. The case for a Scottish Parliament was vociferously made by the biggest-selling tabloids as referendum day approached and discussed at length in the broadsheets. At the very least this cannot have harmed the prospects for a pro-devolution majority in the referendum.

CONCLUSION

The distinctiveness of the Scottish mass media helped to make the 1997 referendum a major event in Scottish politics. Despite the death of the Princess of Wales – a truly sensational news story – the devolution issue and the campaign itself received very substantial coverage. It is difficult to think of a political event or issue, other than a general election or perhaps a referendum on the United Kingdom's role in Europe, which would be covered so extensively and with such passion by the national British press as the referendum was by the Scottish press. Tabloid press treatment was generally very lively, arresting and interesting (albeit heavily biased) while the main broadsheets provided a wealth of discussion and reportage. Television, on the other hand remains hamstrung by doubts as to the meaning of 'balance' in referendums and, especially in the case of the BBC, tended to produce worthy but unexciting coverage.

There is a common tendency to exaggerate the impact of the mass media on the outcomes of elections and referendums (not least by the media themselves). In general, claims of large media effects need to be taken with a large pinch of salt, however, and this is certainly the case with regard to the Scottish referendum. It is true that the press was overwhelmingly in favour of Yes votes on the two questions and that decisive Yes majorities were recorded. In addition, voters who paid close attention to television coverage and read pro-devolution newspapers were indeed more likely to vote for constitutional change than others. Given their pre-existing sense of national identity and attitude towards Scotland's constitutional position, however, they would probably have been more likely to do so anyway, even had they not watched television coverage or read a newspaper.

NOTES

1. Although we use the term 'broadcasting' here, in what follows we deal only with television. There was, of course, a good deal of referendum coverage on radio – especially Radio Scotland but also, more fleetingly, on other Scottish stations. Lack of resources prevented any detailed study of radio coverage but, in any case, radio audiences are much smaller than those for television.
2. This, it might be noted, was not a new complaint. In 1995 the BBC proposed to broadcast a lengthy television interview with the Prime Minister, John Major, on the Monday before the Scottish council elections. This appeared to suggest that decision-makers in London were either ignorant of the forthcoming elections in Scotland or else did not consider them important enough to apply the usual rules related to political broadcasting.
3. These figures and others given later were supplied by the relevant television companies.
4. The winning entry, written by Rody Gorman, an Irishman resident in Skye, and published on referendum day was as follows.

> We'll keep the dividing wall
> A wee whilie yet, and the dyke
> Which is like a border
> Between Scotland and the rest
> Between ourselves
> And the folks next door
>
> But from now on
> Instead of forever flinging
> All our rubbish over it,
> Suppose we keep most of it ourselves,
> For the sake of reconciliation, you understand
> Between us as Jock's wee bairns
>
> And who knows what'll emerge
> From the midden which develops?

5. This analysis was undertaken by John and Dorothy Bochel and involved consulting local newspapers at the National Library in Edinburgh. The nature and extent of devolution coverage in each issue was evaluated and measured (in column centimetres).
6. Our question was, 'During the referendum campaign how much attention did you pay to television news reports about the issue of a Scottish Parliament?' while the Scottish Election Study survey asked, 'People pay attention to different parts of the television news. When you watch the news on television how much attention do you pay to stories about politics?'
7. Some evidence in support of this view is given by the fact that among readers of the four consistently pro-devolution papers, 91 per cent (N=1,321) of respondents who favoured constitutional change thought that the papers were also pro-devolution, compared with 81 per cent (N=193) of those who favoured the status quo. Similarly, among readers of other papers 43 per cent of those favouring change thought that the papers were also in favour compared with 33 per cent of those who preferred the status quo.

5

Local Campaigning in the Referendum

Although it may be overshadowed by the national campaign reported in the media, local campaigning is a familiar and traditional part of elections in Britain. Across the country many thousands of party supporters distribute leaflets and other forms of campaign literature, visit or telephone electors to canvass their support, put up posters and set up and staff street stalls. Candidates walk around shopping centres trying to shake hands with voters, visit schools, hospitals and old people's homes, and address meetings. On polling day, campaign workers knock up tardy supporters, offer lifts to and from the polls and stand outside polling stations taking down the registration numbers of voters or handing out more leaflets. All parties have many members well-versed in running local campaigns and all provide training for campaign organisers and other volunteers on a continuous basis. This reflects the fact that the parties now recognise that local campaigning can have a significant impact on election results. In recent years they have devoted more attention and resources to it, concentrating especially on key marginal seats (see Denver and Hands, 1997a; Denver, Hands and Henig, 1998).

The context for local campaigning in a referendum is different from that of an election, however. Local campaigners and party campaign organisers find themselves in an unfamiliar situation. There is no requirement to have an agent to take responsibility for (and usually also direct) the local campaign. There are no marginal seats into which resources can be poured or safe seats where a party can mount a minimal campaign. There are also no candidates in a referendum. In general and local elections the candidate acts as a focus for campaign activity – the campaign is, as it were, built around projecting the candidate to the voters. In referendums there is simply the question to be decided. Unlike in elections the parties may be divided on the issue in question – internal party divisions may be, indeed, the very reason for holding a referendum, as with the question of membership of the EC in 1975 and Labour's difficulties over devolution in 1979. In 1997, however, the line-up of parties at national level was clear. Labour, the Liberal Democrats and (after some internal discussion) the SNP were on the Yes side with the Conservatives alone campaigning for a No vote. Referendums are also likely to see the emergence of *ad hoc* groups to campaign on the issue in question. These may be independent campaigning groups or else 'umbrella' groups designed mainly to facilitate cross-party co-operation. Thus, as we have seen (Chapter 3), in 1997 Scotland Forward played a significant role in co-ordinating the Yes campaign while the No campaign was organised by Think Twice. The existence of such groups complicates the campaign scene, making for more complex vertical and horizontal relationships among campaigning units. As implied by the previous point, parties may co-operate with one another in a referendum but rarely do so in elections. Whereas in elections the 'enemy' is usually clear – the other parties – in referendums collaboration with erstwhile enemies may be the order of the day. Finally, it is likely that partisan passions will not be as strong in a referendum as they normally are in an election and this might be reflected in less enthusiastic campaigning. Referendums are concerned with a single issue whereas a general election determines the government of the country and the direction of all of public policy for five years.

The rarity of referendums in Britain, as opposed to elections, means that party activists do not have a fund of experience in organising local referendum campaigns on which to draw. It also means that not much has been written on the subject (see, however, Butler and Kitzinger, 1976: ch. 6; Bochel and Denver, 1981). In this chapter we describe and analyse local campaigning in the 1997 Scottish referendum. Although, as with general elections, national-level campaigning dominated during the run-up to the referendum, the political parties attempted to stimulate local activity. This was an uphill struggle as, in addition to the problems mentioned above, the referendum followed shortly after the general election campaign. Even local campaigners who had been successful in the general election were tired and short of financial resources, while among the losers, in particular the Conservatives, there was little enthusiasm for a fight. The *ad hoc* umbrella groups, Scotland Forward and Think Twice, also attempted to encourage local activities, at least initially, both to reinforce the national message and in the hope of encouraging supporters who were not 'partisan' in the party sense of the term.

In order to analyse the extent, intensity and style of local campaigning we made use of two main sources of information. Firstly, we interviewed the Scottish campaign directors of each of the parties in order to ascertain how they organised and encouraged local campaigning.[1] Secondly, we conducted a postal survey of local party campaign organisers in which we asked for details of the nature and extent of campaigning on the ground. Questionnaires were distributed to the constituency secretaries of each of the major parties in each of Scotland's 72 constituencies.[2] We received responses from 48 Labour, 46 Conservative, 42 SNP and 28 Liberal Democrat local parties. The relatively small number of responses from Liberal Democrat associations reflects their organisational weakness in central Scotland where frequently a single party activist acts as secretary for a cluster of constituencies and there are some seats with no organisation at all. We also sent postal questionnaires to all individuals identified by Scotland Forward as local 'contacts' or 'organisers'. However, it was clear that the enthusiasm of, and the role played by, these individuals varied enormously and that there was very little advice or guidance available to them from the central Scotland Forward organisation. Nonetheless, 19 of the 36 returned questionnaires and, although the small number precludes statistical analysis, it allows us to give an impressionistic account of the role of Scotland Forward at local level. Think Twice was also contacted with a view to contacting their local organisers but although the central organisation agreed to distribute the questionnaires none were actually sent out. In fact, at local level Think Twice was almost always the Conservative Party by another name and so analysis of Conservative responses gives an adequate account of local campaigning for a No vote. Using these data we can compare campaigning in the referendum with campaigning at the preceding general election, for which similar data are available,[3] and also with campaigning in the 1979 referendum.[4]

In order to determine the extent to which local campaigning made an impact on voters we included questions relating to it in our post-referendum survey of Scottish electors which is described in more detail in Chapter 7. In addition, however, we sent a one page questionnaire, for completion on the day of the referendum, to assorted and interested colleagues, friends and relatives and also to a random (50 per cent) sample of the 200 Scottish schools which teach Modern Studies, the curriculum for which includes politics. The response was gratifying – we received a total of 383 responses. However, many of these had to be excluded as it was not possible to identify the polling stations observed, or because they were duplicate observations. Despite this, 280 different observations of polling place activity on referendum day remained. These cover, to a greater or lesser extent, 61 of Scotland's 72 constituencies and all but one (Western Isles) of the local government areas in which the referendum count took place. These data are not statistically reliable but do help to convey the atmosphere of referendum day.

THE PARTIES

One of the main differences between the 1979 and 1997 referendums was the unity of parties. Whereas in 1979 Labour had been internally divided and the campaign was characterised by much squabbling among the parties on the Yes side (see Chapter 1), the 1997 campaign was distinguished at national level by the unity of Labour, Liberal Democrats and SNP, both internally and collectively. Indeed, late in the campaign about a million copies of a leaflet bearing the names of all three parties (although not their logos) were distributed.

As far as local campaigning was concerned, the parties' national organisers perceived their main problem as being how to get local activists to co-operate with one another. In particular, in many areas the intense rivalry between Labour and SNP activists, sometimes bordering on hatred, was seen as a potentially serious problem by the national leaderships. Andy Myles, chief executive of the Scottish Liberal Democrats at the time, said that 'there was a great danger that this campaign would end up like 1979 with conflict between supporters of home rule'. Since local party activists are not foot soldiers who obey the commands of generals, the party leaderships took the realistic view that they could not force their local activists to work together, either directly or under the aegis of Scotland Forward, but that they would encourage them to do so. At a meeting involving officials of all three parties it was agreed that the party which had the MP in a constituency would take the lead in local campaigning but where other parties held wards on the local council then they would take responsibility for those wards. Although some difficulties arose where there were marginal wards or local council by-elections were taking place, this strategy generally worked well and in many ways was a model for cross-party co-operation in a referendum. Even in areas where the national officers expected Labour and the SNP to refuse to co-operate – in West Lothian, for instance – there was 'a minor miracle – two mortal enemies agreeing to campaign on the same side together and dividing it up' (Andy Myles).

For the Conservatives and Think Twice the problems were of a rather different nature and consisted mainly of the need to try to mobilise a deeply dispirited and shrinking group of activists into attempting to fight another campaign in which defeat was seen as very likely, less than five months after the general election wipe-out.

In the words of the Conservative Scottish campaigns director, 'our constituency organisations were tired, demoralised ... and when you're twelve people, and eleven of you are demoralised, it's hard to do a lot'. In addition, it was clear from the outset that the No campaign would receive much less support from dissidents in the other parties than was the case in 1979. The Conservatives, therefore, focused their main efforts on the national campaign, through Think Twice, but local associations were encouraged, where they were capable and willing, to obtain and deliver literature from Think Twice. Any local activity was seen as a bonus by the national campaigners, however.

Local decisions

Table 5.1 illustrates the point made above about the difficulties for the central organisations in attempting to control or direct their local organisations. Respondents were asked what advice they received from their Scottish headquarters about relations with other parties and groups in the campaign. Although the national officials of all four parties believed that their advice was clear it was actually interpreted in a number of ways. Nonetheless, although our distinction between co-ordination and integration with umbrella groups may not always have been appreciated by respondents, the data suggest that most constituency parties were aware that they were supposed to co-operate with others – that campaigning in the referendum was to be different from election campaigning.

Table 5.1: Respondents' perceptions of campaigning advice given
by party headquarters

	Con	Lab	Lib Dem	SNP
	%	%	%	%
Campaign on own	2	6	2	4
Co-ordinate with other parties but not SF	0	2	2	4
Co-ordinate with SF/TT	45	47	42	50
Integrate with SF/TT	21	11	5	21
Make own decision	24	19	44	13
No advice	7	15	5	8
(N)	(42)	(47)	(24)	(41)

Note: SF = Scotland Forward; TT = Think Twice.

The actual decisions made by constituency parties in 1997, as compared with decisions made in 1979, are shown in Table 5.2. In both years SNP associations were almost unanimous in deciding to campaign for a Parliament although a small minority of individual members were less keen, seeing the proposed Parliament as an impediment to full independence. Conservative associations appear to have been slightly more likely to actively campaign against devolution in 1997 although, in answer to another question, 19 per cent of associations reported that some of their members worked for the Yes campaign. The proportion of Liberal Democrat associations actively campaigning on the Yes side increased from about two-thirds to more than four-fifths. In this case it is also worth pointing out that whereas the Liberal Party had only three Scottish MPs in 1979 the Liberal Democrats had ten in 1997. It seems likely, therefore, that the number of Liberal Democrat associations which had an active and effective campaigning machine had increased during those 18 years. The most significant change concerns Labour, however. In 1979 a third of Scottish Constituency Labour Parties (CLPs) decided not to campaign but in 1997 all decided to campaign for Yes. The greater unanimity in the Labour Party is also reflected in other data. Whereas in 1979 only 21 per cent of CLPs reported that their decision to campaign was unanimous, in 1997 all except one did so. Moreover, the proportion of Labour respondents saying that some of their members worked for the No side fell from 44 per cent in 1979 to 8 per cent in 1997. This transformation in Labour attitudes to devolution, which included MPs (except Tam Dalyell) as well as activists, is highly significant given Labour's dominant position in Scotland, and reflects the efforts of party officials. In late June and early July 1997 Labour's Scottish headquarters organised five political training seminars, selling the idea of a Scottish Parliament to constituency parties. Following the general election victory Labour's activists were highly enthusiastic and by the end of July Labour had a campaign co-ordinator for the referendum in place in all 72 constituencies.

Table 5.2: Local party decisions about local campaigning in the referendum

	Con		Lab		Lib Dem		SNP	
	1979	1997	1979	1997	1979*	1997	1979	1997
	%	%	%	%	%	%	%	%
Campaign for Yes	0	0	67	100	68	82	97	98
Campaign for No	74	87	0	0	0	0	0	0
Not to campaign	26	13	33	0	32	18	3	2
(N)	(31)	(46)	(43)	(48)	(34)	(28)	(34)	(42)

Note: * = in this and subsequent tables 1979 figures refer to the Liberal Party.

Campaign organisation and activities

While the three parties behind the Yes campaign were recommending to their local organisations that they should work together they also took a fairly relaxed attitude to this. As Labour's Jack McConnell put it to us, 'There were areas where the parties were so antagonistic at a local level that they never would have worked together, so we didn't insist on it. We said we expected people to work together but we understood if they didn't.' Allison Hunter of the SNP concurred: 'At local level, where people were so minded, they were encouraged to work with the other parties. But where they weren't there was no way that you could actually force them – it would be counter-productive.' The Liberal Democrats, in any event, tend to leave a good deal to local intitiative.

The form that local campaigns actually took is shown in Table 5.3. There was a considerable variety of local arrangements but it is striking that only minorities of constituency organisations campaigned on their own. Some form of cross-party co-operation was the norm, at least on the Yes side. The No campaigns involving Think Twice were, as we have noted, almost indistinguishable from straightforward Conservative Party campaigns. Conservative respondents whose campaigns involved Think Twice reported that Conservatives comprised, on average, 95 per cent of active campaigners compared with 3 per cent who were not attached to a party and 1 per cent each from Labour and the Liberal Democrats. In contrast, those actively involved in cross-party Yes campaigns comprised, on average, 49 per cent Labour members, 29 per cent SNP, 15 per cent Liberal Democrats and 6 per cent non-party (with Conservatives averaging less than 1 per cent). Labour people tended to dominate local Yes campaigns, therefore, but members of the other parties on the Yes side were certainly well in evidence. As we have noted, the extent of cross-party collaboration was greater in some areas than expected. In the Ochil constituency, for example, where there had been great rivalry and mutual dislike between Labour and the SNP, these hostilities were suspended during the referendum campaign to the extent that a good working relationship was achieved. To quote Jack McConnell again, 'They just decided it was so important to get a Yes Yes vote that they were going to bite their tongues for four weeks.' However, whilst novel in its extent, the degree of collaboration should perhaps not be overstated. The division of lead roles in constituencies and electoral divisions recommended by the parties nationally meant that in many instances local parties were effectively campaigning on their own in 'their' areas, with genuine pooling of resources and joint working being the exception rather than the rule.

Table 5.3: Co-operation with other groups and parties in local referendum campaigns

	Con	Lab	Lib Dem	SNP
	%	%	%	%
Ran own party campaign	38	37	25	25
Participated in campaign organised by SF/TT	52	28	25	25
Participated in informal cross-party campaign	0	13	17	5
Other involvement with TT/SF	10	22	25	25
Other cross-party involvement	0	0	8	20
(N)	(42)	(47)	(24)	(40)

Note: SF = Scotland Forward; TT = Think Twice.

The data in Table 5.4 suggest that the parties' local campaign organisation was more thorough than in 1979. Almost all Labour campaigns and large majorities of those mounted by the Conservatives and the SNP had an organiser in charge, playing a similar role to that performed by an agent in elections. With the exception of the Liberal Democrats, most also had a central committee room from which to mount their polling day operation. In well-organised general election campaigns the parties also have local committee rooms, usually at ward level but with the exception of Labour these were relatively rare in the referendum campaign. Nonetheless, the basic organisation of local campaigns was clearly better, in all parties, in 1997 as compared with 1979. This might reflect a greater level of professionalism in campaigning generally, or might also reflect the fact that the parties had only recently built up their campaign machines for the general election.

Table 5.4: Local campaign organisation, 1979 and 1997

	Con		Lab		Lib Dem		SNP	
	1979	1997	1979	1997	1979	1997	1979	1997
	%	%	%	%	%	%	%	%
Organiser in charge	23	88	73	93	33	47	56	74
Central committee rooms	35	59	53	68	13	29	61	74
Local committee rooms	22	13	20	42	0	12	38	17
(N)	(23)	(32)	(29)	(41)	(23)	(17)	(33)	(35)

Table 5.5 shows the campaign activities, for which we have comparable data for 1979, undertaken by the parties in the two

referendums. Leaflet distribution was the most common activity in both years although only Labour campaigns show a marked increase in the proportion of parties doing this. The parties on the 'Yes' side sometimes used their own leaflets and posters but also used those produced by Scotland Forward. The result was a combination of materials which varied greatly in the extent to which the different organisations were represented by name. Labour and the SNP both had printed substantial quantities of their own literature which was produced centrally but given to local organisations to distribute – the SNP printed 700,000 of their own 'Yes Yes' leaflets whilst Labour had more than 2 million leaflets produced. These were all distributed by the parties' local organisations.

On the other hand, the data confirm the decline of public meetings as a feature of local political campaigning which has also been observed at general elections. In 1979 these had been a major feature of the local campaign; by 1997, with the exception of Labour, there was little use of this traditional form of activity. In addition, relatively few parties undertook what are often seen as the key mobilising activities of canvassing and knocking up, although it is interesting to note that the relatively new technique of telephone canvassing made what must be its first appearance in a referendum campaign in Britain. The relative infrequency of canvassing (even for Scotland where it is often not a part of the routine in general election campaigns) may reflect the fact that active parties would have had canvass records from the general election but, since only small proportions knocked up voters on referendum day, a more plausible interpretation is that the mobilisation techniques used at elections – at least in marginal seats – were not widely employed. In Labour's case this was a conscious strategy. The party's Scottish secretary commented that devolution was 'the settled will of the Scottish people and the objective was, at local level, to let people know the referendum was on and to turn out ... Voters understood the issues. It was our job to stress the importance of a high turnout and let them know when the referendum was, when to come out and how to actually vote.'

To a large extent, then, local campaigning in the referendum consisted of distributing leaflets and generally 'making a noise' in order to increase public awareness. As part of this effort a variety of 'stunts' were organised and local celebrities involved. Although many of these aspects of campaigning were curtailed by the death of the Princess of Wales (see p.116), there were numerous ceilidhs and 'fundays'; footballers and rock bands (including the rock group Runrig) made campaign appearances and street stalls were common. In Stirling there was an appearance by Hamish the Highland Bull,

Table 5.5: Campaign activities undertaken, 1979 and 1997

	Con		Lab		Lib Dem		SNP	
	1979	1997	1979	1997	1979	1997	1979	1997
	%	%	%	%	%	%	%	%
Distributing leaflets	71	71	63	85	53	57	94	83
Doorstep canvassing	0	4	14	19	18	4	59	19
Telephone canvassing	–	18	–	28	–	0	–	26
Knocking up	19	18	19	26	24	0	21	21
Transport to polls	52	47	23	79	35	29	35	45
Public meetings	42	18	42	47	44	14	44	17

Notes: These are percentages of all responding parties. 'N's vary slightly for the different activities but are close to those reported in Table 5.2 in all cases.

and the unveiling of a statue of William Wallace (bearing a striking resemblance to Mel Gibson, the star of the film 'Braveheart') made national news.

In the anti-devolution camp, most Conservative associations did little or nothing other than perhaps delivering leaflets. Reflecting the lack of financial resources and of willing activists, local Think Twice activities were generally nationally-driven and organised and they were frequently based around the visits of speakers to particular areas. Even finding well-known speakers was a problem, however. Following their general election disaster, the Conservatives had no Scottish MPs to call upon and with many of the big names of the government years apparently lying low, the No campaign was reliant upon a small number of Scottish figures, not all of whom would be very familiar to the public, or imports from outside Scotland. In a few places genuinely local activities were more apparent, however. In Dundee, for example, there was a stall in the city centre for three consecutive Saturdays. Think Twice also utilised advertisements in local papers as well as in the Scottish nationals in order to give the impression of a local base to the No campaign.

All of this local campaigning was carried out with some enthusiasm, at least on the Yes side. Table 5.6 shows the amount of enthusiasm among campaign workers in those associations and parties which decided to campaign on one side or the other. The summary provided by the mean for responses suggests that enthusiasm among Conservatives was somewhat lower compared with 1979 whereas Labour workers were markedly more enthusiastic and the Liberal Democrats somewhat more. SNP workers remained the most enthusiastic of all and, overall, were equally enthusiastic in the two referendums.

Table 5.6: Reported enthusiasm of campaign workers

	Con 1979 %	Con 1997 %	Lab 1979 %	Lab 1997 %	Lib Dem 1979 %	Lib Dem 1997 %	SNP 1979 %	SNP 1997 %
Very enthusiastic	17	9	7	15	8	12	24	31
Quite enthusiastic	52	41	27	58	46	53	64	46
Not very enthusiastic	30	41	57	28	46	35	9	20
Not at all enthusiastic	0	9	10	0	0	0	3	3
Mean (1–4)	2.9	2.5	2.3	2.9	2.6	2.8	3.1	3.1
(N)	(22)	(32)	(30)	(40)	(24)	(17)	(32)	(35)

Note: The mean figure is calculated by assigning scores from 1 (not at all enthusiastic) to 4 (very enthusiastic) to responses.

General election and referendum campaigning compared

For the reasons already given we would not expect local campaigning in a referendum to be as widespread or intense as in a general election. We can investigate this by comparing the results of our survey of constituency parties after the referendum with data on Scottish constituency campaigning collected by Denver and Hands after the general election in May. Table 5.7 makes the comparison in respect of seven aspects of campaigning. As can be seen, canvassing, both on the doorstep and by telephone, was much more common in the general election than in the referendum. This is confirmed by the surveys of the Scottish electorate carried out at the general election and the referendum under the auspices of the Centre for Research into Elections and Social Trends (CREST). These found that whereas 19 per cent of respondents had been canvassed personally at the general election and 9 per cent had been canvassed by telephone, in the referendum only 4 per cent reported having been canvassed on the doorstep and 1.5 per cent by telephone. Our data also show that more constituency associations had local (ward level) organisers in the general election and roughly twice as many used computers in their campaigns. The numbers of volunteer workers, both during the campaign and on polling day, were also significantly smaller for the referendum although grossing the figures for Scotland as a whole suggests that about 9,000 party people were actively involved in campaigning on referendum day – roughly one for every 440 electors. The Conservatives, Liberal Democrats and SNP distributed many fewer posters than in the election but, consistent with their aim of 'making a noise', Labour put out more than twice as many.

Table 5.7: Campaigning in the 1997 general election and referendum compared

| | Con | | Lab | | Lib Dem | | SNP | |
	GE *%*	*Ref* *%*	*GE* *%*	*Ref* *%*	*GE* *%*	*Ref* *%*	*GE* *%*	*Ref* *%*
Doorstep canvassing	83	4	76	19	56	4	75	19
Telephone canvassing	66	18	53	28	20	0	70	26
Had local organisers	43	35	98	81	42	25	54	50
Used computers	81	44	91	46	61	55	84	39
Mean campaign workers	40	17	51	21	37	10	22	18
Mean polling day workers	71	25	92	42	43	37	45	25
Mean posters	1,156	118	2,458	5,995	513	75	1,902	223

Notes: These figures are based on all responding parties. 'N's vary slightly but for the referendum are generally close to those reported in Table 5.2. For the general election the number of responding parties was 47 Conservative, 45 Labour, 41 Liberal Democrat and 44 SNP.

Further evidence that referendum campaigning was less intense than general election campaigning comes from the reports of respondents when asked to compare the referendum effort of their parties with their normal effort in elections. The results, given in Table 5.8, show that very few parties made as much effort as they normally do in a general election. Indeed around three-quarters of Conservative associations and three-fifths of Liberal Democrat associations put in less effort than they normally would in a local election. On the other hand, 41 per cent of CLPs claimed that they made a greater effort than is normal in local elections. Remembering that parties which did not campaign are included in these data and that there were many more of these in 1979 (Table 5.2), it seems that, overall, Conservatives made about the same (not very great) effort in the two referendums while Labour and the Liberal Democrats both worked harder at local campaigning. The apparent decline in effort among local SNP branches may reflect a feeling that Labour was grabbing the glory and took a clear leading role in the campaign.

One way of comparing the intensity of campaigning across parties, constituencies and elections is to compute an index of campaigning (see Denver and Hands, 1997a). Using responses to our survey of constituency secretaries we devised a simple additive index, scoring from 1 to 22, which incorporates seven different dimensions of campaigning – preparation, organisation, number of workers, the use of computers, canvassing, polling day activity and effort put into a

Table 5.8: Effort put into referendum campaigns

	Con 1979 %	Con 1997 %	Lab 1979 %	Lab 1997 %	Lib Dem 1979 %	Lib Dem 1997 %	SNP 1979 %	SNP 1997 %
As in a general election	0	3	0	7	3	5	12	0
More than local, less than general election	17	3	19	34	18	14	55	36
As in local election	7	16	7	27	9	14	21	17
Less than local	33	45	26	29	12	38	6	39
Very little/none	43	34	49	2	59	29	6	8
Mean (1–5)	2.0	2.0	2.0	3.1	1.9	2.3	3.6	2.8
(N)	(30)	(38)	(43)	(41)	(34)	(21)	(33)	(36)

Notes: Figures are based on all constituencies reporting a decision to campaign or not with the latter included under 'very little/none'. The mean figure is calculated by assigning scores from 1 (very little/none) to 5 (as in a general election) to responses.

variety of tasks.[5] For comparison, we calculated the same index for Scottish constituency parties at the general election. Mean scores in the general election and the referendum are shown in Table 5.9. These data confirm that referendum campaigning was generally less intense than in the general election – with a particularly sharp drop on the part of the Conservatives and Liberal Democrats – and that Labour campaigned hardest of all.

Table 5.9: Mean scores on campaign intensity index

	Con	Lab	Lib Dem	SNP
General election campaign	16.1	16.2	11.6	15.3
(N)	(45)	(36)	(36)	(35)
Referendum campaign	8.9	12.7	6.6	10.4
(N)	(38)	(41)	(21)	(36)

In elections, candidates play a key role in local campaigns – the purpose of the campaign is to get them elected. In the referendum one might have expected that MPs would also have played a key role, acting as spokespersons and advocates for their party's policy. In fact our information suggests that their role was relatively limited. This may have been in part due to the nationally led nature of the campaign, and particularly the emphasis on the national media, which meant that for many MPs a significant part of their campaigning role was determined centrally. Another contributing factor may have been that while they might normally expect to be involved in constituency work at weekends, the two weekends immediately before the referendum were affected by the death of the Princess of Wales. In addition, for Labour, almost one-third of MPs held government posts and their activities would have been curtailed by these responsibilities.

THE *AD HOC* GROUPS

As described in Chapter 3, two main *ad hoc* groups emerged to play a part in the referendum campaign – Think Twice and Scotland Forward – but, as far as local campaigning was concerned, the parts that they played were very different. The national headquarters of Scotland Forward initially set out to create a network of local contacts. A series of public meetings were held in the major cities and in some other areas at which those attending were invited to leave their names and addresses and to act as contacts or organisers for local areas. The Scotland Forward web site advertised local events and the availability of campaign literature. In the event, however, the main campaign contribution of Scotland Forward at local level was to act as a clearing house and provide a co-ordinating mechanism – in very few cases was there a Scotland Forward campaign that was distinguishable from the campaigns of the three pro-devolution parties.

We received questionnaire responses from 19 local Scotland Forward organisers and these confirm the fact that Labour Party activists dominated local Scotland Forward groups. When asked to estimate the proportions of people active in their local campaign associated with the different parties, the mean figure (N=17) was 47 per cent for Labour as compared with 24 per cent SNP, 15 per cent Liberal Democrats and 10 per cent non-party people. Arrangements involving Scotland Forward varied a good deal. In some cases there was a single meeting at which an agreed division of duties and areas was reached and then the parties simply got on with the job, never again meeting together. In others, a committee was established which met from time to time to review progress. In some cases there was tension between the parties – especially, as we have noted, Labour and the SNP. As the contact for the Western Isles wrote, 'The atmosphere of meetings was initially strained after years of mistrust and direct opposition.' Nonetheless, almost all of these respondents believed that working through Scotland Forward was an effective way of reducing party rivalry, improving the coherence of the campaign effort and making a cross-party appeal to the electorate. Four also commented that it facilitated non-party input to the campaign.

Where local Scotland Forward groups did actively campaign they generally followed the pattern set by the parties, concentrating on events designed to gain visibility and media attention, rather than the traditional activities associated with election campaigns. Leafleting and the use of posters also featured significantly.

Think Twice was not well-resourced at national level, despite having the services of the Conservative Scottish campaigns director, and failed to establish any local campaigning groups. Both their national and local campaigns were dominated by Conservatives and were portrayed by opponents as simply Conservative campaigns. In marked contrast with the 1979 campaign, the anti-devolution side singularly failed to attract the active support of business leaders or of dissident Labour politicians. For Think Twice the position was, therefore, very different from that of Scotland Says No, the main anti-devolution group in 1979. In 1997 the high level of unity within and between the Yes parties meant that it was unlikely that Think Twice would ever be seen as anything other than a front for the Conservatives, and its potential role as an umbrella group was therefore strictly limited. Even Tam Dalyell, the only Scottish Labour MP to oppose devolution, did not embrace the Think Twice campaign, preferring to take his own independent stance. As discussed above, given the disarray and low morale of the Conservative Party, any local activity for the opponents of devolution was therefore a bonus. Nevertheless, Conservative organisers did believe that Think Twice had been a useful tool for them, enabling them to appear as something more than a Conservative campaign, and also acting as a source for the provision of leaflets for local distribution.

Despite the limited experience of referendums in the United Kingdom it now seems to be established that *ad hoc* umbrella groups will emerge to support one side or the other. The Scottish experience suggests, however, that they can play only a limited role in local campaigning. All the campaigning expertise rests with party activists and there is simply not enough time to recruit significant numbers of new activists and build a campaign machine. As our brief account of Scotland Forward has shown, however, where there is the potential for cross-party collaboration at local levels, the use of an umbrella group can ease the path and enable a greater level of co-operation than might otherwise be the case.

THE DEATH OF DIANA

As discussed in Chapter 3, the death of Diana, Princess of Wales, added a unique factor to the 1997 referendum campaign. There were some calls, largely from the opponents of devolution, for a postponement of the referendum, but the fact that the date was enshrined within legislation made such a move virtually impossible. However, in addition to the immediate halt to the national campaign there was also a virtual cessation of activities at the local level until after the burial.

The impact of Diana's death and the display of public mourning which followed is clearly difficult to measure, as is the extent to which the campaign itself was actually affected. However, we were able to include questions on the issue in our local campaigning surveys. In all parties Diana's death was widely perceived to have affected campaigning, with 63 per cent of Conservative respondents, 87 per cent of Labour, 82 per cent of Liberal Democrat and 67 per cent of SNP reporting this, together with 83 per cent of Scotland Forward contacts. Effects noted included a complete halt to campaigning and disruption of leafleting or arrangements for public meetings. Scotland Forward respondents in particular reported that many events had to be cancelled, particularly concerts, ceilidhs and other fun events. It is perhaps unsurprising that the SNP maintained a higher level of activity during the general lull, although even SNP constituency associations did tone down their operations significantly. Few respondents suggested that the death actually had any negative effect upon their side of the campaign although a number on the Yes side claimed that it led to a loss of momentum or drop in activism. On the other hand, the national Liberal Democrat organiser believed that 'it concentrated campaigning which concentrated minds. It meant that there was a level of excitement generated in the last 100 hours by the Yes campaign by managing to mobilise people on the ground ... It managed to concentrate stuff that would have been spread over ten days and by actually ramming it all together I think that there was a positive effect.'

THE VIEW FROM THE ELECTORATE

Electors experience political campaigns in two main ways. Firstly, they are normally aware of a national campaign conducted through the mass media and the referendum campaign was extensively reported in the Scottish press and on television and radio. Secondly, they may encounter a local campaign in the form of posters, leaflets, street stalls, car cavalcades, being called upon by campaign workers and so on. We have a little evidence concerning voters' impressions in the 1979 referendum. Bochel and Denver (1981) made use of the reports of a number of 'monitors' across the country, who were asked to record their impressions of local campaigning. The following comments capture the flavour of these reports.[6]

> Not much voting; no activity; no cars to polls; no literature; really pathetic.
> It is the quietest political campaign I have witnessed locally.
> Referendum day itself seemed characterised by widespread inertia and numbing apathy. One SNP Yes board was the only visual stimulation to be seen.
> Political activity during the referendum campaign was significantly absent.

In 1997, as explained above, we again asked people to monitor the campaign around Scotland. Their reports confirm the message of our analysis so far – there was more campaigning than in 1979 but much less than is normal at general elections. Thus 65 per cent reported that they observed 'just a little' campaigning with only 5 per cent saying that they saw 'a lot'. By far the most common activity observed was leaflet distribution (44 per cent) and 34 per cent noticed window posters. The next most common sign of local campaigning was publicity stalls but these were noticed by only 8 per cent of monitors. On polling day itself, there were representatives of the parties or *ad hoc* groups at 89 of the 280 polling stations covered by our 'monitors', the bulk of these being Labour or SNP representatives. In well-organised election campaigns party workers at polling stations note the electoral registration numbers of voters so that they can be crossed off previously prepared lists of supporters. In this case, however, representatives were mostly either handing out leaflets or doing nothing. It is, indeed, something of a polling day tradition in Scotland for party workers to stand outside polling places (and for candidates to visit them) to no apparent effect. Another common feature of election days in Scotland is for the parties to place posters at the gates of polling stations – which for minimal effort at least gives the impression that something is going on – and almost half of polling stations observed did have such posters, the great majority of them being from the Yes camp. Overall, the polling day atmosphere at polling stations was described by 20 per cent of monitors as being like a general election while 32 per cent said it was like a local election and

47 per cent that it was very quiet. The overall view was reflected in comments from monitors which included the following:

> Generally very subdued until the last day when the Yes Yes supporters were very much in evidence (Linlithgow).
> Absolutely no sign of the No No campaign. Some Yes Yes window posters. I got the impression that the public had made up their minds long ago on the first question (Edinburgh).
> There was no campaign on the ground at all. Apart from the media you would not have known that there was a referendum (Aberdeen).
> The campaign was almost non-existent. It consisted of one Yes Yes leaflet delivered to the doors. No opposing campaign at all was evident (Lanarkshire).

More statistically reliable data on the impact of local campaigning come from our survey of the Scottish electorate, carried out just after polling day. We first asked respondents whether they had noticed any groups or organisations other than parties campaigning in the referendum. As Table 5.10 shows, only very small percentages mentioned Scotland Forward or Think Twice. Clearly the groups made little impact upon the electorate and this may be explained the fact that people are used to campaigning being done by parties which are a permanent feature of the local political scene. *Ad hoc* groups must find it difficult to register with the voters in the relatively short time available when a referendum is held. On the other hand, almost 70 per cent of respondents recalled seeing a Yes advertising hoarding compared with only 40 per cent recalling a No hoarding, despite the fact that Think Twice made a major effort to get their message across in this way. Every household in Scotland received a government leaflet explaining the devolution proposals but only 46 per cent

Table 5.10: The impact of referendum campaigning on the electorate

Percentage of electorate which noticed:

Scotland Forward	4	'Yes' hoardings	69
Think Twice	5	'No' hoardings	40
Local campaigning:			
Quite a bit	12	Government leaflet	46
A little	46	'Yes' leaflets	76
None	42	'No' leaflets	37

Note: In all cases the 'N's on which these percentages are based are close to 2,300.

recalled seeing this. In the light of this, the figure of 76 per cent who recalled receiving Yes leaflets is highly impressive and clear evidence of local campaigners reaching the voters with their message. Finally, more than half of our respondents (58 per cent) reported that they saw at least a little local campaigning in the referendum. Overall, we would conclude that the efforts made by local campaigners during the referendum were indeed noticed by the electorate.

THE IMPACT ON THE OUTCOME

Perhaps the key question to ask about local campaigning is whether it has any effect on the contest in question. Utilising a variety of methods, recent research has cast serious doubts on the previous academic orthodoxy that in general elections constituency campaigning is little more than a quaint ritual. Rather, it has been shown that local campaigning can make a significant difference to how parties perform (see, for example, Seyd and Whiteley, 1992; Pattie *et al.*, 1995; Denver and Hands, 1997a). It is not clear that the same would apply in referendums, however, in which – apart from the differences mentioned at the outset – the level and intensity of campaigning is not nearly as great as in an election. It is certainly the case that the pro-devolution parties easily out-campaigned the antis in the Scottish referendum and that the result was a triumph for the former but this does not mean that there is any necessary connection between the two.

Trying to provide statistical evidence about local campaign effects in the referendum is fraught with difficulty, however, even though we have an index of campaign effort for each campaigning party. Firstly, our responses relate to constituencies while the results of the referendums were announced for 32 local authorities. Some of these authorities form only part of a constituency, others have the same boundaries as a constituency while yet others (such as Glasgow or Edinburgh) contain a number of constituencies. For each party, therefore, we took the mean campaign intensity score in the counting area concerned as an indicator of the general level of its campaigning. Secondly, it is difficult to find a way of coping with the fact that there were three parties campaigning on one side and only one on the other. The joint impact of the Yes campaigns will surely have been greater than that implied if we consider the parties' campaigns separately. Simply summing the party scores is not helpful, however, as we have scores for all three parties for only six of the counting areas. Finally, the fact that the small number of cases available for analysis (32) is further reduced by non-responses makes it difficult to obtain statistically significant results.

Nonetheless, we show in Table 5.11 the correlation coefficients measuring the association between the campaigning index on the one hand and the percentage voting Yes in the referendum, turnout and the parties' shares of the votes in the general election on the other. For the Conservatives the correlation between campaigning and Yes votes is significant and in the expected direction but in the case of the other parties the relationships are not statistically significant. Similarly, there is no significant association between intensity of campaigning and levels of turnout. The last row shows that the Conservatives, Labour and the SNP campaigned hardest where they were already stronger. This means that even the significant negative relationship between Conservative campaigning and the size of the Yes vote must be treated with caution. Other evidence shows (Chapter 6) that the size of the Yes vote in the various counting areas was strongly related to levels of Conservative and Labour support in the general election. It may be that it was pre-existing Conservative strength (relatively) rather than local campaigning by the Conservatives in these areas that led to a smaller Yes vote.

On this basis, then, we are unable to say whether voting in the referendum was affected by local campaigning. Quite possibly the result would have been the same had there been no local campaigning at all. It remains the case, however, that campaigning for Yes votes was much stronger than in 1979 and very much more widespread and intense than campaigning on the No side. If this was not crucial to the outcome it certainly added to the sense that, this time round, the devolution tide was running very strongly.

Table 5.11: Correlations with campaign intensity index

	Con	Lab	Lib Dem	SNP
Percentage Yes (1st Q.)	-0.73*	0.17	-0.51	-0.37
Referendum turnout	0.32	0.31	0.30	0.01
Percentage vote general election	0.76*	0.46*	0.20	0.51*
(N)	(20)	(19)	(13)	(22)

Note: * = coefficient statistically significant ($p < 0.05$).

CONCLUSIONS

From the preceding discussion we can draw some conclusions that are specific to the experience of the Scottish referendum and some that are likely to apply more generally to referendums in the United Kingdom. Firstly, as far as the 1997 devolution referendum is concerned, local campaigning for a Yes vote was stronger in 1997 than it had been in 1979. To a large extent this was due to a more wholehearted and united effort from the Labour Party, the dominant party in Scotland. Secondly, the local Yes campaigns were, overall, much stronger than No campaigns. This was partly due to the balance of forces but also to the fact that Conservative local campaigners were demoralised and their campaign machines decrepit. Thirdly, Scotland Forward worked fairly effectively in facilitating inter-party co-operation on the Yes side while Think Twice was unable to stimulate autonomous local groups.

At a more general level our analysis suggests, firstly, than local campaigning is less intense in a referendum than it is in a general election. It is also probably less variable geographically as there is no targeting of marginal seats. In Scotland there were specific problems relating to this – the recent general election meant that campaign workers were exhausted and resources depleted and there also appeared to be little doubt about what the referendum result would be. Nonetheless, in future referendums it seems likely that parties will experience problems of organisation and face difficulties in raising the enthusiasm of experienced party campaigners, and this will keep the level of referendum campaigning significantly lower than constituency campaigning in elections. Secondly, cross-party co-operation at local level in referendums takes a variety of forms, but local campaigning specifically by *ad hoc* groups is rare. It is unrealistic to expect such groups to build any significant local campaigning organisation in relatively short periods of time. Parties will continue to dominate local campaigning and the most that groups can generally hope to do is to co-ordinate their efforts and ease the path to co-operation. Finally, measuring the impact of local campaigning in referendums is difficult but it seems likely to be smaller than in elections. In some ways this is surprising since, given the lower turnout and the relative weakness of partisan passions, voters may be more mobilisable. Nonetheless, our evidence suggests that the parties find it difficult to galvanise their activists to mount the kind of all-out campaigns that can have a significant pay-off in terms of votes in elections.

NOTES

1. We are grateful to David Canzini (Conservative), Allison Hunter (SNP), Jack McConnell (Labour) and Andy Myles (Liberal Democrat) for agreeing to be interviewed and to be quoted in this chapter.
2. Recipients were asked to pass the questionnaire to the person in their party who was most involved in organising the local campaign.
3. The general election data are derived from a study of campaigning in the general election undertaken by David Denver and Gordon Hands.
4. In their study of campaigning in the 1979 referendum Bochel and Denver undertook a pioneering but elementary survey of constituency party secretaries in Scotland, the results of which are presented and discussed in Bochel and Denver, 1981.
5. The index comprised the following seven elements:

> *Preparation* – when the constituency began to prepare for the campaign; scored 0–4 from most recent to well in advance.
> *Organisation* – whether there was an organiser in charge, whether there were ward organisers, whether there was a canvassing organiser, postal votes organiser, transport officer, computer officer; scored 0–3.
> *Workers* – the mean number of campaign workers during the campaign and on polling day; scored 1–4 on the basis of quartiles.
> *Computers* – whether computers were used in the campaign; scored 0–1.
> *Canvassing* – whether doorstep canvassing was undertaken, whether there was telephone canvassing; scored 0–2.
> *Polling day* – whether there was a central committee room, whether there was knocking up, whether there were representatives at polling stations, whether cars took voters to the polls; scored 0–2.
> *Effort* – mean effort put into a variety of activities scored on a scale from 1–5.

We can compare this index with respondents' own estimates of the campaign effort made. Those who said it was about the same as for a general election had a mean score of 15.3 (N=5); between local and general elections, 12.4 (N=31); as for local elections, 12.7 (N=26); less than for local elections 9.5 (N=51) and very little effort 7.3 (N=12). These figures show a close correspondence between our index and the subjective appraisals of respondents.
6. These are taken from Bochel and Denver (1981: 54).

The Referendum Results

As we have seen, the Yes campaign had good grounds for optimism about the outcome of the referendum. Most survey and poll evidence on the issue throughout the 1980s and 1990s had suggested that a clear majority of the Scottish electorate favoured a devolved Parliament. The only major political party supporting the constitutional status quo, the Conservatives, had seen their electoral base erode dramatically since 1979. And during the run up to the referendum opinion polls generally suggested that over 60 per cent of the Scottish electorate intended to vote Yes for a Parliament, even including those who were uncertain about how they would vote (see Table 6.1).

The No campaign, meanwhile, had been lacklustre. The Conservatives, still smarting from their record defeat in the 1997 general election, were reluctant to be seen as too closely linked to another defeat in Scotland so soon. Nor did they want to damage the chances of obtaining a substantial No vote by allowing the anti-devolution campaign to be written off by their opponents as simply a Tory campaign. They did not, therefore, play as active or effective a part in the referendum campaign as they might have. The Think Twice campaign itself was at times not very well co-ordinated and presented.

Table 6.1: Opinion polls on the referendum issues, June-September 1997

Should there be a Scottish Parliament?

Company	Sponsor	Publication	Yes %	No %	Don't know %
System 3	Herald	June 1997	64	21	15
System 3	Herald	July 1997	68	21	10
System 3	Herald	August 1997	65	19	16
System 3	Herald	Sept 2 1997	61	23	18
NOP	Sunday Times	Sept 7 1997	63	21	16
ICM	Scotland on Sunday	Sept 7 1997	60	25	15
MORI	STV	Sept 8 1997	67	22	11
System 3	Herald	Sept 10 1997	61	20	19
ICM	Scotsman	Sept 10 1997	63	25	12

Table 6.1: Opinion polls on the referendum issues, June-September 1997 (continued)

Should a Scottish Parliament have tax-varying powers?

Company	Sponsor	Publication	Yes %	No %	Don't know %
System 3	*Herald*	June 1997	53	28	19
System 3	*Herald*	July 1997	56	26	18
System 3	*Herald*	August 1997	54	27	19
System 3	*Herald*	Sept 2 1997	47	32	21
NOP	*Sunday Times*	Sept 7 1997	51	34	15
ICM	*Scotland on Sunday*	Sept 7 1997	45	38	17
MORI	STV	Sept 8 1997	51	32	17
System 3	*Herald*	Sept 10 1997	45	31	24

The result of the referendum could not, of course, be taken as a foregone conclusion, however. In the first place, there was the risk of a surprise result. Predictions of the outcomes of general elections based on opinion polls have twice been seriously in error in the last 30 years. In 1970 the polls predicted re-election for the Labour government but the Conservatives won fairly comfortably. In the 1992 election there was a widespread expectation that the Conservatives would, at best, lose their overall majority, and at worst lose power entirely: in the event, they won with a clear lead in share of the vote and what seemed at the time to be a workable Commons majority. There was no guarantee that a referendum would be more predictable than an election and so both camps had to anticipate the possibility, even if it seemed relatively remote, that the polls were significantly overestimating support for the devolution proposals. Furthermore, referendums are rare in British politics. Both pollsters and voters have little experience of them. There was room for doubt, therefore, on whether and how stated intentions and preferences on the referendum issue would translate into votes on polling day.

Secondly, the structure of the referendum created room for uncertainty. With two questions on the ballot paper, on whether a Scottish Parliament should be established and on whether it should be given tax-varying powers, four different voting patterns were possible – Yes Yes, Yes No, No No and No Yes. The latter might appear illogical but it could be justified as a strategy by those who were opposed to a Scottish Parliament but believed that if it came about then it should be fiscally responsible and have tax powers.[1] In terms of the overall outcome, there were three realistic possibilities – a Yes majority on both issues, a Yes majority for a Parliament, but a No majority on tax-varying powers or a No majority on both questions.

Anti-devolution campaigners had a possible fall-back position in the possibility of a Yes No outcome. While not as good for them as a No No result, this would at least have meant a defeat for the proposal to give a symbolically important element of discretionary power to the new Parliament. As we have seen, the 'tartan tax' argument was used skilfully in the period after 1992 to create doubts in voters' minds about Labour's devolution proposals. Furthermore, opinion polls undertaken in the months before the referendum suggested that the tax question might have been the Achilles' heel of the devolution proposals, and of Labour's strategy of opting for a referendum. Between June and September 1997, opinion polls reported a clear and relatively steady majority of electors saying that they favoured an elected Scottish Parliament (with few exceptions, support varied between 60 per cent and 65 per cent). But support for tax-varying powers was lower and more volatile, dipping below 50 per cent (when 'Don't knows' are included in the figures) in some polls, even in the week of the referendum itself (see Table 6.1). This led some commentators to suggest that on the second question at least the result was still in doubt. In fact, if 'Don't knows' on this question are ignored (as is conventional) all pre-referendum polls predicted that a clear majority would vote Yes to the taxation proposals and most were close to the actual result.

Third, there was the question of what the level of turnout in the referendum would be. In Britain a referendum carries no constitutional force. It is an advisory device – a means by which governments can gauge public opinion on an issue or get the backing of the electorate for its proposals – and the outcome is not binding on government (although in practice it is difficult to imagine a government refusing to accept a referendum result). The division of votes on the questions posed is only part of the process of seeking the assent of the electorate, however. Turnout can be vital. A poor turnout can negate even a strong vote in favour of a referendum proposition. This is in stark contrast to first-past-the-post elections, where the party winning most seats almost invariably gains a generally accepted mandate, irrespective of the turnout. Scotland's previous brush with the referendum experience in 1979 had, of course, hinged on the issue of turnout. The requirement that devolution be supported by 40 per cent of the electorate as well as by a majority of those voting had been sufficient to put an end to the Devolution Bill, despite majority support from those voting. No qualified majority was required in 1997 but the experience of 1979 was important for both camps. For the Yes campaign, a strong vote on a reasonable turnout was seen as important in order to demonstrate that devolution was indeed the 'settled will' of the Scottish electorate. If the referendum produced a poor turnout opponents of change might have been able to argue that even a Yes majority could not be taken as a sufficiently strong mandate for a major constitutional innovation.

As the referendum approached, then, the odds were clearly on a Yes majority on both questions but there remained some doubts and uncertainties about how the results would turn out and how they would be interpreted. Polling took place on 11 September 1997 and proceeded without incident. The counts were mostly conducted quickly in the 32 local authorities with results then being transmitted to Edinburgh where they were formally announced by the chief counting officer, Neil McIntosh, in the international conference centre. The first authority to declare its result, just before midnight, was tiny Clackmannan. An hour later, when the first large authority to declare (South Lanarkshire) produced huge Yes majorities on both questions, there was little doubt that the proposals would be carried easily although it was not until 6am on the next day that the last local authority (Highlands) returned its result following interminable delays. (Full details of the local authority results are given in Appendix 1.)

The results of the referendum were a striking success for the Yes campaign. On a turnout of 60.4 per cent of the electorate, the vote was strongly in favour of devolution. On the first question, a Scottish Parliament was endorsed by 74.3 per cent to 25.7 per cent and there was also a clear majority in favour of giving the Parliament tax-varying powers with 63.5 per cent voting Yes on the second question and 36.5 per cent voting No. These results left no doubt that, as compared with 1979, Scottish opinion had moved decisively in favour of a substantial degree of political devolution. In this and the next chapter, we analyse voting in the referendum in greater detail. Here we focus on the results themselves – in particular on variations across local authorities – while in Chapter 7 we focus on the electorate, making use of data from our survey of Scottish electors to explore their voting behaviour, attitudes and opinions.

TURNOUT IN THE REFERENDUM

Prior to the referendum, there was much speculation in the media and on the part of campaigners about the likely turnout focusing, in particular, on the point raised above – that a poor turnout might weaken the legitimacy of the new Parliament. The No campaign, probably anticipating a likely defeat on the main issue of a new

Parliament, had made much of the possibility of a low turnout. Equally, the Yes campaign was concerned about the risks of voter complacency and aimed to maximise turnout by emphasising that the outcome was far from certain and calling for a resounding Yes vote. Speculation about turnout levels was heightened by the fact that in the general election held in May 1997 turnout fell to a new post-war low point and it was commonly assumed that in part this was because the election result, like the referendum, was widely believed to be a foregone conclusion. In addition, it was always possible that with the referendum following so closely on the election the turnout would be depressed due to an element of 'voter fatigue'.

Much of the media discussion was not very well-informed, however, and the question of what might actually constitute a 'good' or 'satisfactory' turnout was rarely addressed. In fact, at 60.4 per cent, turnout was only slightly lower than in the two previous referendums in Scotland (see Table 6.2). Indeed, the electoral register on which the 1997 figure is based was more than six months older than that used in 1979 and when a standard adjustment is made to take account of deaths and electors who had moved since the compilation of the register, the turnouts in the two referendums were almost identical (for details of the adjustment, see Denver, 1994: 138–9). Not surprisingly, turnout at the referendum was lower than at the previous general election. But this is not unique to the 1997 Scottish referendum. Across a variety of countries and political systems turnout in referendums is almost always lower than turnout in the relevant national elections (see Butler and Ranney, 1994: 16–17). Nonetheless, it is also worth noting that turnout in the referendum was much higher than in either European or local government elections in Scotland. While concerns have been expressed about low turnout in local elections in Britain (see Miller, 1988: ch. 5), until very recently there had been no serious questioning of the electoral mandate that these confer. In comparison, the level of public involvement in the referendum appears healthy. In the event, there was no real cause for concern over the level of turnout.

Table 6.2: Turnout in elections and referendums in Scotland

Elections	%	Referendums	%
General election 1997	71.4	European Community 1975	61.7
Local elections 1995	44.9	Devolution 1979	63.8
European election 1994	37.9	Devolution 1997	60.4

The national turnout level masked quite wide variations across the country, however. The average turnout in the 32 local authorities was 61.5 per cent with a standard deviation of 4.9.[2] The highest turnouts were recorded in west central Scotland (72.7 per cent in East Dunbartonshire; 68.2 per cent in East Renfrewshire, and 66.7 per cent in South Ayrshire). Some of the lowest, meanwhile, were recorded in the Island authorities (51.5 per cent in Shetland, 53.5 per cent in Orkney and 55.8 per cent in Western Isles) and in three of the four major cities (51.6 per cent in Glasgow, 53.7 per cent in Aberdeen and 55.7 per cent in Dundee).

Why did turnout vary so substantially from area to area? One possible explanation might be that areas with low turnout were also areas where enthusiasm for devolution was lowest. Given the particularly low turnouts in three large cities, where a large proportion of the Scottish electorate lives, this interpretation, if true, would constitute a serious set-back for the claim that the referendum demonstrated substantial and widespread support for a tax-varying Parliament. However, this suggestion does not withstand close scrutiny of the referendum results. For instance, one of the largest Yes votes came from the authority with one of the lowest turnouts, Glasgow. More formally, the correlation between percentage turnout and the percentage voting Yes on the first question was extremely weak. At 0.04, the correlation coefficient falls well short of achieving statistical, let alone substantive, significance.[3] There was virtually no relationship between the level of local support for the constitutional package and turnout. The reasons for variations in turnout must lie elsewhere.

An alternative explanation is that variations in levels of turnout at a referendum are produced not by variations in enthusiasm for the measures being addressed at that vote, but by the same sorts of factors that influence levels of political participation more generally (on which see Parry *et al.*, 1992). The factors which give rise to spatial variations in aggregate turnout at conventional elections are well-established and understood (for general elections see, for example, Denver and Hands, 1997b; for local elections see Rallings and Thrasher, 1990). Variations in the social composition of constituencies or wards and in the local electoral context are strongly associated with turnout variation. Thus, Denver and Hands report that in the 1997 general election turnout was higher in more middle-class areas with large proportions of owner occupiers, and also in more marginal seats. Lower turnouts were found in safe seats and in more deprived urban constituencies with larger proportions of manual workers and of council and private tenants.

Simple correlations suggest that, as far as the social composition of local authority areas is concerned, the same broad patterns are found for the referendum (see Table 6.3). The more middle-class the population (as indicated by the percentage of those employed who were professional and managerial workers in 1991), the higher was the referendum turnout, while the more working-class the authority (indicated by the proportion of manual workers), the lower the turnout. The proportions of owner occupiers and council tenants were not significantly related to turnout. On the other hand, areas in which there are large numbers of private tenants tend to have relatively large transient populations (including students) and, as would be expected, there is a significant negative correlation between the percentage of such tenants in a local authority and its turnout. The more private tenants, the lower the turnout. The coefficients for percentage employed in agriculture and persons per hectare (which generally indicates the extent to which an area is urban or rural) are difficult to interpret at first sight. Both are statistically significant but the first (-0.31) implies that the more agricultural workers there were in an area (in other words, the more *rural* an area) the lower the turnout, while the second (-0.38) suggests that the more *urban* an area the lower the turnout. We return to these apparently contradictory results below (see p.131).

Table 6.3: Correlations with local authority referendum turnout

Social composition (1991 Census)		Political context	
% professional & managerial workers	0.34*	% Conservative vote 1997	0.30*
% manual workers	-0.42*	% Labour vote 1997	0.24
% owner occupiers	0.27	% Lib Dem vote 1997	-0.39*
% local authority tenants	-0.11	% SNP vote 1997	0.04
% private tenants	-0.37*		
% employed in agriculture	-0.31*		
% households with no car	-0.28	% turnout 1997 general election	0.87*
% with a degree	0.26	% turnout 1995 local elections	0.57*
Persons per hectare	-0.38*		
Size of electorate 1997	-0.28		

Note: * = statistically significant ($p < 0.05$).

Turning to the local political or electoral context, while the marginality or safeness of a constituency or ward for the various parties importantly influences turnout in elections it should not affect referendum turnout. Whereas in elections the results of the previous contest provides hard evidence of the distribution of party support in a ward or constituency, referendum campaigners have no similar way of knowing the approximate distribution of Yes and No supporters in advance. On the other hand, the general political complexion of an area may be related to turnout and so we also show in Table 6.3 the relationship between the estimated shares of the general election vote obtained by each of the major parties in the 32 local authorities and turnout in the referendum.[4] In general, the stronger the Conservative performance in the election, the higher was the referendum turnout (a correlation coefficient of 0.30). Since the geography of the Conservative vote follows the geography of class and hence of affluence and poverty quite closely, this is what we would expect if turnout were higher among the better off than among those who are poorer. On the other hand, there is a negative correlation between referendum turnout and the Liberal Democrats' share of the 1997 vote (-0.39) indicating that turnout was lower in areas of Liberal Democrat strength than in areas where the party is weak. However, since the Liberal Democrats' strongest areas in Scotland tend to be in some of the most agricultural parts of the country (the Borders, the Highlands and the north-east), this is probably an artefact of the fact that turnout was lower in more agricultural areas. Moreover, turnout in all kinds of elections is traditionally poorer in north-east Scotland.

Perhaps the most telling test of the hypothesis that local variations in referendum turnout reflect pre-existing patterns of political participation, however, is to correlate turnout at the referendum directly with turnout at previous elections. We estimated general election turnout in the 32 local authorities and, as can be seen, this is correlated very strongly and significantly (0.87) with referendum turnout. This is especially striking given that the contextual factor which most strongly influences election turnout – constituency marginality – plays no role, as we have noted, in a referendum. The relatively stable pattern of turnout is further emphasised by the fact that referendum turnout also correlates significantly with turnout in the 1995 local government elections (0.57). It is clear, then, that areas which tend to have high turnouts in general and local elections also produced high turnouts for the referendum, while areas with low election turnouts also had low referendum turnouts. Variations in aggregate turnout at the referendum, it appears, reflect pre-existing variations in levels of political participation.

The correlation coefficients reported in Table 6.3 show the associations between turnout and each variable separately. It is evident, however, that the various measures of the social composition of the different authorities are themselves strongly inter-correlated and, in turn, strongly related to the measures of party strength. Thus areas with large percentages of professional and managerial workers tend also to have large percentages of owner occupiers and to have been areas of relative Conservative strength in the general election. Establishing which variables are statistically more important, and also investigating the effect of combinations of variables, requires multivariate analysis, which enables us to test whether a particular variable is still significantly associated with turnout variation when all others are held constant. We first consider the social composition variables. Multiple regression analysis reveals that three aspects of the social composition are statistically significant, explaining 55 per cent of the variation in referendum turnout across authorities – the percentage of manual workers, persons per hectare and percentage of agricultural workers.[5] The most important social influence on turnout is class composition. Once that is taken into account, turnout was much lower in the most urban areas – especially the densely populated cities – and once that in turn is taken into account some of the most rural areas also had lower turnouts. The answer to the puzzle raised by the simple bivariate correlations in relation to urban and rural areas is that turnout was lower in very urban areas but was also lower in areas which are more sparsely populated and are genuinely agricultural (as opposed, for example, to comprising a scattering of industrial towns and villages).

By far the best 'predictor' of referendum turnout, however, is estimated turnout in the preceding general election. This alone accounts for 75.3 per cent of the variation in referendum turnout and if it is introduced into a multiple regression analysis then no other variable significantly increases the proportion of variation explained. This is not to say that election turnout 'influenced' referendum turnout in the same way as the social composition variables. It is simply that the factors which affected general election turnout (with the exception of constituency marginality) also affected referendum turnout with the result that the two are closely related.[6] Nonetheless, the regression equation predicting referendum turnout on the basis of election turnout can be used to discover those areas which deviated from their 'normal' turnout level in the referendum.[7] Those authorities which deviated by more than three percentage points are shown in Table 6.4. Of the five listed as having lower than expected turnout, four can be easily explained in terms of the expected marginality of constituencies at the general election. Aberdeen contains the highly marginal Aberdeen South and fairly marginal Aberdeen North; Dumfries was a key Labour target seat; Stirling, formerly held by the Scottish Secretary of State, Michael Forsyth, was very keenly contested while Aberdeenshire includes the marginal seats of Gordon and Aberdeenshire West and Kincardine. In all of these seats the local campaign in the general election was very intense and the turnouts were unusually high. It is not surprising, then, that there was a larger than expected decline in September. It is not clear, on the other hand, why there should have been an unexpectedly large decline in the Western Isles, although the constituency witnessed a very strong SNP campaign in the election. Similarly, there is no obvious reason why East Dunbartonshire, Renfrewshire, and Argyll and Bute should have produced larger than expected referendum turnouts.

Table 6.4: Largest deviations from expected turnout

Local authority	Actual turnout %	Predicted turnout %	Actual minus predicted
i) turnout lower than predicted			
Aberdeen	53.7	58.9	-5.2
Dumfries and Galloway	63.4	68.0	-4.6
Stirling	65.8	70.0	-4.2
Western Isles	55.8	59.2	-3.4
Aberdeenshire	57.0	60.2	-3.2
ii) turnout higher than predicted			
East Dunbartonshire	72.7	66.5	6.2
Renfrewshire	62.8	59.6	3.2
Argyll and Bute	65.0	62.0	3.0

The main picture which emerges from the analyses reported here is that there was nothing particularly unusual about patterns of turnout at the referendum. It was higher where we would expect it to be higher, based on past experience, and lower where we would expect that. Other than factors peculiar to an election – such as constituency marginality and the consequent targeting of campaigning – geographical variations in turnout in the referendum were caused by the same sorts of factors that explain variations in election turnout. By implication we would expect the same to be true in future referendums in Britain.

THE VOTE FOR THE SCOTTISH PARLIAMENT

As we have seen, the vote on the first referendum question was a resounding Yes, with 74.3 per cent of all votes cast favouring a Scottish

Parliament. Compared to the previous devolution referendum in 1979, this was an overwhelming majority (Table 6.5). While the 1979 referendum also resulted in a majority Yes vote, it was much narrower, with just 51.6 per cent of votes cast in favour of a Parliament and crucially, was too small to pass the qualified majority threshold of 40 per cent of the electorate. Although there was no equivalent threshold in the legislation governing the 1997 referendum, the 40 per cent mark was an important psychological milestone. In the event, the milestone was passed comfortably: 44.7 per cent of the electorate voted Yes. Since the size of the electorate was vital in 1979 an official adjustment was made to take account of deaths, prisoners, those aged under 18 on polling day and those who were registered in more than one place (for details see Bochel *et al.*, 1981: 8). If similar calculations are made for 1997 then the comparison of the results in the two referendums is more accurate. The adjusted figures show that in 1997 45.7 per cent of the electorate voted Yes to a Parliament compared to just 32.5 per cent in 1979.

Table 6.5: The overall results of the devolution referendums

	% of votes cast	% of electorate	% of adjusted electorate
1979 referendum			
Support a Scottish Assembly			
Yes	51.6	–	32.9
No	48.4	–	30.8
1997 referendum			
Q1: Support a Scottish Parliament			
Yes	74.3	44.7	45.7
No	25.7	15.5	15.8
Q2: Support tax-varying powers			
Yes	63.5	38.1	38.9
No	36.5	21.9	22.4

Another telling comparison between the 1979 and 1997 referendums is in the geography of support for a Parliament. A direct comparison is not straightforward, since the local authorities for which the results were counted and returned in 1997 did not exist in 1979. We can, however, aggregate the results of the 1997 referendums into the Regional and Island Council areas which were the counting areas in 1979 (see Table 6.6). In 1979, a majority of voters opposed the proposed Assembly in six out of the 12 counting areas (the overall outcome was a narrow Yes majority because the most populous areas voted in favour). The areas which voted No were concentrated in two corners of Scotland: the north-east (Grampian, Tayside, Orkney and Shetland), and the south (Borders, and Dumfries and Galloway). In Orkney and Shetland, only just over a quarter of the votes cast were in favour of an Assembly. The Yes majority was very slim indeed in two Regions: Lothian and Highland both recorded Yes votes by the narrowest of margins. The 1979 result suggested, therefore, a country which was deeply divided on the issue of devolution (as indicated by the closeness of the vote), and also split between the central belt and the Western Isles on the one hand, and the rest of the country on the other. The 1979 result, therefore, would have provided a very problematic mandate for change, even if the 40 per cent rule had not applied: an Assembly opposed by almost half of the voters and by half of the national territory would have faced an uphill struggle to establish its legitimacy.

Table 6.6: Referendum results by region, 1979 and 1997

Region	1979 Yes %	1997 Yes (Q1) %	1997 Yes (Q2) %
Western Isles	55.8	79.4	68.4
Central	54.7	76.3	65.9
Strathclyde	54.0	78.1	67.7
Fife	53.7	76.1	64.7
Highland	51.0	72.6	62.1
Lothian	50.1	74.5	63.7
Tayside	49.5	67.6	57.0
Grampian	48.3	67.6	55.6
Borders	40.3	62.8	50.7
Dumfries & Galloway	40.3	60.7	48.8
Orkney	27.9	57.3	47.4
Shetland	27.1	62.4	51.6
SCOTLAND	51.6	74.3	63.5

Note: Regions are listed in descending order of the 'Yes' vote in 1979.

The 1997 result could not have been more different. Even in the most lukewarm local authority area, Orkney, a clear majority of the votes cast (57.3 per cent) were in favour of a Parliament. At the other extreme, more than three-quarters of the voters supported a Parliament in the populous regions of Strathclyde, Central and Fife, as did almost 80 per cent of voters in the Western Isles. There was no question mark over the legitimacy of the Parliament's mandate over any part of the national territory. In contrast to 1979, therefore, there was no doubting that the devolution proposals were heartily endorsed by the Scottish electorate in 1997. By contrast, the 1997 Welsh referendum, while producing a majority for devolution, did so by the narrowest of margins (50.3 per cent). Like the 1979 Scottish referendum, the 1997 Welsh result produced only an equivocal mandate for change.

Although a Scottish Parliament was supported by clear majorities of voters in all regions in 1997, there remained, nonetheless, substantial inter-regional variations in the size of the Yes vote. As Table 6.6 shows, the basic geography of the Yes vote was much the same at both referendums. Although the number of cases for analysis is, of course, very small, the correlation between the 1979 and 1997 regional Yes votes is very strong, with a coefficient of 0.90. Areas which had given the highest levels of support to an Assembly in 1979 also gave the highest levels of support to a Parliament in 1997 and those which had given the lowest support in 1979 still gave the lowest support in 1997. However, while the underlying geography of variations in support for devolution remained unaltered, the overall level of support rose substantially over the intervening years, producing Yes majorities on the first question in all counting areas.

The former Regional Council areas, while allowing comparisons between the 1979 and 1997 referendums, were large and often internally heterogeneous. As a result, they conceal substantial internal variations. Strathclyde, for instance, was in its day the largest local authority in Europe, and covered areas as diverse as Glasgow's inner city, the depressed industrial towns and ex-coalfields of Lanarkshire and Ayrshire, as well as very affluent commuter suburbs and villages such as Bearsden and Drymen, and rural areas (including remote Highland areas in Argyll and islands such as Islay, Mull and Jura). Politically, too, the Regional Councils covered a wide range. Again in Strathclyde, for instance, in addition to numerous Labour strongholds, the region contained the constituency of Eastwood, by a considerable margin the safest Conservative seat in Scotland after the 1992 general election, as well as the Liberal Democrat seat of Argyll and Bute. We need, therefore, a more detailed map to enable us to draw conclusions about the geography of the referendum results. The 1997 results were issued separately for each of the 32 current local authorities, and although this is smaller than the number of parliamentary constituencies (72) it does provide a finer scale of aggregation and allows more scope for analysis than was possible in 1979.

The variations in the Yes vote at this finer scale were even more substantial than at the regional level (see Appendix 1). None of the 32 local authority areas failed to return a Yes majority, but the size of the majority on the question of having a Scottish Parliament varied from

57.3 per cent in Orkney to a remarkable 84.7 per cent in West Dunbartonshire. In total, six areas recorded Yes votes of 80 per cent and above while eight were lower than 65 per cent. What explains these variations?

As we have seen, the Yes and No campaigns were to a large extent politically polarised, with Labour, the SNP and the Liberal Democrats all strongly advocating a Yes vote while the Scottish Conservatives, virtually alone, campaigned against the devolution proposals. With the exception of Tam Dalyell, the Labour MP for Linlithgow, no prominent member of a party publicly advocated voting for the 'opposite' side. Indeed, very few ordinary members actively campaigned in opposition to the party line (see Chapter 5). This was in marked contrast to the cross-party Yes and No campaigns in the 1975 European referendum and the 1979 Scottish referendum, which featured, in particular, a powerful Labour Vote No group (including Tam Dalyell). Given the very clearly polarised and politicised nature of the 1997 referendum campaign, it would be surprising if the geography of the Yes vote were not related to the geography of party support. As Table 6.7 shows, this is certainly true as far as support for Labour and the Conservatives is concerned. The correlation coefficients show that the percentage voting Yes in each local authority was strongly related to how well each of these parties performed there at the general election in May. The way in which the geography of support for Labour and Conservative translated into support for a Scottish Parliament was directly linked to where each party stood on the issue: the bigger the Conservatives' general election vote the lower the percentage voting Yes; the larger Labour's vote share, the larger the Yes vote a few months later. Variations in the size of the Conservative vote at the 1997 election accounted for 52 per cent of the variation in the percentage voting Yes to a Parliament, while variations in the strength of the Labour vote accounted for 68 per cent of the variation in referendum voting. It is clear that Labour areas voted strongly in favour of a Parliament, while areas where the Conservatives retained some support were more lukewarm. That said, of course, even where the Conservatives were strongest there were still majorities in favour of a Parliament.

The correlation coefficient indicating the association between the Liberal Democrat vote share at the 1997 general election and the vote for a Parliament would seem to run counter to the argument about political polarisation. The Liberal Democrats were prominent in the Yes campaign and have had a long-standing commitment to devolution. Yet the relationship between their vote share in May and the Yes vote in September is significant and negative, indicating that

Table 6.7: Correlations with percentage voting Yes to a Scottish Parliament
(first question) in the referendum

Social composition (1991 Census)		Political context	
% professional & managerial workers	-0.55*	% Conservative vote 1997	-0.72*
% manual workers	0.17	% Labour vote 1997	0.83*
% owner occupiers	-0.63*	% Lib Dem vote 1997	-0.59*
% local authority tenants	0.73*	% SNP vote 1997	0.06
% private tenants	-0.69*		
% employed in agriculture	-0.73*		
% households with no car	0.75*		
% with a degree	-0.55*		
% Scottish born	0.73*		
Persons per hectare	0.36*		
Size of electorate, 1997	0.32*		

Note: * = statistically significant at $p < 0.05$.

the higher the party's share of the vote in an area, the lower the Yes
vote. It is worth stressing, however, the important methodological
point that an analysis of voting across geographical areas does not
necessarily tell us anything about how groups of individuals in those
areas might have voted. The negative correlation does not mean that
Liberal Democrat supporters were opposed to a Parliament (indeed,
our survey of individual voters shows them to have been strongly in
favour: see Chapter 7). As noted in our discussion of turnout, Liberal
Democrat support in Scotland is concentrated in the Borders, the
rural north-east, the Highlands, and Orkney and Shetland and these
are also the areas where support for devolution was weakest in 1979.
In other words, the correlation for the Liberal Democrat vote is likely
to be spurious, confirming that areas which were conservative about
devolution in 1979 were still (relatively) conservative in relation to the
question in 1997, rather than telling us anything about the voting
behaviour of Liberal Democrat supporters themselves. Similarly, the
absence of a significant correlation between the SNP vote share in
1997 and the percentage supporting a Parliament does not imply any
ambivalence on the part of SNP supporters for the Labour
government's plans: survey evidence shows that they were more
likely to vote Yes than the supporters of any other party (see Chapter
7). Rather, the weak relationship reflects the fact that in the 1997
general election the SNP did quite well throughout Scotland, in some
traditionally Conservative as well as traditionally Labour areas, hence
their share of the vote does not correlate particularly well with
underlying sentiment on the devolution question.

Levels of support for a Scottish Parliament were also related to the social make-up of the local authority areas (Table 6.7). Given the relationships with party strength, it is not surprising to find that the percentage voting Yes was lower the more middle class the area (there are negative correlations between the proportion voting for a Parliament and both the percentage of professional and managerial workers and the percentage of owner occupiers living there). On the other hand, the more working class an area, the greater the Yes vote (indicated by the strong positive correlations with percentage of local authority tenants and percentage of households with no car).

Areas with a relatively large agricultural workforce, meanwhile, were less likely to vote in favour of a Parliament than others (a strong negative correlation with percentage employed in agriculture) and in this case there is no apparent paradox in the figure for persons per hectare – the more densely populated areas tended to vote more emphatically Yes. This may reflect an anti-central belt element in the voting. Concern about the possibility that the new Parliament might be dominated by the interests of the mainly industrial central Lowlands was a theme played on by No campaigners, who also made much of allegations of sleaze in west of Scotland Labour politics which emerged in the aftermath of the 1997 general election, especially in Paisley, Renfrewshire.

Finally, what may be termed the 'Scottish heartlands' appear to have been more enthusiastic in their support for a Parliament than were areas with relatively high proportions of residents who were not born in Scotland (indicated by the significant positive correlation between percentage Scottish born and the percentage voting Yes). Although feelings of 'Scottishness' probably overlap with some of our other measures (such as class and party supported – see Bennie *et al.*, 1997: 135–41) it seems that the more Scottish a community, the greater the support for the Parliament there. The Yes campaign, it might be suggested, drew more support from areas where a Scottish identity is more likely to be common and, possibly, more intense. This is an issue which will be explored at the level of individual voters in the next chapter.

As with our analysis of turnout, however, the simple correlation analysis reported in Table 6.7 is concerned with the associations between levels of support for a Parliament and each of the social and political factors in isolation. These social and political variables are themselves highly inter-correlated – to an extent some are measuring the same thing. In addition, it is once again unlikely that any one factor is of itself sufficient to account for inter-authority variations in the Yes vote. We turn once again to multiple regression analysis, therefore. Analysing all the social and political variables together, we find that three of the latter (per cent Labour, per cent Conservative and per cent SNP in 1997) and two of the former (per cent professional and managerial and per cent employed in agriculture) are statistically significant and together account for almost 93 per cent of the variation in the percentage voting Yes across the local authorities.[8] Holding the other factors constant, the Yes vote was larger where Labour had been stronger in the general election and also, in contrast to the impression given by the simple correlations, where the SNP vote was higher. On the other hand the Yes vote was smaller, other things being equal, where there were more professional and managerial workers, more agricultural workers and where the Conservatives had performed relatively well in the May election.

The size of the Yes vote in each local authority was, then, considerably more predictable on the basis of social composition and party support than was turnout. Given the very large proportion of variation explained by the regression equation it is not surprising that only in a very few authorities was the percentage which voted Yes notably higher or lower than predicted by the model. The largest deviation towards a lower than expected Yes vote was in Shetland (-3.8). This suggests that, as in 1979, Shetland voters were still more sceptical about change than were Scottish voters as a whole, other things being equal. Interestingly, it also appears that Shetlanders were also more sceptical than their southern neighbours in Orkney since the Yes vote in Orkney was almost exactly as predicted (difference = -0.9). The only other authority in which the Yes vote was over-predicted by more than two percentage points was Dundee (-3.6), which is rather surprising given that one of the city's constituencies had an SNP MP (Gordon Wilson) from February 1974 to 1987, although it is also true that the city's daily newspaper (the *Courier*) was strongly opposed to devolution (see Chapter 4).[9] There were only two authorities in which the Yes vote exceeded the regression prediction by more than three percentage points – West Dunbartonshire (+3.8) which returned the highest Yes percentage of all and, for no obvious reason, Aberdeenshire (+3.6).

Levels of local support for a Scottish Parliament followed the conventional cleavages of Scottish politics closely, therefore. Class and the urban–rural divide were key underlying components, but the primary determinant of how each area voted was how much support it gave to the two major parties, Labour and Conservative, with the level of support for the SNP also playing a more minor role. The main players in the Yes and No campaigns respectively reaped what they had sown in terms of their prior electoral support. It is hard, given these results, to avoid the observation that part of the explanation for the much wider margin of victory for the Yes vote in the 1997 referendum as compared with 1979 was the substantial reduction in the Scottish Conservative vote over the period. Cause and effect are difficult to untangle here. The Scottish Conservatives lost support as the government acquired a reputation for being anti-Scottish, which probably fuelled pent-up demand for a Scottish Parliament. Equally, as Conservative representation in Scotland dwindled, so the party found it harder to get its message across, on the constitution as on other policy areas.

SUPPORT FOR TAX-VARYING POWERS

We suggested above that the outcome of the vote on the second referendum question was a cause for some concern on the part of the Yes campaign (especially among those who had been opposed to the two-question ballot when it was first proposed). Although the scope for control over taxation by a Scottish Parliament was limited, the proposed tax-varying powers were important symbolically. There were certainly grounds for doubt over which way the vote on the second question would go. The conventional wisdom in studies of voting behaviour is that the majority of voters are not usually altruistic. Although survey respondents frequently report that they are willing to see higher taxes in return for better public services it appears that it is other people's taxes, not their own, which they have in mind.[10] Tax increases are often unpopular among those who have to pay them – a view apparently taken on board by New Labour in the run up to the 1997 general election. Although the formula proposed by the government was that a Scottish Parliament would be given tax-*varying* powers, few doubted that the real sub-text would be tax *rises* for Scottish residents. These fears had been played on skilfully by the Conservatives' last Secretary of State for Scotland, Michael Forsyth, before the 1997 election when he raised the spectre of the so-called 'tartan tax'.

When it came to the actual vote, however, Scottish voters gave majority support to the proposal to establish tax-varying powers: 63.5 per cent voted Yes to the second question (see Table 6.5). While this fell some way short of the support for a Parliament, it was still a substantial level of approval. There was no evidence in the actual result of the very close vote which some had predicted on the basis of (an ill-informed reading of) pre-referendum polls. What is more, the majority for tax powers was larger than the 1979 majority for an

Assembly. Applying the 1979 requirement for the support of 40 per cent of the electorate would have resulted in a narrow technical rejection of the proposal for tax-varying powers: only 38 per cent of the registered electorate (39 per cent of the adjusted electorate) expressed support for the measure. However, in the absence of a threshold, and given the size of the majorities on both questions, no questions were raised about the mandate conferred by the referendum.

The pattern of voting on tax-varying powers across local authorities was almost identical to the pattern of voting on whether or not there should be a Scottish Parliament. Comparing the two votes across local authorities the correlation is almost perfect (a coefficient of 0.986). The same sorts of areas which voted heavily in favour of a Parliament also voted heavily in favour on the tax powers question, albeit at a somewhat lower level – at 63.5 per cent, the overall level of support for tax powers was 10.8 percentage points below the level of support for a Parliament. The largest total drop in the Yes percentage between the two questions occurred in Renfrewshire (-15.5 percentage points). This may have been a result of concerns over allegations of corruption in Paisley, which surfaced after the 1997 general election. Some voters there may have been unwilling to trust politicians with more of their money. The smallest drop, however, was in the neighbouring local authority of Glasgow (-8.6 percentage points). If we calculate the difference between the two votes as a percentage of the first Yes vote – thus getting an estimate of the proportion of Yes No voters – the figure is 14.8 per cent nationally. Again this was smallest in Glasgow (10.6 per cent) but on this measure Moray (22.1 per cent) had the largest difference between the two votes.

The majority vote in favour of giving the Scottish Parliament tax-varying powers achieved Tony Blair's goal of giving the government the opportunity to claim a clear mandate for this aspect of its plans. However, interpreting the meaning of the vote is not necessarily so clear-cut. It is unlikely that Scotland became a nation of altruistic voters on the eve of the referendum. Even though there is strong survey evidence that Scots are more likely to favour high public spending, and high taxation to pay for it, than are voters in England (see Pattie and Johnston, 1990; Bennie *et al.*, 1997: 126), this is not the same as saying that Scots are willing to bear an extra taxation burden which is not borne by people resident in other parts of the United Kingdom. It is also worth emphasising that the tax-varying powers on offer to the new Scottish Parliament are limited (a modest three pence in the pound on income tax). Nonetheless, there was a clear recognition on the part of some voters that a Yes vote on the second referendum question would have implications for taxation. In our survey of Scottish electors, conducted in the immediate aftermath of the referendum, 45 per cent of those who voted and who agreed that devolution 'would mean extra taxes for Scotland' nonetheless voted in favour of tax-varying powers. On the other hand, the same survey reveals that 57 per cent of the Scottish public either did not think that an Edinburgh Parliament would mean extra taxes, or were unsure whether it would or would not. Among those who voted in favour of giving the Parliament power to vary tax, 67 per cent fell into these categories. The Yes vote on the second question may represent altruism on the part of some voters, therefore, but by no means all.

On the basis of the referendum results it appears that it was on the tax issue that residual doubts about devolution seem to have been expressed. The only two local authority areas to vote against tax powers, Orkney (with 47.4 per cent voting for the measure) and Dumfries and Galloway (with 48.8 per cent in favour) had both voted against devolution in 1979, as had other areas where the winning margin for the 1997 Yes to taxation powers vote was narrow, such as the Borders (50.7 per cent), Shetland (51.6 per cent) and Tayside (57.0 per cent). At the level of individual voters, as we shall see in the next chapter, it appears that reactions to the tax question were a means of expressing strength of support for the new Parliament. Yes Yes voting was a means of expressing strong support and No No voting indicated strong opposition. Yes No voters were giving qualified support.

A MANDATE FOR CHANGE?

A Yes majority for a new Parliament had been widely anticipated in the run-up to the referendum, although there remained some doubts about the size of the majority and the outcome on the taxation question and, consequently, over the claim to legitimacy that the Parliament would have. These doubts were effectively removed by the referendum results. Turnout, while lower than in a general election, was respectable, and certainly much higher than in second-order elections where low participation has not resulted in serious questioning of the mandate that they confer. The Yes majority on both questions was emphatic, albeit greater for establishing a Parliament than for giving it tax powers. The 1979 referendum had revealed a country sharply divided into opposing camps on the issue of devolution. Almost half the voters on that occasion had come down against an Assembly and half of the counting areas had returned No majorities, but the spectre of a divided country was laid to rest in convincing fashion in 1997.

NOTES

1. Although the anti-devolution MP, Tam Dalyell, announced in a Commons debate that he would be voting No Yes (Hansard, HC, 16 May 1997, col.292), few voters appear to have thought along these lines – our survey of Scottish voters contained only five out of 2,335 respondents who claimed to have voted No Yes.
2. The electorates of the local authorities vary greatly in size, the largest (Glasgow) having an electorate of almost 480,000 and the smallest (Orkney) having just over 15,000 voters. As a result, the mean percentage turnout for the local authorities differs slightly from the overall national figure, because the mean takes no account of the relative size of the different authorities and hence of their differing contributions to the national total.
3. The wide variations in the sizes of local authority electorates can cause problems for correlation analyses since the technique gives equal weight to all cases, thus over-emphasising the importance of the smaller authorities. All correlation coefficients reported in this chapter have been checked controlling for size of electorate: with very few exceptions the results remain unchanged and there is no need to qualify our interpretation of the simple bivariate relationships.
4. Only ten of the 32 Scottish local authorities comprise entire parliamentary constituencies. In the remaining cases boundaries overlap and for these we have calculated estimates of party shares of votes and turnout (see below) in the general election.
5. The regression equation is:
   $$TO = 78.7 – 0.28 \,(MW) – 0.43 \,(PPH) – 0.60 \,(AG)$$
   Adj. $R^2 = 0.550$
   TO = referendum turnout; MW = % manual workers; PPH = persons per hectare; AG = % agricultural workers.
6. For an analysis of turnout in Scotland at the 1997 general election see Denver (1997).
7. The regression equation is:
   $$TO = -8.5 + 0.97 \,(GETO)$$
   Adj. $R^2 = 0.753$
   TO = referendum turnout; GETO = estimated general election turnout.
8. The regression equation is:
   $$YES = 82.7 + 0.14 \,(LAB) -0.31 \,(PMAN) -0.80 \,(AG) -0.36 \,(CON) + 0.12 \,(SNP)$$
   Adj. $R^2 = 0.926$
   YES = % voting Yes; LAB = % Labour 1997; PMAN = % professional and managerial workers; AG = % agricultural workers; CON = % Conservative 1997; SNP = % SNP 1997.
9. Although we would not wish to put too much reliance on the data, since the numbers involved are small, our survey of electors found that the Yes Yes vote among residents of Dundee who read the *Courier* was only 54% (N = 24) compared with 78% (N = 27) for those who read another paper.
10. Interestingly in this context, when the massive Glasgow vote for taxation powers was announced on referendum night a television cameraman commented to one of the authors: 'It's all right for them – they're all on the broo (dole)!'

7

Voting in the Referendum

The analysis of the results of the referendum presented in the preceding chapter tells us a good deal about variations in voting from place to place. What it cannot do is yield information about the behaviour of individuals or groups of electors. In order to find out how people voted, and to try to explain why they voted as they did, we need to make use of survey data. In this chapter, therefore, we use the results of our postal survey of a random sample of the Scottish electorate, which was undertaken immediately after the referendum (for details see Appendix 2), to explore patterns of turnout and the choices made by voters, attempting to explain who supported which options and why the vote in favour of change was so decisive. We begin, however, by considering voting, as opposed to non-voting, in the referendum.

VOTING AND NON-VOTING

We have already seen that turnout in the referendum, at 60.4 per cent, was close to the turnout recorded in the two previous referendums in Scotland. It was lower than general election turnout (71.4 per cent in 1997) but greater than the normal turnout level in local elections (45 per cent). Variations from area to area did not seem to suggest that turnout was related to variations in enthusiasm for the Scottish Parliament and we argued that the pattern of turnout across the country could be described as 'normal'. As with general and local elections, turnout was higher in more affluent areas and lower in more working-class areas, especially inner cities. However, these results tell us where turnout was high and where it was low: they do not tell us about which individual electors voted. To analyse patterns of individual turnout in the referendum we use data derived from our survey of electors.

It is well-established that individual turnout in elections is affected by a relatively small number of social factors, namely age, marital status, length of residence in the community, housing tenure and, to a lesser extent, class-related variables. In addition, strength of party identification has proved to be an important political influence upon turnout levels with stronger identifiers being more likely to vote than those who do not identify with a party or do so only weakly (see Crewe *et al.* 1977; Miller, 1988; Swaddle and Heath, 1989). Past experience and the local activities of the political parties can also affect election turnout. The marginality of a constituency at the previous election gives voters and parties information about how crucial each individual vote is to the overall outcome there: the more marginal the seat, the more important it is to vote, and hence the higher the turnout.[1] Furthermore, local constituency campaigning by the political parties can have an impact on election turnout, especially by encouraging their own supporters to vote (Denver and Hands, 1997a).

Referendums differ from elections in important respects, however, and there is no guarantee that the same factors will be important in the two types of ballot. In the context of turnout, for instance, the previous marginality of constituencies is irrelevant in a national referendum, since the result is calculated on the votes cast over the country as a whole, and targeted party campaigning in particular localities aimed at turning out the vote is almost wholly absent. Hitherto, however, there has been no survey evidence about voting and non-voting in referendums and little is known about the similarities and differences between voting in elections and in referendums. In this section, therefore, we use our referendum survey data to examine, for the first time in Britain, whether the generalisations established concerning voting in elections continue to hold true for voting in a referendum.

All survey studies of non-voting in Britain face a common problem – the over-reporting of turnout by respondents. In all cases the percentage of respondents saying that they voted in the relevant election is far larger than the percentage of the electorate which actually voted. To some extent this arises because surveys usually reach, and receive responses from, people who are actually able to vote while the electoral register (on which the official turnout figure is calculated) contains the names of people who have died or moved away from their area of registration. In addition, the very elderly and infirm are both less likely to vote or to respond to surveys than other people, thus reducing the number of non-voters in the sample. These problems are amplified when a postal survey is used since potential respondents have to make the effort to fill in and post the questionnaire (perhaps a more time consuming task than actually voting). The biggest cause of turnout being exaggerated by surveys, however, is that, for a variety of reasons, respondents tend to say that they voted when in fact they did not (see Swaddle and Heath, 1989).

In some cases people genuinely forget whether or not they voted and tend to assume that they did. In others, since electors are aware that voting is a socially approved activity – that they ought to vote because it is part of their duty as citizens – non- voters are likely to feel guilty and so falsely report that they did indeed vote.

As with previous studies of non-voting, our post-referendum survey of Scottish electors produced very substantial over-reporting of turnout – 82 per cent of our respondents claimed to have voted, which is well in excess of the actual turnout. This does not mean that we are unable to compare voters and non-voters, however. Recent British Election Study (BES) surveys have been able to check survey responses concerning voting against official records (the electoral register on which voters names are crossed off in the polling station) and they find that, although some respondents say that they voted when the records show that they did not, analysis of patterns of non-voting based on survey responses does not produce significantly different results from analysis based on the official records (Swaddle and Heath, 1989). On the assumption that the same applies in this case, we can be fairly confident that our survey gives a reliable picture of the characteristics and attitudes of non-voters in the referendum. In order to bring our figures into line with actual referendum turnout, however, we have weighted the survey data appropriately.[2]

Table 7.1 shows turnout variations by sex, age, occupational class, education and housing tenure (unless otherwise stated, all results reported in this chapter are statistically significant). Men turned out to a slightly greater extent than women, although the difference was not statistically significant. On the other hand, there are clearer differences in terms of occupation, education and tenure than is normally found for elections. Mirroring our aggregate analysis, core middle-class groups (professional, managerial and supervisory non-manual workers) were clearly more inclined to vote than others (although not much more than skilled manual workers) and a rather larger proportion of owner occupiers voted as compared to those who rent their homes from the local council or a private landlord. Education, too, made a difference. Those who had left full-time education at the earliest opportunity were less likely to vote in the referendum (56 per cent) than were those who had stayed on (around two-thirds of those with Highers [the Scottish equivalent of A-levels], A-levels, professional qualifications or degrees turned out). In line with previous research on turnout, however, the social characteristic that most clearly differentiates voters from non-voters is age. Referendum turnout among the youngest age group was very low (44 per cent). This increased to 49 per cent among those aged 25–34 but then there is a sharp step up between those aged 25–34 and those aged 35–44.

Table 7.1: Social characteristics and turnout in the referendum (percentage voted)

	Percentage			*Percentage*	
Men	62	(1,125)	Left school min. age	56	(1,428)
Women	60	(1,165)	Highers/A-levels	69	(219)
			Professional		
			Qualification	66	(207)
Aged 18-24	44	(85)	Degree	68	(424)
Aged 25-34	49	(402)			
Aged 35-44	60	(459)			
Aged 45-54	63	(396)	Owner occupier	65	(1,485)
Aged 55-64	64	(372)	Council tenant	52	(628)
Aged 65+	67	(560)	Other renter	50	(178)
Professional/					
Managerial	66	(608)			
Supervisory					
non-manual	64	(561)			
Other non-manual	55	(238)			
Skilled manual	60	(343)			
Other manual	53	(301)			

Note: These are weighted data.

The apparent apathy of young people so far as voting is concerned has attracted a good deal of journalistic comment. It is not clear that there is anything new in this – young people have always had lower turnout levels than those of more mature years – but it might have been hoped that the referendum would have attracted greater participation from them. Poll figures showed, after all, that young people were enthusiastically in favour of a Scottish Parliament and it is frequently suggested that it is *party* politics which has disillusioned them. Clearly the kinds of factors that depress young peoples' turnout in elections – technical difficulties over registration and voting, greater concern with music, sport, fashion and members of the opposite sex than with politics – continue to operate in a referendum. The fact that the oldest age group had the best turnout is in some ways surprising since this group will contain electors who are infirm or too old to be bothered. But this seems to be outweighed by the simple fact that retired people have plenty of time to vote and going along to the polling station may be something of an occasion for them, a chance to get out of the house.

Table 7.2 focuses on political characteristics. The fact that the pattern of non-voting in the referendum was similar to that found in general elections is emphasised by the fact that only 17 per cent of those who did not vote in the 1997 general election switched to voting in the referendum. In other words a staggering 83 per cent of non-voters in the general election were also referendum non-voters. These might be described as 'core' non-voters and they comprised 12 per cent of our sample. In contrast, 58 per cent of our respondents voted in both the election and the referendum. Putting these together, fully 70 per cent of our respondents made the same decision about whether or not to vote on the two occasions while 28 per cent of our sample voted in the election but not in the referendum and 3 per cent in the referendum but not the election.

There were modest differences in turnout according to the party respondents voted for in the 1997 general election. The highest turnout was among SNP voters (73 per cent) followed by Conservatives (70 per cent), Liberal Democrats (69 per cent), and Labour voters (65 per cent). The figure for Liberal Democrats illustrates the danger of drawing conclusions about individual voters from aggregate correlations. In the aggregate analysis in the previous chapter we found that there was a negative correlation at local council level between turnout and per cent Liberal Democrat in the May general election but we now see that individual Liberal Democrats actually had a relatively high turnout. The aggregate correlation, in this case, is misleading. The fact that supporters of different parties turned out at slightly different rates almost certainly in part reflects differences in the social composition of each party's support. Labour, for instance, gets a large part of its support from working-class voters, who were, as we have seen, less likely to turn out, while the Conservatives and the Liberal Democrats have more solidly middle-class support bases and these groups were more likely to vote. The high referendum turnout among SNP supporters is more likely to reflect the greater importance that they attach to the issue of self-government for Scotland.

The likelihood of someone voting in elections is strongly influenced by whether and how strongly he or she identifies with one of the parties. Strong party supporters are much more likely to vote than those who are not. They are generally more interested in politics, care more about the outcome of elections and have no difficulty in deciding which party to support. In the Scottish referendum the major parties were clearly ranged on one side or the other and so the conditions making for higher turnout among strong party supporters were present. As the table shows, very strong party supporters had the highest turnout (72 per cent) but were not markedly more inclined to vote than fairly strong supporters (70 per cent). On the other hand, the turnout of weak supporters (55 per cent) and of those who did not consider themselves to be party supporters (49 per cent) was, as anticipated, much lower.[3]

The corollary of the points discussed in the previous paragraph is that those who describe themselves as interested in politics should be more likely to turn out than those who are not much interested. This comes close to being tautological but it is possible that people with a general interest in politics might not be interested in the particular issue at stake in a referendum – perhaps even regarding it as a distraction from 'real' politics (the politics of class, for example). As our data show, however, this was certainly not the case in the Scottish referendum. Almost three-quarters of those who said that, in general, they were 'very interested' in politics voted in the referendum and participation drops steeply as interest in politics wanes: over two-thirds of those who said they were 'not at all interested' in politics did not vote.

Table 7.2: Political characteristics and turnout in the referendum (percentage voted)

	Percentage			*Percentage*	
Voted in GE	68	(1,962)	*General interest in politics*		
Did not vote in GE	17	(328)	Very interested	76	(407)
			Quite interested	67	(1,211)
Voted Con	70	(327)	Not very interested	41	(581)
Voted Lab	65	(1,018)	Not at all interested	31	(89)
Voted Lib Dem	69	(198)			
Voted SNP	73	(374)			
Strength of party support					
Very strong	72	(306)			
Fairly strong	70	(774)			
Not very strong	54	(506)			
None	49	(646)			

Note: These are weighted data.

Would it have made any difference to the outcome of the referendum if all non-voters had voted? The evidence of Table 7.3 suggests not. A slightly larger proportion of non-voters would have voted Yes for a Parliament (79 per cent) than did those who voted, and although the majority for taxation powers is smaller (52 per cent) among non-voters than among voters, the proposal would still have been passed comfortably even if all non-voters had voted.

Nonetheless, the lower level of support for taxation powers suggests, contrary to the impression given by the aggregate analysis, that non-voters were less strongly committed to devolution than were voters. This is confirmed by the figures relating to attitudes towards the proposed Scottish Parliament. Whereas 46 per cent of voters were *strongly* in favour only 27 per cent of non-voters were; 14 per cent of non-voters appear to have been indifferent compared with 3 per cent of voters. On the other hand, non-voters were also less likely to be strongly against (5 per cent) than voters (9 per cent). Recalculating these data shows that there was a turnout of 73 per cent among both those strongly in favour and those strongly against, 62 per cent among those simply against, 52 per cent among those in favour and 27 per cent among those who were indifferent. We can conclude, therefore, that strength of feeling about the issue (whether in favour or in opposition to change) clearly affected peoples' decisions about whether or not to vote in the referendum: strong feelings either way encouraged participation, while indifference discouraged it.

Table 7.3: Opinions of voters and non-voters on devolution

Would have voted/did vote	Non-voters	Voters
	%	%
Yes Yes	52	66
Yes No	27	11
No No	21	23
	(322)	(1,816)
Opinion on Scottish Parliament		
	%	%
Strongly favour	27	46
Favour	42	29
Neither	14	3
Against	12	12
Strongly against	5	9
	(368)	(1,708)

Although we have shown that a number of variables were associated with differential turnout levels in the referendum, interpretation remains difficult because there are clear overlaps between them. Young people, for example, tend also to have weak party identification; owner occupiers are disproportionately Conservative. In order to gain a clearer picture of the main determinants of turnout we need to turn to multivariate analysis. This enables us to test whether a variable remains a significant influence on turnout once the other relevant factors are taken into account, and also to examine the total effect of combinations of variables.[4] Since the dependent variable is a dichotomy (voted or did not vote) the statistically more appropriate form of multivariate analysis to use is logistic regression but for ease of interpretation – and because the substantive results are very similar[5] – we present here the results of ordinary least-squares regression analysis (see Table 7.4).

Table 7.4: Regression analysis of referendum turnout

Variable	Equation 1		Equation 2	
	Regression coefficient	*'t' statistic*	*Regression coefficient*	*'t' statistic*
Age	0.180	6.98	0.136	5.23
Education	0.120	4.73	0.112	4.42
Tenure	0.100	4.19	0.102	4.21
Interest in politics	–	–	0.188	7.40
Strength of opinion on Parliament	–	–	0.144	6.30
Strength of party support	–	–	0.120	5.20
Constant	0.344	11.81	0.141	4.37
(Adj.) R²	0.047		0.152	

Note: The coefficients shown are unstandardised regression coefficients ('b's). Variables with non-significant coefficients (sex and occupation) are not shown.

The first equation in Table 7.4 shows that age, education and tenure were significantly associated with variations in voting (sex and occupation are not shown as they were not statistically significant). Those aged 35 and over were more likely to vote than those under 35; those who completed their education after the minimum school-leaving age were more likely to vote than those who left school at the first opportunity, and owner occupiers were more likely to do so than tenants. To repeat, this means that each of these variables independently affected voting even when the other social variables are taken into account. The R^2 figure shows, however, that these three variables together explain only about 5 per cent of the variation in individual turnout. When we add the political variables to the analysis (equation 2) the proportion of variation explained increases to about 15 per cent. The coefficients and associated 't' statistics show that, on the whole, the most important influences on the decision to vote were not social but political. Interest in politics is the strongest influence, comparing those who were very or fairly interested with others, followed by strength of opinion on the issue of a Scottish Parliament – those strongly in favour or strongly against were more likely to vote than those with less firm opinions. Strength of party identification, comparing very strong or fairly strong party supporters with others, has a similar effect to age, which is the most important of the social variables. Nonetheless, education and housing tenure are also significantly associated with variations in voting and non-voting (in the expected directions), when all the other variables are held constant. So, if an elector was very or quite interested in politics, was strongly in favour or opposed to a Scottish Parliament, was aged 35 or over, was a very or fairly strong supporter of one of the parties, left school after the minimum leaving age and was an owner occupier, then the probability that he or she voted in the referendum is very strong. Those who had none of these characteristics were very likely to be non-voters.

What general lessons can be drawn about voting and non-voting in referendums from our analysis and discussion of these data? Firstly, it seems likely that, as in elections, non-voting will continue to be more prevalent among some socially defined groups – in particular the young, the less well-educated and those who live in rented accommodation. The factors which inhibit turnout among these groups at elections continue to apply at referendums. Secondly, where the parties take clear stands on the issue in question it seems likely that strong party identifiers will turn out in greater numbers than those who are not strongly aligned with a party. The converse of this is, however, that if the parties are divided or not clearly identified with one side of the question then turnout may be low, as strong identifiers will have no extra incentive to go to the polls. Third, and perhaps most intriguingly, our analysis has shown that strength of feeling on the issue concerned is an important determinant of turnout. If an issue is put before the people on which they do not have strong feelings either way – reforming the electoral system, perhaps – then it seems that a low turnout should be anticipated.

VOTING ON THE SCOTTISH PARLIAMENT

As previously explained, voters in the referendum were asked to record their preferences on two issues – whether they favoured a Scottish Parliament and whether they favoured such a Parliament having tax-varying powers. The reported votes of our sample of voters were 77 per cent Yes on the first question and 68 per cent Yes on the second question. These are relatively close to the actual figures (74 per cent and 64 per cent respectively) so that in this case there is no need to weight the survey data.

We can divide respondents into three main groups – those who voted Yes Yes (65 per cent of voters), those who voted Yes No (11 per cent) and those whose choice was No No (23 per cent) – although we also had five respondents who claimed to have voted No Yes. As with turnout, we begin by examining how different social groups voted.

Social characteristics
Table 7.5 shows how voting in the referendum varied according to sex, age, occupational group, education, housing tenure and religious denomination. It is worth noting, first of all, that in every social group that we have identified in the table a majority voted Yes to both questions. There are, nonetheless, variations across groups in the size of the majority. Women appear to have been slightly more hesitant than men about supporting a Scottish Parliament. This is not an artefact of the different age structures of the male and female population as the difference is found among every age group. Enthusiasm for the new Parliament clearly diminishes with age. Although there is a slight reversal of the trend among those aged 45–54, there is generally a decline in the proportion voting Yes Yes as one moves up the age range. This may reflect the generally greater conservatism (with a small 'c') of older people. In addition, it is worth remembering that the oldest groups of voters had shared with others in the United Kingdom several key experiences which had helped maintain a common sense of Britishness: the Second World War and the coronation of Queen Elizabeth II are probably particularly significant in this respect but we return to the question of national identity below. Younger voters, on the other hand, came of age during a long period of rule by Conservative governments apparently insensitive to Scottish concerns. Occupational differences are also evident with manual workers giving very strong support to devolution and professional and managerial workers giving least. To an extent these patterns are reflected in the figures for education and housing tenure – the strongest Yes Yes majorities are among those who left school at the minimum age and council tenants. There is an interesting variation in the education figures, however, in that the most highly educated were least inclined to vote Yes No and were more supportive of devolution than those who have a professional qualification or who left school after taking Highers and did not go on to university. This may reflect a tendency for graduates to see the proposals as a coherent package to be accepted or rejected as a whole.

We have included figures for religious denomination because, although religious practice in Scotland – as elsewhere – has declined, religious issues continue to be more important than in other parts of Britain (see Bennie *et al.*, 1997: ch. 8). In the 1979 referendum the Church of Scotland urged a Yes vote (although ministers of the Church were prominent in both the Yes and No camps). In 1997, the Church's voice was much more muted. Officially it was in favour of the Scottish Parliament and a number of members had been prominent in the Constitutional Convention but the Kirk had a low profile during the campaign. No formal statement of support was read out from pulpits as had happened in 1979. Politically uninterested Church attenders could have been forgiven for not knowing the Church of Scotland's position on the question of Scotland's constitutional status. In addition, it used to be argued that Scottish Catholics were chary of having a Parliament in Edinburgh because they feared that they would be disadvantaged in a society dominated by Presbyterians (see Brand, 1978: 130). By 1997, however, the figures show that Catholics voted overwhelmingly for the new Parliament. The proportion of Catholics in Scotland is greater than in the United Kingdom as a whole and it may be that they saw a Scottish Parliament as possibly being more inclined to restrict the availability of abortion than the United Kingdom Parliament. That said, two other factors were probably at play here. First, many Scottish Catholics are of Irish descent, and do not share the British Unionist sympathies of many Scottish Presbyterians: Ireland's struggles for home rule and (ultimately) independence may have an echo here in their support for a Scottish Parliament. Second, and again in part because of the historic links between Presbyterianism and unionism in Scotland, Catholics have overwhelmingly supported Labour and are influential in the party, especially in the west of Scotland, and Labour was, of course, strongly behind the Yes campaign in 1997. Voters with Church of Scotland affiliations were solidly in the Yes Yes camp but not overwhelmingly so. The lowest level of support for devolution was among Episcopalians (the Scottish equivalent of the Church of England) and Anglicans. This is not surprising as many Anglicans in Scotland are English or the descendants of English immigrants. Although details are not shown here, the difference in voting between Catholics and Church of Scotland adherents was more marked among the middle class. Among those with a non-manual occupation 77 per cent of the former voted Yes Yes compared with 51 per cent of the latter – a difference of 26 points – whereas among manual workers the figures were 91 per cent and 79 per cent – a 12 point difference.

Table 7.5: Social characteristics and referendum vote (row percentages)

	Yes Yes %	Yes Yes %	No No %	(N)
All	66	11	23	(1,814)
Sex				
Men	70	9	21	(902)
Women	62	14	25	(893)
Age				
Aged 18–24	77	6	17	(48)
Aged 25–34	72	13	16	(254)
Aged 35–44	67	15	18	(369)
Aged 45–54	69	11	21	(329)
Aged 55–64	66	9	26	(311)
Aged 65+	58	10	31	(472)
Occupation				
Professional/Managerial	56	12	33	(530)
Supervisory non-manual	59	12	29	(474)
Other non-manual	68	13	19	(166)
Skilled manual	82	8	10	(262)
Other manual	82	10	8	(203)
Education				
Minimum age	71	11	19	(1,026)
Highers	52	15	33	(202)
Professional qualification	57	12	31	(180)
Degree	64	9	26	(381)
Housing tenure				
Owner occupiers	62	12	27	(1,268)
Council tenants	78	11	12	(411)
Other renters	67	13	20	(97)
Religion				
None	72	10	18	(461)
Church of Scotland	59	13	28	(866)
Roman Catholic	83	7	10	(282)
Episcopalian/Anglican	53	9	38	(45)
Other Protestant	54	17	29	(113)

Subjective identities

Among the most basic identities that people have is a sense of national identity – a sense of being part of a national community (see Keating, 1988). Conventional notions of national identity suggest that the state and the nation are coterminous and that national identity is a relatively simple matter for most citizens. While this is sometimes true it is clearly not the case in the United Kingdom where people might feel themselves to be English, Scottish, Welsh or Irish as well as being part of a British 'nation'. Although feelings of national identity may vary from time to time – involvement of the state in a conflict such as the Falklands War in 1982 or even a royal marriage may heighten feelings of Britishness while the success of the film 'Braveheart' may have made Scots feel more Scottish – there is evidence that in Scotland since the 1970s Scottish identity has increased in importance and intensity (see Bennie *et al.* 1997: 132–3). Table 7.6 shows the national identities of our respondents at the time of the referendum with comparable figures from the 1992 Scottish election study. In 1997 a rather larger proportion of voters felt themselves to be simply Scottish, fewer felt equally Scottish and British and the same (small) proportions were more inclined to describe themselves as British.[6]

Table 7.6: National identities in Scotland, 1992 and 1997

	1992 %	1997 %
Scottish not British	19	28
More Scottish than British	40	35
Equally Scottish and British	33	29
More British than Scottish	3	3
British not Scottish	3	3
None of these/DK/other	2	2
(N)	(957)	(2,307)

Sources: Bennie *et al.* (1997: 133); survey of electors 1997.

If national identity is in some sense fundamental to people then, in the context of United Kingdom politics, class identity used to be just as important. For most of the post-war period the class cleavage underlay the United Kingdom party system. In recent years the influence of class upon party choice in general elections appears to have declined across the United Kingdom as a whole, but in Scotland class identity continued to be important (Franklin, 1985; Johnston and Pattie, 1992; Bennie *et al.* 1997, pp. 101-5; but see Heath *et al.* 1985, 1991). Scots, therefore may have two identities of potential importance for voting in the referendum – nation and class – which, as discussed in Chapter 1, may cut across or reinforce one another.

Table 7.7 shows the relationships between these identities and the referendum vote. Unsurprisingly, national identity is strongly related to voting patterns. The proportions voting Yes Yes decline very

Table 7.7: National and class identity and referendum vote (row percentages)

	Yes Yes %	Yes No %	No No %	(N)
All	66	11	23	(1,814)
National identity				
Scottish not British	89	8	4	(491)
More Scottish than British	75	12	14	(640)
Equally Scottish and British	42	15	43	(526)
More British than Scottish	21	8	71	(48)
British not Scottish	18	13	69	(55)
Class identity				
Working class	74	10	15	(844)
Middle class	46	12	43	(285)
Neither	63	13	25	(666)

sharply, and those voting No No increase sharply, as identities become less Scottish and more British. Class identity also makes a difference with those describing themselves as working class being much more supportive of devolution than the self-described middle class. We can explore the impact of subjective identities further by examining the voting patterns of electors in the light of both kinds of identity. This is done in Table 7.8. In general, national identity was a more important determinant of referendum voting than class identity. Within each class category the proportions voting Yes Yes drop off very sharply among those who are prepared to accept some form of British identity. On the other hand, among those who feel equally Scottish and British the effect of class identity is substantial – and much more evident than in any other national identity group. Another significant feature of the data in this table is that, among

Table 7.8: Percentage voting Yes Yes by class identity and national identity

	Working class %		Middle class %		No class identity %	
Scottish not British	88	(260)	77	(44)	93	(180)
More Scottish than British	80	(313)	65	(89)	72	(232)
Equally Scottish and British	58	(226)	20	(95)	34	(199)
More British/British	26	(23)	24	(45)	9	(34)

Notes: The 'More British than Scottish' and 'British not Scottish' categories have been combined in this table. The figures in brackets are the numbers on which the percentages are based.

those who reject a class identity, national identity produces very dramatic differences in voting. Fully 93 per cent of those who had a purely Scottish identity and no class identity voted Yes Yes; only 9 per cent of those with a British identity and no class identity did so.

Political characteristics

As has been seen in previous chapters, the political parties in Scotland eventually took very clear stands on the issue of a Scottish Parliament. Voters are not at the beck and call of their party headquarters, however, and the question remains as to how voters' previous political affiliations were associated with their referendum votes. The relevant data are given in Table 7.9.

Table 7.9: Party support and referendum vote (row percentages)

	Yes Yes %	Yes No %	No No %	(N)
All	66	11	23	(1,814)
General election vote				
Conservative	10	14	76	(303)
Labour	81	10	9	(856)
Liberal Democrat	51	18	31	(182)
SNP	88	8	4	(359)
Party supporters				
Conservative	8	11	81	(253)
Labour	85	8	7	(715)
Liberal Democrat	55	19	26	(112)
SNP	90	7	3	(292)
None	53	18	29	(413)
Very/fairly strong supporters				
Conservative	7	6	87	(166)
Labour	89	7	4	(551)
Liberal Democrat	59	22	18	(49)
SNP	91	6	3	(226)

The first part of the table uses party voted for in the 1997 general election as an indicator of party affiliation and it is clear that referendum voting was strongly related to party choice in May. Although a quarter of Conservative voters supported a Parliament, three-quarters of them voted the No No ticket. Among Labour and SNP voters the Yes Yes vote was very large. Liberal Democrat voters were more divided than voters for the other parties – just over half voted Yes Yes and a large minority voted No No. This is somewhat surprising given the historic commitment of the party and its predecessors to home rule but it probably reflects the fact that the Liberal Democrat vote is more diffuse than that for other parties – it is more likely to be negative (arising from a dislike of the other parties rather than a particular liking for the Liberal Democrats) and less likely to reflect the voters' policy preferences than is the case with the major parties (see Curtice, 1996). The second part of the table groups respondents according to the answers that they gave when asked: 'In general, do you think of yourself as a supporter of one of the main parties.' This, we hoped, would identify 'core' party supporters rather than those who happened to vote for a particular party in May. As can be seen, the pattern of referendum voting is very similar to that for party voters but in each case is more in line with the party's policy. Thus the No No vote increases to 81 per cent for Conservative supporters while the size of the Yes Yes vote also increases among supporters of the other parties. Taking this analysis a stage further, we show the referendum votes of those who described themselves as very or fairly strong supporters of their party. Once again the proportions voting in line with their parties increase – reaching around nine out of ten for the Conservatives, Labour and the SNP and six out of ten among Liberal Democrats.

We do not have exactly comparable data from the 1979 referendum but a System Three poll undertaken just before polling day on that occasion reported that 91 per cent of SNP supporters intended to vote Yes compared with 21 per cent of Conservative supporters and 66 per cent of Labour supporters (see Chapter 1, Table 1.2). Clearly the major change in 1997 was among Labour supporters. The Labour Party itself was much more united behind devolution and so were the party's supporters.

In their explanation of the result in the 1979 referendum Bochel and Denver (1981: 144) argued that support for devolution fell away during the run-up to the vote at least partly because of the unpopularity of the then Labour government and the Prime Minister, James Callaghan – for reasons quite unconnected with devolution. In February 1979 Gallup's figures for Britain as a whole showed that the government's approval rating (per cent approve minus per cent disapprove of the government's record to date) was -40; the Prime Minister's satisfaction rating (per cent satisfied minus per cent dissatisfied) was -25. In 1997 the situation was very different. In August, the comparable Gallup figures put the government's approval rating at +36 and satisfaction with Tony Blair at an astonishing +70. Among our sample of Scottish voters in September, the government's rating was +54 and Tony Blair's +64. To the extent that the popularity of a government affects its ability to carry its proposals in a referendum, the decision of the government to opt for a referendum only five months into its term of office, while still in its 'honeymoon' period with the electorate, was a good strategy.

Table 7.10: Government record/Tony Blair and referendum vote (row percentages)

	Yes Yes %	Yes No %	No No %	(N)
All	66	11	23	(1,814)
Overall approval of govt. record				
Approve	79	9	12	(1,250)
Disapprove	28	17	55	(237)
No opinion	41	16	43	(310)
Satisfaction with Tony Blair				
Satisfied	76	11	14	(1,347)
Dissatisfied	28	13	59	(186)
No opinion	41	14	46	(352)

As Table 7.10 shows, approval of the government's record and satisfaction with Tony Blair were strongly associated with referendum voting. Large majorities of those who approved and were satisfied – themselves constituting a large majority of voters – voted Yes Yes. Among those who disapproved or were dissatisfied, on the other hand, majorities voted No No. These differences also persist when the figures are broken down by party support. For example, the Yes Yes vote was 83 per cent among Labour voters who were satisfied with Tony Blair and 35 per cent among those who were dissatisfied; it was 77 per cent among SNP voters who disapproved of the government's record but 93 per cent among those who approved. We can conclude, then, that the popularity of the new government and of Tony Blair were important elements in producing the decisive Yes Yes vote in 1997.

Opinions on the constitutional question and the Parliament
The preferences of Scottish voters with reference to the various options for constitutional arrangements defining the relationship between Scotland and the United Kingdom have been documented with some regularity over the past 25 years or so. In broad terms there have been three options – no change, a devolved Assembly or Parliament and outright independence. Although the figures have fluctuated a bit, a devolved Parliament has generally been the most favoured option. Thus, at the time of the 1992 general election, among

those expressing a view, the status quo was favoured by 24 per cent of electors, devolution by 52 per cent and independence by 24 per cent (Bennie *et al.*, 1997: 155). In our sample, at the time of the referendum in 1997, the proportion favouring independence was very similar (25 per cent) but support for no change had declined to 20 per cent and the proportion in favour of a devolved Parliament had risen to 55 per cent.[7] We also asked our respondents to indicate the strength of their opinion on the proposed Scottish Parliament and 43 per cent said that they were strongly in favour, 31 per cent in favour, 5 per cent had no preference, 12 per cent were against and 8 per cent strongly against (N=2,089).

It almost goes without saying that these opinions and preferences were strongly related to voting in the referendum (see Table 7.11). Among those favouring complete independence a few (3 per cent) apparently thought that devolution would hinder progress towards their goal and voted No No, but the Yes Yes vote was nonetheless overwhelming. Among those favouring devolution there was more hesitation about taxation powers but the No No vote was very small. Those in favour of no change were, unsurprisingly, virtually unanimous in voting No No. In terms of attitudes towards the Scottish Parliament, Yes Yes voting varied dramatically from 94 per cent among those strongly in favour to 0 per cent among those strongly against, with the No No vote ranging from less than 1 per cent to 100 per cent. In an obvious way, then, voting in the referendum was a product of electors' views on the constitutional question and the Parliament. Our task is, therefore, to explain why opinion was so strongly in favour of the Parliament.

Table 7.11: Constitutional preference, attitude to Scottish Parliament and referendum vote (row percentages)

	Yes Yes %	Yes No %	No No %	(N)
All	66	11	23	(1,814)
Constitutional preference				
Independence	93	4	3	(465)
Devolved Parliament	78	19	3	(968)
No change	0.5	0.5	99	(373)
Attitude to Scottish Parliament				
Strongly favour	94	6	0	(765)
Favour	73	25	2	(476)
No preference	15	23	62	(52)
Against	0.5	1	99	(210)
Strongly against	0	0	100	(147)

Sentiment in favour of devolution clearly strengthened between 1979 and 1997 for reasons discussed above. Here we consider how variations in support for the Scottish Parliament were related to opinions about what the Parliament might or might not achieve and about Scotland's treatment in the United Kingdom context. For ease of analysis and presentation we have converted respondents' positions on the Parliament into a five-point scale running from 1 = strongly against, to 5 = strongly in favour and present mean scores (see Table 7.12). The mean score for all respondents was 3.9, that is close to 'in favour'.

Table 7.12: Against/favour a Scottish Parliament (mean scores) according to opinions

A Scottish Parliament would:	Agree	Disagree	Difference
Harm the Scottish economy	2.0	4.6	2.6
Create unnecessary extra government	2.3	4.6	2.3
Mean that Scotland might be run by corrupt politicians	2.5	4.3	1.8
Mean extra taxes	3.3	4.5	1.2
Give voters more say in Scottish affairs	4.3	1.8	2.5
Mean that Scots could solve their own problems	4.5	2.1	2.4
Make Scotland more democratic	4.5	2.2	2.3
Conservative governments paid little attention to Scottish opinion	4.1	2.2	1.9
London and the south-east get too much attention on television	4.1	2.7	1.4
English sporting achievements get more praise in the media than Scottish	4.0	3.0	1.0
Scotland benefits from being part of the United Kingdom	3.2	4.7	1.5

The first four statements in Table 7.12 about the potential effects of a Scottish Parliament suggest undesirable consequences and those who disagreed with them, on average, strongly favoured devolution with a mean score of between 4.3 and 4.6 on the five-point approval scale. Those who agreed with them, as might be expected, tended to be against having a Parliament (especially those who thought that devolution would harm the Scottish economy – mean score 2.0) except in the case of the assertion that the Parliament would mean heavier taxation in Scotland (mean, 3.3). This is to be explained by the fact that many voters agreed that the Parliament would raise taxes but saw this as part and parcel of being self-governing – they positively approved of the possibility of increased taxation as a concomitant of having a powerful Scottish Parliament. The next three statements relate to issues of citizenship and democracy and suggest that in these areas a Parliament would improve matters. In this case those who agreed that devolution was a step in the direction of greater democracy and self-government strongly favoured a Scottish Parliament (scores of 4.3 to 4.5) while those who did not were opposed (scores of 1.8 to 2.2). The last four statements relate to more general views which might influence attitudes to home rule. Reactions to the suggestion that recent Conservative governments paid little attention to Scottish opinion were clearly related to opinion on devolution, the mean approval scores being 4.1 for those who agreed and 2.2 for those who disagreed. The complaints heard frequently in Scotland that London and the south-east get too much coverage in the United Kingdom-wide media (scores of 4.1 and 2.7) and that Scottish sport does not get a fair deal (scores of 4.0 and 3.0) also seem to have played a part in shaping devolution attitudes, although the differences here are not very large. Finally, those who disagreed with the most general statement of those listed – that Scotland benefits from being part of the United Kingdom – provided the strongest support of all for a Scottish Parliament (mean score 4.7) while those who agreed were, on balance, slightly in favour (3.2). The latter may appear paradoxical but it is, of course, perfectly consistent to accept that Scotland benefits from being part of the United Kingdom and also favour a devolved Parliament in the United Kingdom context.

There are problems in untangling the nature and direction of the causal relationships involving respondents' general approval or disapproval of establishing a Scottish Parliament and their more specific opinions about the likely effects of the Parliament or Scotland's treatment within the United Kingdom. It appears, nonetheless, that those who viewed devolution as a means of remedying the 'democratic deficit' in Scotland, who rejected specific criticisms of the Parliament, who resented the Conservatives' handling of Scottish affairs and believed that Scotland did not receive fair treatment were much more inclined to favour – and favour strongly – the proposed Scottish Parliament than were those who took different views on these questions.

Reasons for voting Yes and No

Thus far we have sought to describe and explain voting in the referendum by reference to the social and political characteristics and opinions of voters. It might be suggested that a more direct method of approaching an explanation is simply to ask voters why they made the choices that they did. Accordingly, we included in our survey an open-ended question asking respondents to give in their own words the main reasons for their vote. Table 7.13 displays the main reasons given for voting Yes Yes. A great variety of reasons were offered but by far the most important was a simple belief in the virtues of self-government. Over 40 per cent of Yes Yes voters explained their vote in this way. Typical responses were: 'I think that the Scottish people should have more of a say in running their own affairs'; 'We should have control over our own destiny.' A closely related sentiment, that devolution would improve democracy, was mentioned by 10 per cent of Yes Yes respondents. The suggestion that 'Scotland is different from the rest of the United Kingdom' (4 per cent) also carries connotations that self-government is a logical consequence. If some saw self-government as a virtue in itself, others saw it as a means to a better future for Scotland – 18 per cent said that it would lead to a better economy, better public services or just a better future in general. Some negative reasons for voting Yes Yes figure in the responses. Firstly, 12 per cent were dissatisfied with government from Westminster, seeing it as remote and insensitive ('Scotland has not been listened to') while 6 per cent expressed a vague dissatisfaction with the status quo. More specifically 12 per cent referred to Margaret Thatcher and Conservative policies (especially the poll tax) as harming Scotland, which illustrates the extent to which the experience of Thatcherism had strengthened opinion in favour of home rule since Thatcher had long ceased to be Prime Minister. A significant minority (16 per cent) saw devolution as a step on the road to full independence, which they

Table 7.13: Reasons for voting Yes Yes (percentage of Yes Yes voters)

	%
Autonomy: greater say in own affairs, control over finances	43
Better future – economy, public services etc.	18
Step to independence	16
Dissatisfaction with government from Westminster	12
Anti-Conservative/Thatcher	12
Improve accountability/democracy	10
Vague dissatisfaction with status quo	6
Taxation powers give Parliament credibility	6
Scotland is different from rest of United Kingdom	4
Anti-English	4
Patriotism	3
Support pro-devolution party	2
Other	18
(N)	(1,022)

Note: Up to three reasons were coded and for that reason percentages total more than 100.

favoured. In contrast, anti-English references, mentions of Scottish patriotism and indications that the respondent was simply following a party line were relatively rare.

Among the reasons for voting No No (Table 7.14) two stand out. Half of No No voters said that they supported the United Kingdom ('I'm against the break-up of Britain'; 'I'm British') while 31 per cent commented on what they perceived to be the excessive and unnecessary (and expensive) bureaucracy which would arise if the Parliament was established. There was also a significant minority fearful of increased taxation (17 per cent) while 11 per cent believed that the Parliament would be run by low-calibre politicians. This reason is probably also linked to fears about Labour domination (6 per cent) and the possibility of corruption (4 per cent) – issues which figured to a considerable extent in the campaign.

Table 7.14: Reasons for voting No No (percentage of No No voters)

	%
Support United Kingdom/status quo	50
Excessive/unnecessary bureaucracy	31
Higher taxation	17
Low-calibre politicians	11
Scotland is too small	8
Bad for economy	7
Scheme rushed/ not thought out	7
Labour/central belt dominance	6
Possibility of corruption	4
Talking shop	4
Other	22
(N)	(372)

Note: Up to three reasons were coded and for that reasons percentages total more than 100.

The reasons given by those who split their vote – being for a Parliament but against taxation powers – are not shown in detail here. They comprise, not surprisingly, a mixture of the reasons given by those who voted Yes Yes and those who voted No No. In fact, however, only two reasons stand out. The desire for Scots to have a greater say in their own affairs was mentioned by 38 per cent of this group while being fearful of higher taxes was given as a reason for their vote on the second question by 52 per cent. No other category of answer (except a vague feeling of being unsure about taxation powers, mentioned by 11 per cent) was referred to by more than 10 per cent of Yes No voters.

Multivariate analysis of referendum voting

The preceding analysis of our survey data has shown that voting in the referendum was associated with various social characteristics, with party supported, with subjective identities and with general attitudes towards how Scotland should be governed. As with turnout, however, several of the characteristics associated with voting in the referendum are themselves inter-related. For instance, which party individuals support will be related to their social backgrounds and their opinions, among other things. Once again, we need to employ multivariate statistical analyses to find out which factors were most important, which continue to be significant when other variables are held constant and what are the cumulative effects of a number of different factors.[8]

The results, derived from an ordinary least-squares regression analysis, are given in Table 7.15 in which, as before, only significant coefficients are reported.[9] Three separate analyses are described in the table. The first contrasts those who voted Yes to both referendum questions with all other voters. The second contrasts those who voted No to both questions with all other voters and the third contrasts those who voted Yes on the first question and No on the second with Yes Yes voters. For each analysis three equations are reported. The first includes only 'social' variables – sex, age, occupational class, education, housing tenure and religious denomination – and these have been scored to differentiate groups which were more likely to vote Yes (scored 1) from those which were less likely to do so (scored 0). In the second equation three variables measuring national identity, class identity and party identity, and scored in the same way, are added. Finally, attitudes towards the government and the Prime Minister are added to make a third equation.

Considering first Yes Yes voters in comparison to the rest (analysis 1), the first equation shows that five of the social variables had significant effects on Yes Yes voting. Holding other social characteristics constant, men were more likely to vote Yes Yes than women, younger people more than older people, manual workers more than non-manual workers, council tenants more than owner occupiers or private renters and Catholics and those with no religious affiliation more than Protestants. Religion and occupation were the most important social variables structuring the vote (as shown by the 't' statistics). Level of education (excluded from the table) on the other hand, is not significant when the other variables are taken into account. Taken together, however, social characteristics explain only about 9 per cent of the variation in Yes Yes *versus* other votes (as indicated by the R^2 figure). In other words, social characteristics alone

Table 7.15: Regression analyses of referendum voting

	Equation 1		Equation 2		Equation 3	
	Regression coefficient	't' statistic	Regression coefficient	't' statistic	Regression coefficient	't' statistic
Analysis 1						
Yes Yes vs all other voters						
Sex	0.051	2.23	–	–	–	–
Age	0.063	2.60	–	–	–	–
Occupation	0.175	6.16	0.074	2.86	0.062	2.47
Tenure	0.078	2.63	–	–	–	–
Religion	0.163	6.88	0.106	4.99	0.098	4.60
National identity	–	–	0.128	4.73	0.080	3.03
Party identity	–	–	0.613	19.51	0.473	14.63
Government record	–	–	–	–	0.241	7.23
Blair	–	–	–	–	0.070	1.99
Constant	0.421	15.27	-0.142	-3.24	-0.199	-4.64
(Adj.)R^2	0.089		0.283		0.343	
Analysis 2						
No No vs all other voters						
Age	-0.118	-5.45	-0.064	-3.37	-0.076	-4.10
Occupation	-0.158	-6.26	-0.058	-2.61	-0.048	-2.20
Education	-0.053	-2.17	-0.047	-2.17	-0.046	-2.21
Tenure	-0.073	-2.76	–	–	–	–
Religion	-0.109	-5.20	-0.057	-3.12	-0.048	-2.69
National identity	–	–	-0.092	-3.94	-0.057	-2.50
Party identity	–	–	-0.614	-22.66	-0.506	-18.02
Government record	–	–	–	–	-0.114	-3.92
Blair	–	–	–	–	-0.140	-4.56
Constant	0.459	18.71	0.993	26.32	1.053	28.21
(Adj.)R^2	0.092		0.334		0.378	
Analysis 3						
Yes No vs Yes Yes voters						
Sex	-0.056	-2.75	-0.043	-2.19	-0.039	-1.99
Age	0.044	2.01	–	–	–	–
Occupation	-0.049	-2.01	–	–	–	–
Religion	-0.089	-4.40	-0.072	-3.63	-0.066	-3.37
National identity	–	–	-0.073	-2.77	–	–
Party identity	–	–	-0.475	-8.64	-0.382	-6.83
Government record	–	–	–	–	-0.181	-5.58
Constant	0.206	7.77	0.714	11.03	0.752	11.43
(Adj.)R^2	0.026		0.084		0.118	

Notes: The coefficients shown are unstandardised regression coefficients ('b's). Only significant coefficients are shown and variables with non-significant coefficients in all three equations are not listed.

do not differentiate very well between Yes Yes voters and others. When the interconnected variables of class, national and party identity are added (equation 2), class identity does not reach statistical significance but the other two make a substantial difference. Feeling more Scottish than British and not identifying with the Conservative party were significantly associated with Yes Yes voting even taking account of social variables. The percentage of variation explained rises to 28 per cent and only religion and occupation of the social variables remain significant. Finally, approval or disapproval of the government and satisfaction with Tony Blair are added to make equation 3. These variables are also statistically significant and the equation explains 34 per cent of the variation in voting. Political factors are clearly predominant in differentiating Yes Yes voters from others. Not identifying with the Conservative Party was by far the most significant characteristic of Yes Yes voters and, even when this is taken into account, it was followed by approving of the record of the government. Being a Catholic or having no religion, and having a more Scottish than British national identity come next on the list with having a manual occupation and being satisfied with Tony Blair also playing a part.

The second set of equations (Analysis 2), contrasting No No voters with the rest show the same sorts of patterns in reverse, although the social variables tend to remain significant after the introduction of the others. As the final equation shows, however, party identification was also the most important influence on No No voting followed, in this case by attitude towards Tony Blair, age and approval or disapproval of the government's record. Taken together, the variables shown explain almost 38 per cent of the variation in No No versus other voting.

Differentiating Yes No and Yes Yes voters (Analysis 3) is more difficult, however, the best equation only accounts for 12 per cent of the variation. This suggests that Yes Yes and Yes No shared broadly similar characteristics. Nonetheless, Yes No voters were significantly more likely than Yes Yes voters to be Conservative supporters, to disapprove of the government's record, to be Protestants and to be women.

CONCLUSION

Table 7.15 provides a wealth of detail about what sorts of people chose the different options on offer in the referendum. It does not tell us why the Yes Yes camp won such a resounding victory but this is not difficult to explain. The experience of the years from 1979 to 1997, under a Conservative government, convinced a large majority of Scots that self-government was desirable. Scotland, it was believed, was not well-treated and the answer was for Scots to have more control over their own affairs. In addition, and at least partly in consequence, a sense of Scottish identity became more powerful. When the new Labour government offered a devolved Parliament with taxation powers this was warmly approved. The main exceptions to this general picture were Conservative supporters. As well as having an historic attachment to the Union and the United Kingdom, they could not be expected to be highly critical of how the Conservatives had treated Scotland during their 18 years in office and consequently did not believe that there was a need to change the constitutional position. Voting in the referendum thus correlated strongly with party and, in turn, with the social characteristics that are themselves linked to party choice in Scotland. The problem for anti-devolutionists was that Conservatives now constituted a small minority of Scottish voters.

On most variables that we have looked at, Yes No voters fall somewhere between those who voted Yes Yes or No No. The reasons that these voters gave for their choice suggest that they too were convinced about the need for some form of self-government. But they were less strongly in favour of a Scottish Parliament and their sense of national identity was less strongly Scottish. On the other hand, this group clearly thought that granting tax-varying powers would mean increased taxes and they were not prepared to go that far. If Yes Yes voting represented a full vote of confidence for a Parliament with teeth, and No No voting expressed clear opposition, then Yes No voting represented a partial endorsement.

In a much-quoted phrase John Smith, Labour Party leader from 1992 to 1994, asserted that devolution was 'the settled will of the Scottish people'. It is tempting to conclude that this view was confirmed by the results of the referendum. What was 'settled' by the referendum, however, was that Scotland's position in the United Kingdom had to change and our analysis suggests that this view prevailed to a large extent because of hostility to the Conservatives generated during their long period in office. There remains a substantial body of opinion which sees devolution as simply a first step and favours further change – to independence. Within Scotland, the constitutional issue is likely to remain unsettled for the foreseeable future.

NOTES

1. The strength of the aggregate relationship between constituency marginality and turnout in general elections has proved somewhat variable, however, and survey studies have not been able to demonstrate a significant relationship between individual voting and constituency marginality (see Denver, 1995; Pattie and Johnston, 1998).
2. The responses of non-voters in the sample were weighted at 2.188 and those of voters at 0.737. These are derived by dividing the proportions of non-voters and voters in the referendum itself by the proportions in the sample.
3. Comparing the turnout of very and fairly strong supporters with weak supporters of the different parties, the figures are as follows:

	Strong		*Weak*	
Conservatives	81%	(N=155)	55%	(N=112)
Labour	68%	(N=631)	51%	(N=119)
Liberal Democrats	88%	(N=42)	63%	(N=70)
SNP	68%	(N=253)	58%	(N=88)

4. For this purpose we first converted the social characteristic variables used in Table 7.1 (sex, age, occupational class, education and housing tenure) into a series of dichotomous variables scoring 0 and 1 and entered these into a regression equation with whether or not respondents voted in the referendum as the dependent variable. The scores assigned to the variables are: Sex: (0 = female, 1 = male); Age (0 = aged up to 34, 1 = remainder); Class (0 = other manual, 1 = remainder); Education (0 = minimum age, 1 = remainder); Tenure (0 = tenant/renter, 1 = owner occupier). The dependent variable, Vote, is scored 0 = did not vote, 1 = voted. We then added the 'political' variables – strength of party identification, strength of opinion about the Scottish Parliament and level of interest in politics in general, again scored as 0 or 1 – to the regression equations. Whether respondents voted or not in the general election is not included in the analysis since, although voting in the election correlates strongly with voting in the referendum it cannot be conceived of as a variable explaining referendum turnout in the same way as the others. The scores assigned to the political variables included are: Strength of party support (0= not very strong/none, 1 = very/fairly strong); Strength of opinion on a Scottish Parliament (0 = favour/neither/against, 1 = strongly favour/strongly against); Interest in politics (0 = not very/not at all interested, 1 = quite/very interested).
5. The results of a logistic regression of the data (showing statistically significant variables) are as follows:

Variable	*Regression coefficient*
Interest in politics	0.810
Strength of opinion on Parliament	0.704
Strength of party support	0.591
Age	0.659
Education	0.567
Housing tenure	0.497
Constant	-0.171
N	1,887
Improvement (df)	307.60 (8)
Percentage correctly predicted	69.9%

6. The figures for national identity produced by the NOP/BBC telephone survey at the time of the referendum are similar to those found by our survey. They are:

	%
Scottish not British	20
More Scottish than British	37
Equally Scottish and British	32
More British than Scottish	4
British not Scottish	6
None of these/DK/other	1
(N)	(2,006)

7. Other surveys undertaken in 1997 produced similar results. Thus the NOP/BBC referendum survey found 55 per cent for a devolved Parliament, 26 per cent for no change and 19 per cent for independence. The figures from the Scottish Election Study survey in May are 55 per cent for devolution, 18 per cent for no elected Parliament and 27 per cent for independence (N = 800).

8. The variables which seem to be related to how people voted have once again been turned into dichotomous variables scoring 0 and 1, with a score of 1 being assigned to the category which was more likely to vote Yes. The scores assigned to 'social' variables are as follows: Sex: (0 = female, 1 = male); Age (0 = aged 55 and over, 1 = remainder); Occupational class: (0 = professional, managerial and supervisory non-manual, 1 = remainder); Education (0 = Highers/professional qualifications/degree, 1 = minimum age); Housing tenure: (0 = owner occupiers/other renters, 1 = council tenants); Religion: (0 = Church of Scotland and other Protestant denominations, 1 = Catholic and no religion). The scores on the 'identity' variables are: National identity (0 = equal Scottish and British/more British than Scottish/British not Scottish/none of these, 1 = Scottish not British/more Scottish than British); Class identity (0 = middle class; 1 = remainder); Party identity (0 = Conservative, 1 = other parties and none). Attitudes to the government and the Prime Minister are scored as government record (0 = disapprove/no opinion, 1 = approve); Tony Blair (0 = dissatisfied/no opinion, 1 = satisfied).

9. As with turnout, we repeated the analysis using logistic regression. The final equations were as follows (non-significant variables have not been reported).

Variable	Yes Yes v. Others Regression coefficient	No No v. Others Regression coefficient	Yes No v. Yes Yes Regression coefficient
Age	–	-0.667	–
Occupation	0.392	-0.474	–
Education	–	-0.408	–
Religion	0.622	-0.436	-0.615
National identity	0.468	-0.505	–
Party identity	2.992	-2.549	-1.817
Government record	1.298	-0.822	-1.248
Blair	0.452	-0.900	–
N	1,554	1,554	1,188
Improvement (df)	591.61 (11)	563.56 (11)	120.68 (11)
Percentage correctly predicted	80.7	86.0	86.3

A more advanced and extended statistical analysis of voting in the referendum, based on our survey data and using logistic regression techniques, can be found in Pattie *et al.* (1999).

8

The Referendum in Context

By late 1998 seven significant referendums had been held in the United Kingdom.[1] The first-ever (and so far only) United Kingdom-wide referendum took place in June 1975 on the question of the country's membership of the European Community. It was followed in 1979 by votes on devolution in Scotland and Wales but thereafter, with the Conservatives in power, there was no recourse to a referendum for 18 years. The new Labour government elected in May 1997 was much more interested in constitutional reform than the Conservatives had been, however, and more willing to hold referendums. The 1997 Scottish referendum was the first in a series initiated by the government. In little more than 12 months, in addition to the Scottish case, referendums were held on the creation of an Assembly for Wales (18 September 1997), reforming the government of London to allow for an elected mayor and a Greater London Authority (7 May 1998) and on the proposals for Northern Ireland contained in the 'Good Friday Agreement', which related to the system of government as well as to other matters (22 May 1998). Further referendums are promised on other issues including reform of the electoral system, United Kingdom entry into European economic and monetary union and, possibly, the setting up of regional assemblies within England.

As the constitutional commentator Geoffrey Marshall has remarked, this new-found enthusiasm for referendums is 'a curious turn of events' (Marshall, 1997). It is curious because most British politicians and most constitutional experts have, in the past, been hostile to the use of the referendum, seeing it as inconsistent with parliamentary democracy and an abdication of responsibility by elected representatives. It might also be argued that referendums undermine a fundamental element in the British constitution – the sovereignty of Parliament. To circumvent this suggestion, all referendums held in the United Kingdom have been, in theory, advisory only, leaving the final decision on the matter concerned to Parliament. In practice, however, Parliament has never legislated in defiance of a referendum result conforming to agreed rules, and the chances of its ever doing so must be very slim indeed.

The theoretical case for referendums is relatively straightforward – they are democratic (see Butler and Ranney, 1994: ch. 2). Indeed, advocates of direct or participatory democracy suggest that decision-making by referendums is preferable to decision-making by elected representatives since it involves two democratic ideals – popular sovereignty and popular participation. In this view, 'the only truly democratic way to make decisions on matters of public policy is by the full, direct, and unmediated participation of all citizens' (Butler and Ranney, 1994: 12) and referendums allow this. A less extreme view sees referendums as useful supplements to the normal workings of parliamentary democracy. In certain circumstances and under certain conditions a referendum, because it allows the public to participate in decision-making, can confer a greater legitimacy on a policy than would be the case if the decision were made by elected politicians alone. Thus in Britain, where there is no written constitution, it is always possible that an incoming government will reverse any constitutional changes made by its predecessor. When the changes have been approved in a referendum, however, they have a greater chance of being permanent since few politicians would dare to challenge the clearly expressed will of the people.

Among the major political parties in Britain, the SNP and the Liberal Democrats are perhaps most closely identified with participatory democracy but these ideas have also influenced Labour's thinking. Within the party there have been moves to broaden participation by extending voting rights to all members and by holding membership ballots on, for example, the revision of Clause IV of the party constitution and the draft manifesto for the 1997 election. In relation to local government, too, there has been a concern to increase participation – both by voting and in other ways. A government consultation paper, *Modernising local government: Local democracy and community leadership* (DETR, 1998), implied support for a greater degree of direct democracy at local level. Nonetheless, we have suggested (Chapter 2) that the decision to hold a referendum in Scotland on the question of devolution owed more to practical politics than to theoretical considerations. It was a means of defusing the problems raised by the issue of taxation powers for a Scottish Parliament for the duration of the general election campaign. Moreover, it was a decision that was controversial within the party. On the other hand, there is no doubt that, *post hoc*, the referendum achieved the ends claimed by proponents of the device. A substantial proportion of the Scottish electorate participated and added legitimacy was conferred not only on the new Parliament but also on the decision to allow the Parliament to vary income tax rates. Without a referendum a future government could have felt justified in rescinding the devolution legislation; the referendum result made it very unlikely that any future government would make significant alterations to the government of Scotland without first consulting the people.

Table 8.1: United Kingdom referendums

	% Turnout	% Yes	% No
EC membership 1975	64.5	67.2	32.8
Scottish devolution 1979	63.8	51.6	48.4
Welsh devolution 1979	58.8	20.3	79.7
Scottish Parliament 1997 Q.1	60.4	74.3	25.7
Scottish Parliament 1997 Q.2	–	63.5	36.5
Welsh Assembly 1997	50.1	50.3	49.7
Reform of London government 1998	34.1	72.0	28.0
Good Friday Agreement 1998	81.0	71.1	28.9

It is not clear, however, that the same can be said about the other referendums instigated by the Blair government, the results of which are summarised (with the Scottish case and the referendums of the 1970s for comparison) in Table 8.1. The referendum on the establishment of an Assembly in Wales followed one week after the Scottish referendum. Having agreed a referendum for Scotland it would have appeared illogical not to hold one in Wales as well, so that once again the decision to have a referendum arose from practical considerations rather than any special commitment to participatory democracy. Moreover, providing for a week's delay between the two referendums reflected a political calculation that a good result (for the government) in Scotland would produce a momentum for change which would carry over into the Welsh vote. On the surface, the two referendums were similar – both were on devolution proposals made by a Labour government which had received strong support in the two countries, Labour campaigned strongly for Yes votes in both, as did the Nationalists and Liberal Democrats, with the Conservatives being opposed. As in Scotland, umbrella groups emerged to campaign in the Welsh referendum ('Yes for Wales' and 'Just Say No'). In fact, however, the contexts of the two referendums and, as it proved, the results, were very different.

Support for Plaid Cymru in Wales had never been as strong as that for the SNP in Scotland. At the 1997 election Plaid won only 9.9 per cent of the Welsh vote compared with 22.1 per cent for the SNP in

Scotland. In the 1979 referendum devolution had been roundly rejected in Wales with only 20 per cent of votes cast in favour. In part, the weakness of home rule sentiment in Wales reflects the relative weakness of a specifically Welsh identity[2] which in turn may be a consequence of the fact that fewer Welsh residents were born in Wales (77.2 per cent) as compared with Scottish residents born in Scotland (89.1 per cent).[3] Partly also, it is the case that nationalism in Wales has taken cultural and linguistic, rather than political, forms (see Miller, 1984). Even among the Welsh-born population there are significant differences of opinion and interest between Welsh speakers (living mainly in north and west Wales) and those who speak only English. Furthermore, the Welsh counties which border England are more closely connected to neighbouring English areas – in terms of accessibility, transport and access to mass media – than to other parts of Wales. In recognition of the weaker demand for devolution in Wales, the government proposed not a Parliament but an Assembly with no legislative or taxation powers. Ironically, this led to accusations that the Assembly would be little more than a 'talking shop'. Whereas the proposals for Scotland had emerged over many years of cross-party discussion and negotiation (see Chapters 1 and 2), those for Wales resulted from a Labour policy commission which reported in 1993 and were endorsed by a special Welsh Labour conference in February 1997. Even so, Labour activists were prominent in the 'Just Say No' campaign and several Welsh Labour MPs voiced criticisms. The unanimity of Labour in Scotland was not evident in the Welsh referendum campaign (McAllister, 1998).

Wales voted by a very narrow margin in favour of an Assembly (see Table 8.1). This represented a major shift in opinion from 1979 but hardly constituted a ringing endorsement of the government's proposals. Moreover the turnout, at just over 50 per cent, was significantly lower than that in Scotland the week before. Although the result was enough to allow the government to proceed with devolution legislation, the referendum had not attracted a high level of participation and did not provide substantial added legitimacy to the government's policy. The result also shows that United Kingdom referendums are not simply polls on the popularity of the government or Prime Minister. The Yes campaign in Wales focused strongly on appeals to 'back Blair' and to traditional Labour loyalties but the poor turnout and very narrow victory were actually something of an embarrassment for the government.

A referendum in London on the government of the capital was promised in Labour's 1997 election manifesto. The change proposed – to a system involving an elected mayor with executive powers and a London-wide assembly – was radical, introducing, for the first time at any level of government in the United Kingdom, a directly elected executive. In this case there seems no reason to believe that political or tactical considerations were involved in the decision to hold a referendum. Rather, this referendum seems to have arisen from a genuine desire to involve and consult the public on local government and it could be the forerunner of similar votes in other cities. The referendum was held on the same day as the local elections in May 1998. Although the proposed changes were heavily endorsed, as an exercise in participatory democracy the referendum was a flop. Just over a third of the electorate voted (Table 8.1). This suggests that the London electorate was simply not very interested in the issue. The structure and activities of local government rarely excite widespread interest among the voters and the London experience does not bode well for any future referendums concerned with these matters. The low level of participation also reflects the fact that there was no significant opposition to the proposals for London. All three major parties supported them so that the passions generated by partisan divisions were absent and there was little campaigning on the referendum issue.

The referendum in Northern Ireland on May 22 1998 could hardly have been more different. Following lengthy and difficult negotiations the parties to the 'peace process' reached an agreement on Good Friday. This involved, among other things, re-establishing a legislature for Northern Ireland (elected by proportional represen-tation) and setting up cross-border, all-Ireland institutions. In a deeply divided society it was clearly important to demonstrate popular support for these measures, to establish some sort of consensus which could form the basis of a way forward and an end to violence. It was widely anticipated that the Nationalist community would over-whelmingly endorse the agreement but the Unionist community was divided. It was important for the proponents of the peace plan that a majority of Unionists should also back the agreement since otherwise no consensus could be claimed. In other words, there was an implicit hurdle in the referendum – a vote of 51 per cent in favour would not have been enough to provide a basis for progress. Following a vigorous campaign, however, the proposals were decisively carried on a very high turnout of voters.[4] The referendum allowed ordinary citizens to have their say and clearly settled the question of whether the proposals agreed by the negotiating parties should be pursued. Citing the referendum results would prove to be an effective way of countering the arguments of diehard opponents of change.

Recent United Kingdom experience of referendums, then, has been mixed. The main reason for holding them has varied – to defuse a contentious issue for electoral purposes, to try to involve the electorate in local government reform, to establish a consensus in a divided society. Unlike the referendums of the 1970s, however, the need to paper over internal party divisions has not been a major motivating factor in the decisions to have referendums. The level of participation has also varied. From this point of view, the Northern Ireland referendum has been the most successful followed by the referendum in Scotland, but the Welsh case must be considered as only a partial success while the attempt to involve voters in deciding the future government of London clearly failed. Partly as a consequence, only the Scottish and Northern Irish referendums have clearly and decisively conferred legitimacy on the proposals made by the government. The results in the other two – unconvincing even at a time of considerable government popularity – should give governments pause for thought before calling further referendums on issues on which they have a clear preference as to the outcome.

The role of the political parties and the nature and extent of campaigning in the referendums are further examples of variation in the four referendums. In Scotland and Wales the parties lined up three to one in favour of devolution and were heavily involved in campaigning. Crucially, however, there were divisions in the Labour Party in Wales. In London, all three parties were on the same side and there was virtually no campaigning. In Northern Ireland, on the other hand, while the British parties all favoured acceptance of the proposals and the main Nationalist and Republican parties were solidly behind them, the Ulster Unionists were bitterly divided and the Democratic Unionists implacably opposed. The referendums witnessed, therefore, varying forms of cross-party co-operation and resulted in some strange bedfellows, especially in Northern Ireland. The most extensive and intensive campaigning took place in Scotland and Northern Ireland and it is significant that these two areas have distinctive mass media – much more so than is the case in Wales or London (or any English region). The Scottish and Ulster media gave great prominence to their respective referendums and it is unlikely that a sub-national referendum in any other part of the United Kingdom would receive as much coverage. In that respect, Scotland and Northern Ireland are very atypical.

In one way, however, the first four referendums of the Blair government did not vary. All endorsed the government's policy and produced majorities for change. It is sometimes argued that referendums are conservative devices in that the mass of the population 'instinctively' prefer things to stay the same. Geoffrey Marshall (1997: 307) cites a nineteenth-century opponent of referendums, Sir Henry Maine, as arguing that if popular opinion had its way there would have been 'no reformation of religion, no change of dynasty, no toleration of Dissent, not even an accurate calendar. The threshing machine, the power loom, the spinning jenny and possibly the steam engine would have been prohibited.' In the recent referendums, however, the electorate has approved radical innovations.

THE UNITED KINGDOM REFERENDUMS IN COMPARATIVE CONTEXT

Many democracies have much greater experience of referendums than the United Kingdom. Between 1970 and 1995, for example, there were six national referendums in Denmark, 14 in Ireland, 39 in Italy and no less than 215 in Switzerland (Gallagher, 1996: 231). In addition, the 1990s have seen the spread of referendums to the new democracies of Eastern Europe (White and Hill, 1996). Further afield, a number of referendums have taken place in Australia and New Zealand (Hughes, 1994) while referendums are permitted – and frequently used – in just over half of the states in the United States (Magleby, 1994). Writing in 1994, Butler and Ranney (1994: 258) found only five major democracies which had never had a nation-wide referendum – India, Israel, Japan, the Netherlands and the United States. The fact that referendums have been regularly and widely used in a great variety of political systems and political cultures, and the intimate connection between the ideas underlying their use and democratic theory, have interested political scientists and given rise to a small comparative literature on the subject (see, for example, Butler and Ranney, 1994; Gallagher and Uleri, 1996; Budge, 1996). What they have found, in general, is that referendums around the world are characterised by immense variety. As Gallagher (1996: 233–5) notes, 'the search for generalisations is indeed difficult … perhaps in the end we simply cannot avoid treating each country as *sui generis*'. Nonetheless we can locate British referendums, and the Scottish referendum in particular, in a comparative context by considering briefly the main ways in which referendums vary across different political systems.

Constitutional status
In many countries the use of referendums is specifically mentioned in the constitution. In some cases (France, Denmark, Australia, for example) a referendum is required for, or is one way of ratifying,

certain changes to the constitution. In other cases, referendums are also used more widely. In Italy since 1970, for example, a referendum can be held if 500,000 citizens or five regional councils call for it and the device can be used to repeal, either partially or totally, a piece of legislation (Sassoon, 1986) while in Switzerland citizens can initiate referendums on a wide variety of topics (Trechsel and Kriesi, 1996). Apart from the United Kingdom, only three of the 16 West European states surveyed by Bogdanor (1994) do not provide for referendums in their constitutions – Belgium, the Netherlands and Norway – although only the Netherlands has never held a referendum.

The United Kingdom has an uncodified constitution based on the principle of parliamentary sovereignty. There is, therefore, no constitutional requirement to put any question to a referendum. On the other hand, Parliament – in effect the government – can submit any issue that it chooses to a referendum. British referendums are instituted, therefore, by specific Acts of Parliament. Moreover, as we have seen previously, such referendums can only be consultative and not binding. Implementation of the results requires further decisions by Parliament. In practice, of course, the results of all 'official' United Kingdom referendums have been accepted by the government of the day. In most cases too – the problems associated with the '40 per cent rule' in the 1979 Scottish devolution referendum notwithstanding – opposition parties have also accepted the referendum results. This was certainly the case with the 1997 Scottish referendum. Following the vote, the relevant devolution legislation was passed quickly and with little significant opposition (see Chapter 9). The Conservatives had opposed devolution but were forced by the substantial Yes Yes vote (and by the realities of Scottish politics) to accept the result and the establishment of the Scottish Parliament. By mid 1998 the party leadership had taken a stance that they should aim to make devolution work. Effectively, then, the use of referendums in the United Kingdom has allowed the government and Parliament to relinquish their decision-making powers to the people on particular issues.

The trigger

In systems in which referendums are mandatory in order to change the constitution it is the normal process of constitutional amendment which triggers a referendum. In most countries, however, there are special provisions giving governments the authority to call referendums. In some cases, such as Greece, Ireland and Portugal, the President alone can call a referendum in certain circumstances while other countries make it possible for minorities in the legislature to trigger a referendum. Only in a few systems (Italy, Switzerland and some states of the United States being the best known examples) can citizens acting alone set the referendum process in motion.

Clearly, the United Kingdom falls into the category in which the government alone has the power to initiate referendums which have any legal status. Given the British system of government, of course, political parties can make commitments relating to referendums while they are still in opposition. This is what happened in the cases of the Scottish, Welsh and London referendums. Labour's commitment to a Scottish referendum was made for internal party purposes (as with the previous referendums in 1975 and 1979) and the trigger, as it were, was the party's victory in the 1997 election and the government's subsequent decision to give the issue high priority. Moreover, as we have seen, Labour is committed to hold further referendums and both major parties have given public undertakings to hold a referendum on any move to take the United Kingdom into a single European currency, while still maintaining their 'wait-and-see' attitude to the substantive issue involved. Neither party has suggested extending the use of referendums to non-constitutional issues, however, and neither has shown very much interest in the idea of citizen initiatives, even at local level.

Frequency
With the exception of Switzerland and some individual states in the United States, it is clear that nation-wide referendums are not frequent events – far less frequent, for instance, than general legislative elections. It is less easy to say, however, whether the use of referendums is increasing or decreasing – the answer given depends on the countries involved in the count and on the time-scale used. Thus in the 1970s Butler and Ranney (1978: 221) identified a trend towards the increasing use of the device whereas in the early 1990s they concluded that 'the major democratic polities … have not significantly increased their use of referendums in recent years' (Butler and Ranney, 1994: 262). Bogdanor (1994: 90ff.), on the other hand, is clear that as far as Europe is concerned referendum use has increased since the 1970s, and he attributes this to the decay of party systems and the emergence of a generation of voters more interested in participating directly in politics than their predecessors. On the basis of his argument Bogdanor suggests that 'we may confidently expect a more widespread use of the referendum in the twenty-first century than we have seen in the twentieth' (p. 97).

Bogdanor's argument is persuasive as far as the United Kingdom is concerned. While there has been only one nation-wide referendum so far, it seems likely that others will take place in the near future. There has also been, of course, a flurry of sub-national referendums since 1997. Moreover, the electorate strongly supports the use of referendums. The 1997 British Election Study survey asked respondents whether decisions on joining the European single currency, setting up a Scottish Parliament and introducing proportional representation should be made by elected politicians or by means of a referendum. An average of only 15 per cent preferred to leave the decisions to politicians while 71 per cent opted for referendums. It is worth remembering, however, that it is only under Labour governments that referendums have been held. Although in some cases the party resorted to a popular vote in order to deal with internal problems it is also the case that under Tony Blair New Labour appears to have a greater interest in constitutional innovation than either 'Old' Labour or the Conservatives. As long as they remain in power further referendums are likely. Despite their commitment to a referendum on Europe (which also reflects internal party problems) it seems likely that the return of a Conservative government would see referendums once again becoming rare events in British politics.

Subject matter
The types of issues which are put before citizens in referendums can be placed into one of three main categories. Firstly, there are constitutional or territorial issues. As we have seen, in some political systems amendment of the constitution requires the assent of the citizens in a special vote while in others it is one among a number of ways of doing so. Thus in France, although a three-fifths majority of both Houses of Parliament can change the constitution, seven of the eight referendums held since 1958 have concerned important constitutional matters – the adoption of the constitution itself, the status of Algeria (twice) and New Caledonia, the method of electing the President, reform of the senate and creation of regions, and France's position in the European Union.[5] A common type of referendum in this category involves cases of regime change. When a dictatorship is succeeded by a democratic system, for example, (as in Spain in 1978 or in Eastern Europe in recent years) the new arrangements are frequently put to a popular vote. In addition, changes to borders and questions relating to sovereignty are often the subjects of referendums. Thus the development of the European Union has generated a number of referendums. Between 1970 and 1995, 15 of the 36 referendums held in Western Europe (excluding Italy and Switzerland) concerned the EC/EU (Gallagher, 1996: 232). Fitzmaurice (1995) notes that there are quite specific reasons for the

use of referendums on EU issues – decisions on accession to the EU, or which cede sovereignty, are controversial and effectively irreversible. They also tend to divide political parties and cross traditional cleavage patterns.

The second category of subjects that are frequently the subject of referendums comprises moral or social issues such as limits on the sale of alcohol, divorce and abortion. Opinion on these sorts of issues frequently cuts across party lines and, since they often sharply divide the electorate, parties are unwilling to identify themselves with one side or the other. As Budge (1996) notes, moral issues, together with those relating to the environment and nuclear power,

> are often not covered by the ideology of established parties ... Thus they raise threats of factionalism and splits. To avoid this, leaders of normally hostile parties have a common interest in agreeing on a referendum, evading intra-party conflict by allowing all sectors a free voice in expressing their opinions, and defining the conflict as a non-partisan one. (pp. 86–7)

Finally, there is a mixture of other issues that have been put to a popular vote. These are most likely to arise where citizens have the power to demand a ballot as in a number of US states, Italy and Switzerland, and have ranged from hunting to traffic laws, taxation and the adoption of daylight saving time.

All but one of the United Kingdom referendums have been concerned solely with constitutional and/or territorial matters. In that respect the 1997 Scottish referendum was not unusual. The (partial) exception is the Northern Ireland referendum. In this case, the voters were asked to indicate whether or not they accepted the Good Friday Agreement and while the agreement included proposals for constitutional change, as noted above, it also extended to other matters, including reform of the police and the release of prisoners jailed for terrorist offences, which are not strictly constitutional. It is unlikely, however, that this will set a precedent for the future in the United Kingdom. Although calls are occasionally made for referendums on other issues, such as capital punishment, nuclear power and fox hunting, it seems likely that their use will remain largely confined to constitutional matters.

The party system
In all democracies political parties play a number of key roles. Most obviously, they develop policies, compete for votes in elections and form governments. It is not difficult to argue that referendums tend

to undermine party dominance of the political process. In circumstances where they are not compulsory, they allow parties and governments to 'wash their hands' of an issue and transfer decision-making from the normal political and parliamentary processes to the electorate. Referendums, and in particular citizen initiatives, undermine the parties' control of the political agenda; they also undermine their unity as *ad hoc* alliances emerge which cross party lines. Thus, Blondel suggests that referendums 'tend to reduce somewhat the role of parties and can therefore be regarded as contributing to the decline of the weight of parties in the political system' (Blondel, 1990: 350) while Bogdanor (1994) suggests that, on the issue of Europe at least, recent referendums highlight an emerging division between the people and the political class. From another perspective, however, the use of referendums may maintain the party system by avoiding damaging splits in established parties; they enable the party system to manage controversial issues which have the potential to destroy the existing system.

The latter interpretation seems more appropriate in the case of the United Kingdom referendums of the 1970s. At that time the major parties were deeply divided on Europe and devolution, and referendums enabled the issues to be resolved without splitting the parties permanently. In the 1990s the question of Europe remains divisive and is thus likely to provoke further referendums. On Scottish devolution in 1997, however, there were no significant internal party divisions and it would be difficult to argue that these referendums weakened the party system. On the contrary, the parties clearly aligned themselves on the issue and campaigned vigorously. The referendums provided popular backing for a policy that was proposed by the government and supported by the Liberal Democrats and Nationalist parties. Given their infrequency, limited scope and government control over whether or not to hold them, it seems unlikely that the use of referendums in the United Kingdom, will significantly weaken the party system.

Results

As we have already noted in Chapter 6, turnout in referendums is usually lower than turnout in national elections and all United Kingdom referendums, with the exception of that in the very special circumstances of Northern Ireland, have conformed to this generalisation. Voters, it seems, ascribe more importance to the general question of who will govern their country than to specific constitutional or other issues. This again suggests that referendums have not replaced or weakened representative government through the medium of political parties. In the United Kingdom, as in most democracies, electors are used to voting for parties in general elections and less experienced in voting on issues that may be complex, obscure, delicate or peripheral to their concerns. We have shown, however (Chapter 6), that the pattern of turnout in the 1997 Scottish referendum was very similar to patterns of turnout in general elections. The referendum did not attract a new type of participant in politics; those more likely to vote in elections were also more likely to turn out in the referendum.

It is difficult to generalise about the outcomes of referendums. The argument that they tend to produce conservative results does not withstand serious scrutiny. Over the period from 1945–95 more referendums in Western Europe produced votes for change than for the status quo (Gallagher, 1996: 236). As noted above, all of the recent United Kingdom referendums have also resulted in votes for change. There is some evidence, however, that opinion tends to become more conservative during referendum campaigns. Using examples from Ireland and the USA, Darcy and Laver (1990) argue that the absence of a strong lead from parties provides fertile ground for conservatives to play upon voters' uncertainties and fear of the unknown (see also Cronin, 1989). This may well have applied in the devolution referendums of 1979 and, to a lesser extent, in Wales in 1997 but there is little evidence of increasing conservatism during the latest Scottish referendum.

A second generalisation – that governments usually win government-sponsored referendums – has a stronger empirical basis. Butler and Ranney (1994: 261) note that 'the vast majority of referendums have been sponsored by governments and have produced the voting outcomes desired by those governments'. Although governments in various countries lose occasionally, only Australia stands out as an exception to the general rule. Franklin *et al.* (1995), on the basis of studying a small sample of cases, go so far as to suggest that, as a device for ascertaining the attitudes of the people on specific issues, referendums are largely useless since voters use them simply to indicate their approval or otherwise of the government. There is something in this argument as far as the United Kingdom experience is concerned. The only two referendums lost by governments (in Scotland – under the 40 per cent rule – and Wales in 1979) were held at a time of extreme government unpopularity. On the other hand, government popularity alone cannot account for the results of the 1997 Scottish referendum, was not enough to avert a close shave in Wales and can have played little part in the Northern Ireland vote. When a government is closely identified with one side in a referendum then its level of popularity can influence the outcome, but such influence is not likely to be decisive when strong views on the issue concerned are widely held.

Voting behaviour

Nilson and Bjorklund (1986) offer a tentative typology of voting behaviour in referendums. They suggest that it is either party-structured (voters' choices being determined by their party allegiance), group-structured (votes being determined by the influence of interest groups) or unstructured. This is an over-simple categorisation to apply in the British context. Firstly, although there has certainly been a relationship between party support and referendum vote in most of those held so far, the relationship has been far from perfect. Labour supporters were deeply divided on the EC in 1975 (see Butler and Kitzinger, 1996: 252) and also in Wales in 1997 (58 per cent supporting devolution and 42 per cent opposing), for example.[6] Moreover, in proposing Scottish devolution the Labour party was merely bringing itself into line with the pre-existing demand among its own supporters. Labour supporters voted for a Parliament not because their party backed it but because they supported the policy for other reasons. Secondly, even if we redefine campaign groups which spring up during referendums as 'interest groups' there is little evidence that such groups play an important part in structuring votes. The overwhelming mass of voters are not members of these sorts of groups and although business and union groups sometimes have made their views known their influence on voters is questionable. An exception in this case might be the Northern Ireland referendum, however, in which the Orange Order (which has a large membership in the province) advised its members to vote No.

It would be wrong to conclude, however, that voting in British referendums is largely unstructured. As we have shown in our detailed analysis of voting in Scotland (see Chapter 7) voter reactions to the ballot were structured by cleavages – class, party and national identity. We have argued, indeed, that the growth in home rule sentiment and hence the massive Yes votes in the referendum were largely due to a progressive overlapping of class and national identities which occured during the 1980s. This suggests that the typology offered by Nilson and Bjorklund needs to be expanded to include cleavages relevant to the issue at hand.

If future referendums in the United Kingdom are held on issues of low salience then it may be that votes are more likely to be cast on the basis of party loyalty (or the popularity of the government as discussed in the preceding section) than was the case in Scotland. So far, however, there has been only one referendum on an issue of low salience (London government). As long as they are confined to issues perceived as important and relevant by the electorate, it seems likely that factors other than party loyalty will influence voters' decisions.

CONCLUSION

Referendums in the United Kingdom have, on the whole, partially fulfilled the hopes of those who advocate their greater use. They have made a contribution to the opening up of the policy process by allowing popular participation and helped to resolve issues that governments might have found difficult to handle. They have generally bestowed greater legitimacy on the decisions made than might have been the case if politicians alone had made them. On the other hand, there is no evidence that British referendums have undermined the system of representative government, weakened the party system or destabilised the polity. All of this is true, in particular, of the Scottish referendum which is the concern of this book. In this case, an electorate which was well-informed about the issue made a clear decision which led to a major constitutional change. Government policy on the issue was triumphantly vindicated. As our brief review of the referendum experience elsewhere has shown, things do not always work out so neatly but the Scottish experience shows clearly how referendums can be a very valuable supplement to the normal workings of representative democracy. This success is encouraging for proponents of referendums and also increases the expectation among both voters and politicians that major constitutional issues should be submitted to a vote by the people. To that extent it may be said that, on a limited range of constitutional issues, the referendum appears to be becoming entrenched in British politics.

NOTES

1. The seven are listed in Table 8.1. As noted in Chapter 1 there was also a referendum in Northern Ireland in 1973, on the constitutional status of the province, but it was boycotted by Nationalists and was not, therefore, very meaningful. In addition there have been a number of local plebiscites in Scotland and Wales relating to licensing laws and occasional unofficial referendums organised by local authorities. The latter have no legal status, however.
2. At the time of the Welsh referendum a CREST survey of Welsh voters found that only 42 per cent felt themselves to be either Welsh not British or more

Welsh than British (N = 686). The comparable figure for Scottish identity is 63 per cent (see Table 7.6).

3. These figures are from the 1991 census.
4. A simultaneous referendum on the peace proposals was held in the Irish Republic. On a turnout of 55.6 per cent, they were supported by 94.4 per cent of voters.
5. The exception, in 1972, was on approving the enlargement of the European Community.
6. The figures quoted for Wales (N=223) are derived from the CREST survey of Welsh voters at the time of the referendum.

9

The Aftermath of the Referendum

Following the decisive result of the referendum, the Scotland Bill ('To provide for the establishment of a Scottish Parliament and Administration') was formally introduced into the House of Commons on 17 December 1997 by Donald Dewar, Secretary of State for Scotland. The contents of the Bill were little different from the White Paper that had been published before the referendum. It defined the powers of the Parliament and the method of election of the 129 members, specified which powers were to be reserved to the Westminster Parliament, established the executive arm of the Parliament, prescribed financial arrangements and dealt with taxation powers.

The second reading of a bill involves approving it in principle and in the case of the Scotland Bill this took place on 12 and 13 January 1998. In this debate, the chief Conservative spokesman, Michael Ancram, announced that the Tories would not oppose the principle of the Bill, respecting 'the democratically expressed view' of the Scottish people, but would 'oppose the manner in which the Bill attempts to establish them' (HCDeb, 12 January 1998, vol.304, col.35). To that end, he moved a 'reasoned amendment' which 'while accepting and respecting the clear decision of the Scottish people' (*ibid.*) summarised the grounds for the Conservatives' opposition to devolution. The amendment was overwhelmingly defeated (411 votes to 148) with all parties other than the Conservatives voting against. This was an early indication of the fact that, given the much reduced position of the Conservatives in the House, the Bill would, in all essentials, pass in the form that the government wished.

Eight days were allotted to the committee stage of the Bill and a further three to the report and Third Reading. As with most constitutional matters, the committee stage was taken on the floor of the House with debates being held on 28 and 29 January, 10, 12 and 23 February, and 4, 30 and 31 March. In these debates, the Conservatives generally attempted to restrict the powers of the Parliament, trying to make it explicit, for example, that taxation powers related only to income tax. There were two exceptions, however. On the seventh day of debate the Tories proposed that the Scottish Parliament should have powers over drug trafficking and abuse, and on the next day proposed that abortion law should be a devolved, rather than reserved, matter. Their argument relating to abortion was that it would be inconsistent to have this as a reserved matter while all other health policies were devolved, but the real intent was to embarrass the government. Dewar responded that if there were different abortion laws in Scotland this would lead to a problem of 'cross-border traffic'. In a division (which was a free vote on the Labour side) the amendment was defeated by 278 to 160. The SNP, the Liberal Democrats and Plaid Cymru supported the amendment, as did three Scottish Labour MPs – Tommy McAvoy (Glasgow Rutherglen), John McFall (Dumbarton) and Dennis Canavan (Falkirk West).[1]

During the committee stage of the Bill, the SNP and the Liberal Democrats generally argued for, and put amendments about, increasing the powers of the Parliament by reducing the list of reserved powers (the licensing of public service vehicles, for example) or making other, more symbolic changes. The SNP, in particular, focused on the powers of the Parliament in relation to 'cross-border' public bodies, such as the BBC and the Equal Opportunities Commission, on improving Scottish representation in the European Union and extending the legislative competence of the Parliament to include the activities of the Crown Estates Commissioners, which related to the sensitive issues of land reform and 'the right to roam'. None of the various amendments proposed by the opposition or by the smaller parties were successful. On the other hand, the government itself introduced and passed a raft of amendments during the committee and report stages. Some of these made small adjustments to the division between reserved and devolved powers (devolving powers under the Theatres Act and the Hypnotism Act, for example) while others dealt with a variety of technical matters. Some government amendments attempted to deal with concerns raised during debates. Thus, it was agreed that the Crown Estates in Scotland would be subject to the Parliament in relation to devolved matters (including land reform) and in response to worries about sleaze the post of Auditor General for Scotland, accountable to the Parliament, was established. During the committee and report stages of the Bill there were 26 divisions all of which were won easily by the government. Forty-nine government amendments were passed without a division (many being grouped together). Finally, on 19 May, the Bill passed its third reading without a division.

On 20 May the Scotland Bill was introduced into the House of Lords and received its first (formal) reading. The second reading debate was held on 17 and 18 June and the Bill was passed without a division. Whereas the Commons had devoted eight days to the committee stage of the Bill, in the Lords – sitting like the Commons as a committee of the whole House – this took ten days, straddling the summer recess.[2] The substance of the debates in the Lords reflected those in the Commons with, for example, the question of abortion again being raised. The Conservatives moved a large number of amendments most of which were withdrawn with the remainder being defeated in divisions. The government lost a vote, however, on a Liberal Democrat amendment relating to the scrutiny of bills in the Scottish Parliament (28 July). The report stage in the Lords lasted four days[3] and involved two further defeats for the government. The first (22 October) was on a Liberal Democrat proposal to allow the Scottish Parliament control over the number of members[4] that it had while the second (2 November) concerned limiting its power to sack unfit judges. On 9 November the Bill received its third reading and returned to the Commons with the amendments that had been passed.

The amendments proposed by the Lords were considered by the Commons on 11 and 12 November. Those relating to the scrutiny of bills and the number of members in the new Parliament were swiftly and decisively reversed. The latter debate was noticeable, however, for the fact that the Scottish Labour MP, Dennis Canavan voted against the government. This was the first and only dissenting vote cast by a Labour member against the government during the entire passage of the Bill.[5] On the sacking of unfit judges, the government proposed a compromise amendment and this was accepted. At this stage the government also took the opportunity to introduce a number of yet further technical amendments dealing with, for example, relations between the Parliament and the courts, further tightening regulations governing the conduct of members, clarifying tax and residency requirements and decreeing that no Member of the Scottish Parliament (MSP) could be a member of the United Kingdom government. Perhaps fittingly, the closing debate concerned the regulation of the Tweed and Esk fisheries, the rivers which form part of the border between Scotland and England.

The revised Bill was accepted by the Lords, thus completing the parliamentary process, on 17 November, just before the end of the parliamentary session. It had been debated for just under 192 hours, taking up more time than any other bill during the session, during 15 days in the House of Commons and 17 in the Lords. More than a million words had been spoken in these debates and 2,075 amendments had been tabled, 670 of them by the government. Finally, on 19 November 1998, described by Donald Dewar as 'a truly historic day for Scotland' (*Guardian*, 20 November 1998) the Scotland Bill received the royal assent and passed into law. At the same time it was announced that the new Parliament would be opened by the Queen on 1 July 1999.

This brief account of the passage of the Scotland Bill through the House of Commons suggests a number of comments. First, compared with the legislation in the 1970s, the legislative progress of the devolution proposals was very smooth. In part this was a consequence of the fact that the referendum had produced a decisive result before the legislation was debated. As Michael Ancram acknowledged, this made it very difficult for anyone to oppose the main principles of the Bill and opponents had to be content with sniping over details. In addition, smooth progress was ensured because, as already mentioned, the size of the government's majority left no doubt that it would be passed easily – one might say 'steamrollered' – through the House. Although minor concessions were made along the way, the government did not really need to make concessions to anyone else. It might be argued, however, that the combination of the huge government majority and the pre-legislative nature of the referendum led to scrutiny of the Bill being less detailed and searching than might otherwise have been the case. Secondly, in marked contrast to the passage of the Scotland Act in 1978, there was a notable absence of dissent on the Labour side. Only one dissenting vote was cast by a Labour MP throughout (the issue of abortion being a free vote). Thirdly, and not surprisingly, a feature of the parliamentary debates was the focus on the nation-wide implications of devolution and especially the likely impact on Westminster itself, which had been largely absent from the debate in Scotland during the referendum. Finally, it is clear that the Bill was a highly complex piece of legislation. This largely explains why the government itself had to introduce numerous amendments. Moreover, the debates illustrated the considerable difficulty involved in drawing the line between matters that were to be reserved to Westmister and those to be devolved. This is a problem that would be certain to re-appear when the Scottish Parliament came into operation.

PREPARING FOR THE PARLIAMENT

Legislating for a new Parliament is one thing; having it up and running by May 1999 was another matter entirely. The Scotland Act left many important issues to be determined by the Parliament itself and, in order to make progress on these, the government established an all-party Consultative Steering Group (CSG).[6] The remit of the group included 'to bring together views on and consider the operational needs and working methods' of the Parliament and 'to develop proposals for the rules of procedure and Standing Orders'. It first met in January 1998 and was assisted by several expert panels. A very extensive programme of consultation was undertaken. Interested parties were invited to make submissions and the general public were able to have their say in a series of 'Open Forums', held at various locations throughout Scotland, or via an interactive web site.

The CSG considered and made recommendations about a great variety of issues. Weighty topics included the pre-legislative process, the legislative process itself, parliamentary committees, procedures for appointing the Scottish Executive and financial regulations. In addition, numerous details were attended to – the form of the opening ceremony, days and hours of business, whether there should be prayers and what form they should take, the use of electronic voting, how MSPs would address each other, and so on (see Scottish Office, October 1998).

It is clear from its report and recommendations that the CSG did not intend the new Parliament to be a small-scale version of the Westminster Parliament and this view was widely shared among the political community. The Parliament was to be 'accessible, open, responsive'. There seems to have been a desire to remove some of the stuffiness of Westminster (allowing members to refer to one another by name rather than as 'the honourable member'), to make procedures 'transparent', to encourage 'a participative approach to the development ... of policy' (especially through more extensive use of committees) and to be modern (using computers for voting). In addition the Parliament is to be in session during normal office hours (with no all-night sessions) and recesses will coincide with Scottish school holidays. What is planned is a radical departure from the Westminster model. Time will tell whether these aspirations relating to participation and openness will come to fruition. A more basic question to be decided, however, was where the Parliament should be housed.

Finding a home
At the time of the 1979 devolution referendum the government intended that the new Scottish Assembly would meet in the former Royal High School building in Edinburgh and work was undertaken to turn it into a suitable home for the new body. Even before the 1997

referendum took place, however, it was apparent that the building was now unsuitable for the new Parliament, with both size and security risks posing major difficulties. The building lacked sufficient office space to support the Parliament and was said by security experts to be insecure against potential terrorist attacks. The Scottish Office decided that a new building should be constructed comprising a debating chamber, committee rooms, office space for members and other facilities such as secure car parks. A TV viewing gallery was also included in the specification. A number of sites were put forward for consideration including Calton Hill, Leith Docks and Haymarket, all in Edinburgh. The clear preference among Scottish politicians (including the Liberal Democrats and the SNP) and media was for a site near the centre of Edinburgh and Calton Hill appeared to be the favoured option.

Following the referendum, pressure both to decide on the site and to make progress with the plans for the building increased. In response, Donald Dewar issued a 'user brief' (accompanied by complaints from the Liberal Democrats and the SNP that he was retreating from the cross-party co-operation that had been a feature of the referendum campaign) which stated that the intention was to provide a Parliament building which would last well into the twenty-first century and beyond, and which would be accessible in a whole variety of respects. The expenditure limit on the building was originally set at £40 million although it was clear that cost was not to be an overriding factor.

Since the new building would not be ready in time for the first sitting of the Parliament interim arrangements had to be made. The local authority in Glasgow put forward a case, arguing that the new Parliament should meet there temporarily, in the former Strathclyde Regional Council building. This helped to stir up the rivalry between Scotland's two largest cities but it was always a long shot and it was eventually determined that the temporary home of the Parliament would be in the Church of Scotland Assembly Halls at the top of the Mound in Edinburgh. This meant that members entering the chamber would have to pass under a forbidding statue of John Knox, hero of the Scottish Protestant Reformation – not, perhaps a very welcoming sight to Roman Catholic representatives.

In late 1997 a new site, next to Holyrood Palace at the 'bottom' end of the 'Royal Mile', began to emerge as a front runner when the Scottish Office released figures suggesting that the previous favourite, Calton Hill, would cost at least £15 million more than Holyrood, Leith or Haymarket. Donald Dewar confirmed that the site at Holyrood

Road, formerly housing the administrative headquarters of Scottish & Newcastle Breweries, had become a 'strong entrant' providing an open, flat site in a heritage area close to the centre of Edinburgh. By this time the likely costs of the building were expected to be between £50 million and £65 million.

Holyrood was finally chosen as the designated site for the Parliament building and a competition for design teams of 'proven ability' was announced in January 1998. Donald Dewar suggested that 'This is a unique opportunity to create an exciting building within the dramatic setting of a world heritage site of which we and future generations to come can be proud … We are looking in particular for architects who, we can be confident, will produce suitable designs for a dignified, modern, operationally efficient Parliament building incorporating innovative features in a historical setting' (*Scotsman*, 27 January 1998).

The arrangements for the competition were criticised by many architects for effectively excluding small and medium-sized firms. Nevertheless, over 70 applications were eventually received from across Europe as well as America and Australia, frequently including twinning arrangements with Scottish architects to provide a local base. In July 1998 the winning architect was announced – Enric Miralles, a 43-year-old Catalan who would work in association with an Edinburgh firm (RMJM (Scotland) Ltd) and whose controversial design was based on the theme of upturned boats. Those who disapproved drew comparisons between the proposed building and the Titanic. It remains to be seen whether they will be mollified and whether the Scottish people will come to identify with the new building when it is completed.

THE ELECTORAL SYSTEM

The establishing of the Scottish Parliament breaks new constitutional ground not just in terms of the devolution of power from Westminster but also in terms of its electoral arrangements. The traditional first-past-the-post method of election has been partially retained but, for the first time in the United Kingdom, it is complemented by an 'additional members' system. (The same system was adopted for the Welsh Assembly.) Since a similar system was suggested by the Jenkins Committee as an alternative to first-past-the-post in a future referendum on an electoral system for Westminster, the Scottish (and Welsh) experience in the first elections held in May 1999 provided some important lessons for the rest of the country (see Chapter 10).

The new electoral system creates two routes for election to the Scottish Parliament. Just over half of all MSPs (that is 73 out of 129) are elected by the familiar first-past-the-post system in single member constituencies. The constituencies are the same as those used for Westminster elections except that the Orkney and Shetland Westminster seat has been split into two separate seats for the Scottish Parliament. In addition to voting for a constituency MSP, however, voters also vote for a regional party list. The regions used correspond to the European Parliament constituencies as redrawn in 1996 and each of them elects seven additional MSPs giving a total of 56 'additional members' in the Parliament. The purpose of this system is to secure a closer match between votes received and seats won in each region, and hence in the Parliament as a whole, than is possible using first-past-the-post alone.

The process by which additional members are allocated is relatively straightforward. After the constituency seats have been decided, the total number of votes cast for each party list within each region are counted. These are then divided by the number of constituency seats already won *plus one*. (Thus if a party has won no seats its total is divided by 1.) The party with the highest total of list votes after this calculation gets the first additional MSP, who will usually be the first-named candidate on that party's regional list. This party's total is now divided again, to take account of the fact that it now has a seat (or an extra seat) and the party which now has the largest number of list votes gets the second additional seat. This process continues until all seven additional places have been filled.

In practice, this means that in regions where a party is strong its MSPs will mostly be elected via the constituency route and few, if any, will be added from the regional list. Glasgow provides a telling example. The city is one of the 'regions' employed for the Scottish Parliament elections, with ten constituency MSPs, and seven regional additional members to be elected. Labour dominates Glasgow politics (winning 60 per cent of the vote there in the 1997 general election, for example) and would usually expect to win all of the constituency seats. It is unlikely, therefore, to win any via the 'regional additional member' route since its list votes would initially be divided by 11 (if all ten constituency seats were won) while the other parties' votes would start off by being divided by one. The additional members in Glasgow would, therefore, be shared among the other parties.

The Conservatives remain firmly opposed to proportional representation but, ironically, the additional member system provides them with a path back into the mainstream of Scottish politics after their whitewash in the 1997 general election. It also offers the SNP a better chance of converting its electoral support into parliamentary representation than has been the case in nation-wide elections. The system will not, of course, produce exact proportionality of representation but it is considerably more proportional than first-past-the-post. As a consequence, in all but the most unusual circumstances, coalition governments will be the norm in Scotland for the foreseeable future.

PUBLIC OPINION IN SCOTLAND

The Labour Party, not unreasonably, must have expected to earn some kudos from the Scottish electorate for successfully carrying through the policy of devolution. Establishing the Parliament was a major constitutional innovation and it was enthusiastically backed by the voters. Monthly figures for voting intentions in a Westminster general election show that at first this proved to be the case (see Table 9.1). Labour obtained 46 per cent of the votes in the general election but in the first five months after the referendum their share of voting intentions was 50 per cent or more. Thereafter, they fell back a little but the percentage saying that they would vote Labour in a general election hovered around the level achieved in the 1997 general election. In contrast, in the latter part of 1997 and throughout 1998 the Conservatives were even more unpopular in Scotland than they had been at the general election. The Liberal Democrats did not benefit from (and perhaps were actually weakened by) their identification with the Yes campaign. After the referendum their support was always lower than it had been in May.[7] The opposite was the case with the SNP. Although the referendum did not produce an immediate boost in SNP support, their share of voting intentions throughout 1998 was consistently well above the 22 per cent that they had obtained in the general election.

Much the most intriguing aspect of party support in Scotland in the aftermath of the referendum, however, was the contrast in voting intentions for a United Kingdom general election and for the Scottish Parliament elections, especially in relation to Labour and the SNP. The voting intention figures for the Scottish Parliament are given in Table 9.2, and Figure 9.1 compares the Labour 'lead' over the SNP for the two elections. It is clear that voters were less inclined to support Labour and more inclined to support the SNP for the Scottish elections. In the early summer of 1998, indeed, the SNP was ahead in the latter polls. Without more detailed survey evidence it is difficult to know why there should be such a difference. It may be that some voters were happy to see a Labour government at Westminster but believed that specifically Scottish interests would be more strongly

Table 9.1: Voting intentions in a United Kingdom general election, 1997–98

	Conservative %	Labour %	Liberal Democrat %	SNP %
General election	18	46	13	22
1997				
September	13	55	9	23
October	14	55	8	22
November	12	51	12	24
1998				
January (early)	12	50	10	27
January (late)	11	50	12	25
February	14	46	11	28
March	12	48	9	28
April	14	44	11	30
May	14	46	10	29
June	14	43	9	33
July	13	48	8	28
August	13	46	8	31
September	13	45	10	31
October	14	43	12	29
November	13	42	13	31

Source: System Three polls published in the *Herald*.

pursued if there were a strong SNP presence in Edinburgh. More generally, the Scottish Parliament elections might have been seen by voters as 'second-order' elections, simply not as important as general elections. Characteristically, in second-order elections turnout is lower and voters are more inclined to desert their 'normal' party, using their votes to register their current reactions to the performance of the government, or to indicate some sympathy with another party, in the knowledge that they are not deciding whether or not the government should remain in office.

On the other hand, paralleling the increase in support for the SNP in opinion polls there was also an increase in support for outright independence for Scotland. At the time of the referendum, independence was favoured by 24 per cent of our survey respondents and polls had found a similar figure over a number of years. From June to November 1998, however, ICM asked respondents to their Scottish polls how they would vote in a referendum on Scottish independence and in each case the results suggested an outcome in favour of independence. In the six polls concerned 51 per cent on

Table 9.2: Voting intentions for the Scottish Parliament election, 1997–98

	Conservative %	Labour %	Liberal Democrat %	SNP %
1997				
November	13	48	9	29
1998				
January	9	44	13	33
February	12	39	10	38
March	8	40	10	40
April	11	36	10	41
May	10	35	10	44
June	9	37	8	45
July	10	40	9	41
August	11	41	8	38
September	12	40	9	39
October	11	39	12	37
November	11	38	12	37

Source: System Three Polls published in the *Herald*.
Notes: From June 1998 System Three asked respondents separately how they would cast their constituency and regional list votes. The figures shown are for constituency voting intention.

Figure 9.1: Labour lead over SNP, January–November 1998

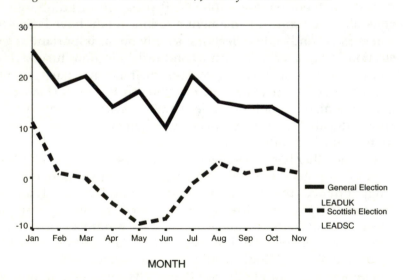

MONTH

average claimed that they would vote 'Yes' and 39 per cent that they would vote 'No' (the remainder being uncertain). There is, of course, no independence referendum on the horizon but these data suggest that the expectation that devolution would dampen the demand for independence has not been fulfilled.

Other indicators of the electorate's attitudes towards the parties in Scotland tell the same story of a decline in support for Labour and a buoyant SNP. In 21 local government by-elections held during 1998 Labour lost eight (six of them to the SNP) retained five and gained none. In November the SNP retained the north-east Scotland European Parliament seat in a by-election, with an increased share of the vote while Labour slipped to third place, behind the Conservatives, with a vote share reduced by ten points.

Labour's response to the apparent growth in independence sentiment and to the electoral threat of the SNP was to launch a strong attack on the SNP and 'separatism' towards the end of the year. The Prime Minister himself visited Scotland in November and both he and the Chancellor, Gordon Brown, defended the Union in high profile speeches. Nonetheless at the start of 1999, according to the polls, the two parties were still running neck and neck in the Scottish Parliament stakes.

THE FUTURE: AN EXPECTATIONS GAP?

When Prime Minister Lord Salisbury invited the Duke of Richmond and Gordon to become the first Secretary of State for Scotland in 1885, he warned him that 'the work is not heavy, but measured by the expectations of the people of Scotland it is approaching the Archangelic' (quoted in Ross, 1978: 4). Half a century later, an official enquiry into the work of the Scottish Office noted that Scots tended to look to the Scottish Secretary on all matters, regardless of whether the office actually had responsibility for the area concerned (Mitchell, 1989). The idea that expectations have outstripped the capabilities of Scottish political institutions has been a recurring theme in Scottish politics and the extent to which the new Scottish Parliament is capable of meeting the expectations of the Scottish people will be a crucial determinant of the future course of constitutional politics in the United Kingdom. If expectations are not met, it is conceivable that more devolution or even independence will be demanded. It is, therefore, important to identify what Scots expect from the Parliament they voted for in September 1997 as well as whether it is institutionally capable of delivering what is expected.

Throughout the 1980s, Scottish public opinion became polarised on the issue of constitutional change. A relationship developed between support for a Scottish Parliament and support for broadly left-of-centre politics. This is not surprising as devolution came to be seen as a way of avoiding or opposing the imposition of 'Thatcherite' policies on Scotland. The association between the two was confirmed in the referendum. Conservatives and those of a right-wing disposition were least likely to support a Scottish Parliament while those favouring state intervention, identifying with the working class and left-leaning political parties were most likely to do so. In essence, support for a Scottish Parliament went hand in hand with support for more left-inclined policies.[8] The rhetoric surrounding debates on Scotland's constitutional status also suggested this.

Some evidence concerning the expectations that Yes Yes voters had about the future impact of the Scottish Parliament is given in Table 9.3, which is derived from a survey undertaken by CREST. Just 11 per cent thought that there would be some increase in unemployment while 70 per cent believed that taxes would rise a little – evidently this was thought to be a price worth paying. The most interesting figures, however, are those which show that very large majorities believed that the economy would be improved and that there would be better standards in the health service, education and social welfare.

Table 9.3: Expectations of Yes Yes voters on the impact of the Scottish Parliament

	A lot	A little	Total
The Scottish Parliament would:	%	%	%
Increase unemployment	2	9	11
Increase taxes	2	68	70
Improve the economy	26	60	86
Improve the standard of the NHS	36	46	82
Improve the quality of education	39	50	89
Improve the standard of social welfare	19	52	71

Source: CREST referendum survey.
Note: Ns vary from 311 to 314.

When the powers of the Scottish Parliament are examined, it is far from clear that the expectations of the Scottish people, at least those they had at the time of the referendum, will be realised. Table 9.4 provides a list showing the broad division of responsibilities between the Scottish and Westminster Parliaments. On the face of it the Scottish Parliament has very considerable powers, covering important aspects of national life. Having responsibility for something is not the same as having power to effect change in that area, however. A more useful way of conceiving the powers of the Scottish Parliament, which both takes account of its real power potential and equates broadly with the kinds of expectations of it that we have identified, can be derived from public policy analysis (Lowi, 1964). The traditional four-fold classification of policy types, initially introduced into the literature almost 40 years ago, offers a useful typology for our purposes:

1. Redistributive policies: policies designed to redistribute wealth amongst individuals. The main tools to achieve this are taxation and social security.
2. Distributive policies: policies designed to distribute grants to groups of people, farmers for example or public expenditure on education.
3. Regulatory policies: policies involving little or no public spending but which involve public control of private activities in the public interest, such as environmental or consumer legislation.
4. Policy-making process: the processes through which policies are made which, though strictly speaking not a policy type as such, can impact on the output of policies (See Mitchell (1998) for a fuller account of these).

These are ideal types and reality is more complex. It is possible, for example, that distributive types of policies will have redistributive consequences, although distributive policy instruments are rather blunt weapons in any attempt to redistribute wealth. Nonetheless, skilful politicians can have some success in using one policy instrument to achieve ends other than those for which they are primarily designed. In the context of considering the powers of the Parliament and the expectations of the Scottish people it is worth considering each of the policy types outlined above in turn.

The Scottish Parliament's redistributive powers are almost non-existent. The tax-varying power, which was the reason for having the referendum in the first place, is of dubious fiscal value. Even if it were used, it would not have a particularly redistributive impact and it would not raise very much money. It is also conceivable that the Treasury would react to a rise in taxes in Scotland by lowering the grant made available to the Scottish Parliament. The 'tartan tax' was of great political significance but fiscally it is feeble. It is also worth noting that social security payments and pensions are reserved powers. The main policy-making tools used to redistribute wealth are simply not available to the Scottish Parliament. This does not mean

Table 9.4: Powers of the Scottish Parliament

Reserved powers (not devolved)	Areas not reserved (responsibility of Scottish Parliament)
	Agriculture, Fisheries and Forestry
Common Market for United Kingdom	Economic Development
Goods and Services	Education
Constitution of the United Kingdom	Environment
Defence and National Security	Health
Employment Legislation	Housing
Fiscal, Economic and Monetary	Law and Home Affairs
System	Local Government
Foreign Policy including relations	Research and Statistics
with Europe	Social Work
Health (in some areas), Medicine	Training
Media and Culture	Transport
Professional Regulations (in certain	
cases)	
Protection of Borders	
Social Security	
Transport Safety and Regulation	

that redistributive ends cannot be pursued by other means but it does mean that the Scottish Parliament will find it difficult to have a major impact on the socio-economic structure of Scotland.

The Parliament will have distributive powers, almost entirely derived through the grant from the Treasury. However, the scope for making changes in levels of public expenditure will be limited. As the total amount of the grant will be outwith the control of the Parliament, it will have little power to meet the pressures for more money coming from various interest groups in Scotland. If revenues coming into the Treasury rise then, of course, the Scottish Parliament would expect to benefit accordingly. On the other hand, Scotland's share of national public expenditure has become a sensitive issue, with pressure coming from outside Scotland for a reduction in Scotland's share. In late 1998 statements by Ken Livingstone and Jeffrey Archer, each hoping to become Mayor of London, suggested that pressure will mount to reduce Scotland's share of the national cake. The Parliament will have the power to re-prioritise its spending patterns. Theoretically at least, more money might be spent on housing if less money were spent on some other item. This power of *virement* exists for the Scottish Office but can only be used incrementally. Small changes have been possible which, in the long run, might make a substantial difference, but there are political costs involved in shifting priorities in public expenditure, potentially very considerable, and reducing public expenditure in any area is notoriously difficult. In essence, little is likely to change from the situation before the establishment of the Scottish Parliament except that debates are likely to be more public and the issue of Scotland's share of expenditure more controversial.

Regulatory policies probably offer the Scottish Parliament the best chance to carve out a distinctive role for itself. It has been argued that we have witnessed the 'rise of the regulatory state' in Europe as states have privatised government agencies and transformed state functions (Majone, 1994). The most notable example of an institution with negligible redistributive and distributive policy-making capacity which has, nonetheless, acquired a prominent role for itself is the European Commission. However, it should be noted that in the field of economic regulation the Parliament will be extremely constrained in what it can do. The United Kingdom's fiscal, economic and monetary system are retained powers under the terms of the Scotland Act.

It is, perhaps, in the way in which policies are made that the greatest changes are likely to occur. Though this should not be exaggerated, the policies pursued in the areas devolved to the Parliament will not emanate from a party with little support in Scotland (as during 1979–97). Rather the party or parties determining policy will have very significant support and might, therefore, be more in step with the Scottish public mood and expectations. However, this may simply result in the MSPs themselves becoming frustrated.

This brief examination of the autonomy and powers of the Scottish Parliament appears to suggest that it will be frustrated in important respects. However, it would be wrong to assume that public opinion and expectations as they were in September 1997 are static. One possible scenario is that expectations will alter, that it will be possible to lower them. If this transpires, then it is conceivable that a stable and lasting constitutional order will have been achieved. Even if expectations are not lowered, however, this need not mean that Scots will demand greater devolution or independence. They would have to be convinced that greater autonomy would allow aspirations and expectations to be realised. This takes us to current debates in Scottish politics. Those opposed to further constitutional turmoil are seeking to lower expectations, to promise little and to deliver on all that is promised. This conforms with the approach adopted by New Labour across Britain in the run-up to the 1997 general election. Scottish Labour's campaign for the Parliament aimed to present the party as responsible, refusing to make rash and unrealistic promises. In addition, given that a devolved Parliament is now the status quo, they question whether further constitutional change would increase the capacity of governmental institutions to meet expectations. The argument that Scotland is too poor for independence is a central part of this strategy. On the other hand, Nationalists and those who seek to increase the powers of the Parliament argue that only through acquiring new powers will the Scottish Parliament be able to meet the aspirations of the Scottish people.

The gap between popular expectations and the capacity of the Scottish Parliament to meet these expectations is likely to prove the key determinant of the future course of Scottish politics. New Labour seeks to bridge that gap, as will the Conservatives. The public statements of the Conservatives during the years leading up to the referendum suggested that they doubted whether this could be achieved. The Liberal Democrats find themselves in an unusual position of seeking both to develop devolution and to oppose the demands of the SNP. The SNP seek to argue that the gap exists and cannot be bridged other than through radical constitutional change. One interpretation of polls since the referendum is that Scots do not believe that the *new* status quo will fulfil their expectations, but neither do they believe, or at least are as yet not convinced, that independence will do so either. If this interpretation is correct, then the referendum on devolution may prove to have been a very important watershed in Scottish politics but by no means a defining moment in Scotland's constitutional status.

NOTES

1. A fourth Labour MP, Kevin McNamara (Hull North) accidentally voted against the amendment, having arrived in the House just in time for the division. Having anti-abortion views, McNamara had intended to support the amendment but on realising his mistake immediately went into the other lobby to cancel out his first vote.
2. The dates of these debates were 8, 14, 16, 21, 23, 27, 28 and 30 July, and 6 and 8 October.
3. The report stage was taken on 22 and 28 October and 2 and 3 November.
4. The Bill laid down that 71 MSPs would be directly elected from existing parliamentary constituencies together with one each from Orkney and Shetland. It was anticipated, however, that the next review of parliamentary constituencies would reduce the number in Scotland with a consequent reduction in the number of MSPs.
5. Canavan, a veteran of Labour's 'awkward squad' was in dispute with the party over the fact that he had been excluded from the list of approved candidates for the Scottish Parliament. Another Scottish Labour MP, John McAllion deliberately abstained on this vote.
6. The initial members of the CSG were Jim Wallace MP (Liberal Democrat), Alex Salmond MP (SNP), Paul Cullen QC (Conservative), Keith Geddes

(representing the Convention of Scottish Local Authorities), Canon Kenyon Wright (Constitutional Convention), Professor Alice Brown (Edinburgh University), Dr Joan Stringer (Principal of Queen Margaret's College), Joyce MacMillan (writer and journalist), Esther Robertson (Constitutional Convention), Deirdre Hutton (Scottish Consumer Council), Andrew Cubie (lawyer and former chair of the CBI in Scotland) and Campbell Christie (General Secretary of the STUC).

7. It should be said, however, that the Liberal Democrats regularly tend to receive less support in opinion polls than they do in actual elections.

8. On a left–right scale running from 1 (left) to 5 (right) which summarises attitudes on political issues, the CREST referendum survey found that the mean score for Yes Yes voters was 2.4 (N=314) while for Yes No voters it was 2.6 (N=52) and for No No voters 2.9 (N=106).

10

Postscript: The First Elections to the Scottish Parliament

The Scottish devolution saga, which had involved two referendums, brought about the downfall of a government in 1979 and dominated political debate in Scotland for a generation, entered a new phase on 6 May 1999 when the first elections to the newly-established Parliament were held. The elections attracted attention well beyond Scotland. Partly this was because of their historic significance – they would determine the composition of the first Parliament to sit in Scotland for almost 300 years – but it was also because, as described in Chapter 9, the electoral system which had been adopted involved, for the first time in Britain (along with the elections to the Welsh National Assembly held on the same day), an element of proportional representation. There was considerable interest, therefore, in how voters would react to an unfamiliar system and on how the system would affect the make-up of the Parliament.

TRENDS IN PUBLIC OPINION

As seen in Chapter 9, polls reporting voting intentions for the Scottish Parliament suggested that at the start of 1999 Labour and the SNP were running almost neck and neck. This situation changed in the new year. Table 10.1 shows that Labour opened up a seven point gap in January and, although this narrowed a little in February, the SNP's share of vote intentions fell to around 30 per cent as the election approached. Labour support, on the other hand, remained buoyant and was at or above the level achieved in the 1997 general election. For the other parties, the polls brought little comfort.

It is difficult to be certain about why support for the SNP declined during this period. On the one hand, this may simply be another example of the 'homing' tendency of voters as an election drew nearer. Having flirted with the SNP during the 'phoney war' after the referendum, this hypothesis would suggest that voters' minds were concentrated when the election became imminent and they tended to

Table 10.1: Voting intentions in the Scottish Parliament election, January–May 1999

	Conservative	Labour	Liberal Democrat	SNP
	%	%	%	%
January (2)	11	43	10	36
February (3)	11	42	10	37
March (4)	11	46	10	32
Early April (5)	11	47	10	30
Late April/May (7)	12	45	10	31

Notes: The figures are the mean percentages for voting intentions in constituency contests from polls conducted by the major polling firms in the period

return to their traditional party homes. On the other hand, there were two specific events which may have influenced the voters. The first was the decision by the SNP following the Budget on 9 March that the one penny cut in the standard rate of income tax announced by the Chancellor should be foregone in Scotland, the money saved to be used to increase the funding for public services. An ICM poll to test public reaction to this suggestion found that while 12 per cent of respondents said that the proposal would make them more likely to vote SNP, 16 per cent said that it would make them less likely to do so. At the start of April, according to a MORI poll reported in the *Herald* (2 May 1999), Labour had a lead of 12 points over the SNP as the party most preferred on taxation but by the end of the month this had stretched to 15 points. The second event of possible significance occurred at the end of March when, in a well-publicised party election broadcast, Alex Salmond described the NATO bombing campaign in Yugoslavia as 'an act of unpardonable folly'. This does not seem to have gone down well with the electorate. MORI found in early April that only 11 per cent of their respondents said that on the war in Kosovo the party that they most agreed with was the SNP while 45 per cent chose Labour.

The Scottish press, which was overwhelmingly anti-SNP, pilloried the party over these events, portraying them as serious campaign errors which indicated a lack of judgement on the part of the party's leadership. They also provided convenient sticks which the other parties used to beat the SNP and it is certainly the case that they coincided with a clear decline in SNP support. Whether this was any more than coincidence is difficult to tell, but the income tax and Kosovo issues provided an excuse for 'soft' supporters to desert the party and it seems safe to conclude that they certainly cannot have improved the SNP's prospects.

THE RESULT OF THE ELECTION

In the event, the outcome of the election proved something of an embarrassment for the polls. Table 10.2 shows, firstly, the result of the constituency contests. In terms of vote share, both the Conservatives and the Liberal Democrats did better than the polls had suggested while Labour's vote was well below expectations and the SNP's slightly below. Compared with the levels of support for the SNP recorded throughout 1998, the fact that the SNP failed to obtain 30 per cent of votes must have come as a disappointment. Despite Labour's decline in vote share, the election would have resulted in a clear victory for them if it had been conducted under first-past-the-post rules alone – they captured 53 of the 73 seats at stake in constituency contests. For the second successive election the Conservatives were unable to win a single first-past-the-post seat in Scotland. With just 14.2 per cent of the votes, the Liberal Democrats won 12 seats but the SNP, with more than double the number of votes took only seven. The 'Other' seat was won by Dennis Canavan, the dissident Labour MP in Falkirk West, who had been denied the opportunity to stand as a Labour candidate but contested the seat as an Independent and won an overwhelming victory with 55 per cent of the vote to Labour's 18.8 per cent.

The results of the regional list voting are also shown in the table and the figures suggest that many electors who had voted for one of the major parties in the constituency elections switched to minor parties in the list voting. Especially noteworthy is the fact that whereas Labour obtained 38.8 per cent of the constituency votes they fell to 33.6 per cent of the list votes. 'Others' appear to have been the beneficiaries of this switching especially the Green Party (which did not contest any constituency seats but got 3.6 per cent of list votes), the Socialist Labour Party (2.4 per cent) and the Scottish Socialist Party (2 per cent). The allocation of 'top up' seats on the basis of list votes worked as anticipated with the SNP winning 28 seats, the Conservatives 18, the Liberal Democrats five and Labour only three. In addition, the Scottish Socialist Party won a list seat in Glasgow and a Green Party candidate was elected in Lothians. As a result, and as intended, the distribution of seats in the Parliament was much more representative of the distribution of party support among the voters than would have been achieved using only a first-past-the-post system. As a consequence, no party had an overall majority and immediately after the election Labour and the Liberal Democrats set about working out an agreement that would enable the two to govern Scotland together.

Table 10.2: The distribution of votes and seats in Scotland, 1999

| | Constituencies | | Regional lists | | |
	Share of votes	Seats won	Share of votes	Seats won	Total seats
	%		%		
Conservative	15.5	0	15.4	18	18
Labour	38.8	53	33.6	3	56
Lib Dem	14.2	12	12.4	5	17
SNP	28.7	7	27.3	28	35
Others	2.7	1	11.3	2	3

LIST VOTING

The novel aspect of the Scottish Parliament election was the use of a list voting system to supplement the constituency votes in order to achieve greater proportionality. It is appropriate, therefore, to consider how voters reacted to the list system in a little more detail. It is worth noting first that almost all voters made use of their two votes. Across Scotland, just under 3,700 fewer votes were cast in the list election (out of more than 2.3 million) than in the constituency contests. Excluding the Edinburgh West constituency, where there was a surprisingly large and unexplained decrease in the number of votes cast in the list election,[1] the difference in votes cast in the two types of elections in Scotland as a whole was only 1,633. Few voters appear to have been deterred by the lengthy list ballot papers that were required and the complicated counting arrangements involved.

One of the arguments frequently used by proponents of proportional representation is that it minimises 'wasted' votes. Under first-past-the-post a large number of votes can be said to be wasted. Thus, the votes of those who vote for any candidate other than the winner in a constituency do not contribute to electing a representative and hence to the make-up of the legislature. Even votes which are cast for a winner but only serve to increase the majority beyond a single vote can be viewed as 'wasted' in that they were not required to elect the candidate concerned.

The system adopted for the Scottish election was only partly proportional, however, and was not designed to make all votes count. The fact that victories in the constituency contests were taken into account before allocating seats to the list candidates meant that a party which won a lot of constituencies would have little chance of obtaining a top up seat, no matter how many list votes it had. There was, therefore, plenty of scope for tactical or strategic voting as far as the lists were concerned. If a voter was sure that his or her favoured party would win enough constituency seats to make it unlikely that it would secure more *via* the lists, then a rational strategy would be to choose another party with which he or she had some sympathy in the list voting. This might enable the second-favoured party to secure list seats at the expense of a party to which the voter was strongly opposed. As noted in Chapter 9, in Glasgow, for example, Labour was more or less certain to win at least nine of the ten constituencies and unlikely, therefore, to qualify for a list seat. To maximise the impact of their list votes the strategy of Labour voters would be to give them to the party they preferred second. Nonetheless, all the major parties urged their supporters to vote for them twice – in the list elections as well as in the constituency contests.

Table 10.3 shows the difference between the results of the constituency and list voting in the regions used to allocate additional member seats in the Parliament. As far as the major parties are concerned, the figures suggest that most voters chose the same party in both the constituency and list contests. There are ups and downs between the two votes, of course, but no evidence of really massive defections or huge increases in support.

Table 10.3: Differences between constituency and list votes for parties (regions)

	Con	Lab	Lib Dem	SNP	Soc Lab	SSP	Green	Others
Central Scotland	-0.4	-7.3	-0.4	-2.1	+1.9	+1.4	+1.8	+5.0
Glasgow	+0.2	-5.4	-0.9	-2.4	+1.5	+1.0	+4.0	+2.1
Highlands & Islands	+0.6	-1.9	-6.8	-0.8	+1.4	+0.9	+3.8	+2.9
Lothians	-0.1	-10.0	-1.3	-1.1	+3.3	+0.9	+6.9	+1.4
Mid Scotland & Fife	0	-3.0	-0.1	-2.8	+1.4	+1.0	+3.9	-0.4
North-east Scotland	+0.4	-0.7	-3.7	-0.7	+1.2	+0.3	+2.8	+0.4
South of Scotland	-1.2	-5.9	-2.7	-0.4	+4.4	+1.0	+3.0	+1.8
West of Scotland	-0.7	-5.0	-0.3	-1.0	+1.4	+1.3	+2.6	+1.5
Scotland	-0.1	-5.2	-1.8	-1.4	+2.2	+1.0	+3.6	+1.8

Notes: SSP = Scottish Socialist Party; Soc Lab = Socialist Labour Party. The Green Party did not contest any constituency seats and so all of their list votes count as an increase.

Nonetheless, these data can be interpreted as showing that at least some voters made the kind of calculation described above. Since the Conservatives could not be sure of winning constituency seats in any region, the strategy of their supporters should have been to stick with them in the list vote and, as can be seen, across all of the regions their support barely changed. It is also the case, however, that the Conservatives are rather isolated in Scottish politics and none of the other parties appear to be an obvious second choice for Conservative supporters. The Liberal Democrats would have been expected to win a majority of constituency seats in the Highlands and Islands and to have had a good chance of winning some in north-east Scotland. In both regions, as would be expected on the rational voting hypothesis, their list vote was clearly down on their constituency vote while in other areas they retained the great bulk of their constituency vote, as they needed to. Changes in the SNP vote do not conform so clearly to the expected pattern, however. While their biggest drop was in mid Scotland and Fife, where they already held two United Kingdom Parliament seats, they lost hardly any support in north-east Scotland where they also held two seats. In both cases, however, their chances of gaining additional list seats were good. The decline in Labour support in the list voting was much the largest of all the parties. This is not surprising as Labour would be expected to take almost all constituency seats in almost all regions. However the smallest declines were in the regions where they had the smallest proportions of United Kingdom MPs – Highlands and Islands and north-east Scotland – which is again consistent with a rational list voting strategy.

It is impossible to be sure, however, that these patterns were produced by some voters working out how to cast their votes most effectively. It may be, on the other hand, that some voters mistakenly believed that they were *required* to vote for a different party in the list contests (the list vote was frequently described in the media as a *second* vote) and the data are also consistent with that interpretation.

It is also impossible to be precise about the extent and nature of switching between constituency and list votes from these data. The election results reflect the net effects of movements between parties and some switching will have been self-cancelling. Thus some switching from Labour to the SNP, for example, will have been cancelled out by switching in the opposite direction. Nonetheless, the figures suggest that the bulk of voters who switched parties in their list vote appear to have opted for the Green Party or one of the small Socialist parties. The sharp increase in 'Other' votes in central Scotland indicates support for the stand taken by Dennis Canavan across constituencies other than his own.

We can explore list voting in a little more detail by examining the difference between list and constituency votes in individual constituencies. In Table 10.4 we show how changes in the parties' vote shares were related to one another. Changes in the level of Conservative support were not significantly related to changes in the performance of the other parties except for the Liberal Democrats.

Here there was a negative relationship (-0.242) – where the Conservative share went up, the Liberal Democrat share went down and *vice versa*. The same was true of changes in the Labour and Liberal Democrat votes but in this case the relationship was stronger (-0.466). A coalition between the two was widely touted as the most likely outcome of the election and it seems that in appropriate areas supporters of one switched to the other. It is not surprising that the Socialist Labour Party appears to have benefited from Labour defections (-0.382) but the coefficient for Labour and the Scottish Socialist Party (SSP) (-0.229) just fails to achieve statistical significance. There were also significant associations between the size of the decline in Labour's list vote and the increases obtained by 'Others' and the Green Party. The strongest association of all relates to the Liberal Democrats and the SNP (-0.501) suggesting that these two parties were in competition for 'second' votes. In some constituencies the SNP reaped the benefit and the Liberal Democrat vote fell away while in others it was the Liberal Democrats who received these votes rather than the SNP. The SNP also did less well where 'Others' garnered a significant proportion of list votes (notably in the constituencies in central Scotland where Dennis Canavan was on the list).

Table 10.4: Correlations between changes in constituency and list share of votes for parties (constituencies)

	Con	Lab	Lib Dem	SNP	Soc Lab	SSP	Green
Lab	0.000						
Lib Dem	**-0.242**	**-0.466**					
SNP	0.050	0.067	**-0.501**				
Soc Lab	-0.091	**-0.382**	0.187	0.062			
SSP	-0.073	-0.229	0.026	-0.093	0.073		
Green	0.171	**-0.293**	-0.058	-0.054	0.003	0.046	
Others	-0.191	**-0.400**	-0.087	**-0.304**	-0.112	0.051	-0.104

Notes: The Edinburgh West constituency is omitted from this analysis for reasons explained in the text. N = 72. Significant coefficients are printed in bold.

TURNOUT

It is worth mentioning briefly the level of turnout in the election since some commentators made much of the fact that, at 58.8 per cent, the turnout of voters was 12.6 per cent down on the 1997 general election and 1.6 per cent lower than in the 1997 referendum. Although there was wet weather across much of Scotland until the early afternoon of polling day, this was interpreted as indicating that voters were apathetic about the new Parliament. In fact, it would be unrealistic to expect turnout in the election to be close to general election levels. In all political systems turnout is higher in elections for the national legislature than in those for subordinate institutions and although the Scottish Parliament has considerable powers it is certainly subordinate to the United Kingdom Parliament. On the other hand, the Scottish Parliament is more important than local councils and it would have been surprising if turnout in the election had fallen to local government election levels. Bad weather notwithstanding, therefore, it is not surprising to find that the turnout was almost exactly half way between what is normal in general and local elections.

The pattern of turnout across constituencies was very similar to that seen in the 1997 general election. The correlation coefficient measuring the association between constituency turnouts in 1997 and 1999 was 0.897 which indicates a very strong relationship. Perhaps surprisingly, changes in constituency turnout between the general election and the Scottish election were not systematically related to changes in the parties' shares of constituency votes , except in the case of the SNP. The larger the decline in turnout the better was the SNP perfomance (correlation coefficient -0.370). It would be unwise to read too much into this, however, as turnout declined most and the SNP did best in safe Labour seats.

CONCLUSION

As is customary after elections, all parties claimed some success in the first Scottish Parliament election. They were able to do this because they used different criteria to determine what counts as success. In fact all had a mixture of success and disappointment. The Conservatives put themselves back on the Scottish political map by winning some representation in the Parliament and their performance in terms of votes was not as bad as opinion polls had suggested. On the other hand, their vote declined even further as compared with the catastrophic result in the 1997 general election and they once again failed to win a first-past-the-post seat. Labour also saw its support slip significantly (at a time when nation-wide opinion polls suggested that they were riding high). They had the consolation of winning most seats in the Parliament and retaining almost all of the seats won in their general election triumph. The Liberal Democrats slightly strengthened their position in both share of the vote and constituencies won and certainly did better than the polls suggested they would. On the other hand, they remain the fourth party in Scotland in terms both of popularity among the voters and seats in the Parliament. The SNP saw its vote increase and emerged from the election with a sizeable number of MSPs. Compared to expectations, however, their performance was a disappointment.

The election of May 1999 marked the end of a long road and ushered in a new style of politics in Scotland. In the first place, women will play a more prominent part in the Parliament than they do in the House of Commons. A total of 49 women were elected – 28 Labour, 16 SNP, three Liberal Democrats and two Conservatives – so that they comprise 38 per cent of the members. Perhaps more importantly, the electoral system ensured that no party could govern on its own and within a week of the election an agreement had been reached between Labour and the Liberal Democrats that they would work together in a coalition, with two Liberal Democrats holding cabinet positions.

The new Parliament assembled on Wednesday 12 May. Members were sworn in by Winnie Ewing, the veteran SNP representative, who was the oldest person elected. Lord (formerly David) Steel was chosen as the Presiding Officer and Donald Dewar confirmed as First Minister. A new political adventure was under way. It remains to be seen, however, how the new politics will work in practice and whether the Scottish Parliament will fulfil the high hopes and expectations of those who struggled long and hard to bring it into existence.

NOTE

1. The figures given by the returning officer for Edinburgh imply that 2,059 fewer people voted for the party lists in Edinburgh West as compared with the constituency contest. The next largest reduction was only 802 (Glasgow Anniesland) while the change in the other five Edinburgh constituencies ranged from a decline of 42 to an increase of 101. It seems not unreasonable to conclude that about 2,000 votes were somehow 'lost' in counting the list votes for Edinburgh West.

APPENDIX 1

The Referendum Results

The results of the referendum were announced for each of the 32 local authorities in Scotland. This appendix gives full details of the results for each authority and for Scotland as a whole – electorate and turnout, Yes and No votes and percentages for each question. We also show the numbers and proportions of ballots that were excluded as being 'spoiled' (Table A1.4). Although we have not analysed the distribution of spoiled ballots in the text, it is interesting to note that they were slightly more common on the second question (0.79 per cent of the total) than on the first (0.50 per cent). In both cases there were more spoiled ballots than is usual in general elections. In the 1992 election, for example, there were only 2,586 rejected ballots in Scotland (0.09 per cent of the total). This suggests that electors might be slightly more confused about the mechanics of voting in a referendum than they are in elections.

Table A1.1: Electorate and turnout in the referendum

Local authority	Electorate N	Turnout %	Local authority	Electorate N	Turnout %
Aberdeen	169,683	53.7	Glasgow	476,886	51.6
Aberdeenshire	170,310	57.0	Highland	165,751	60.3
Angus	86,582	60.2	Inverclyde	67,660	60.4
Argyll & Bute	69,995	65.0	North Lanarkshire	246,704	60.8
East Ayrshire	93,958	64.8	South Lanarkshire	235,108	63.1
North Ayrshire	106,511	63.4	East Lothian	69,615	65.0
South Ayrshire	90,433	66.7	Midlothian	61,135	65.1
Borders	83,674	64.8	West Lothian	114,836	62.6
Clackmannan	35,725	66.1	Moray	64,235	57.8
Dumfries & Galloway	116,411	63.4	Perthshire & Kinross	104,138	63.1
East Dunbartonshire	81,153	72.7	East Renfrewshire	67,363	68.2
West Dunbartonshire	72,744	63.7	Renfrewshire	139,269	62.8
Dundee	117,101	55.7	Stirling	65,075	65.8
Edinburgh	362,245	60.1	Orkney	15,579	53.5
Falkirk	109,723	63.7	Shetland	16,954	51.5
Fife	274,384	60.7	Western Isles	22,733	55.8
			SCOTLAND	3,973,673	60.4

Table A1.2: Votes cast on first question (establishing a Scottish Parliament)

Local authority	YES		NO	
	N	%	N	%
Aberdeen	65,035	71.8	25,580	28.2
Aberdeenshire	61,621	63.9	34,878	36.1
Angus	33,571	64.7	18,350	35.3
Argyll & Bute	30,452	67.3	14,796	32.7
East Ayrshire	49,131	81.1	11,426	18.9
North Ayrshire	51,304	76.3	15,931	23.7
South Ayrshire	40,161	66.9	19,909	33.1
Borders	33,855	62.8	20,060	37.2
Clackmannan	18,790	80.0	4,706	20.0
Dumfries & Galloway	44,619	60.7	28,863	39.3
East Dunbartonshire	40,917	69.8	17,725	30.2
West Dunbartonshire	39,051	84.7	7,058	15.3
Dundee	49,252	76.0	15,553	24.0
Edinburgh	155,900	71.9	60,832	28.1
Falkirk	55,642	80.0	13,953	20.0
Fife	125,668	76.1	39,517	23.9
Glasgow	204,269	83.6	40,106	16.4
Highland	72,551	72.6	27,431	27.4
Inverclyde	31,680	78.0	8,945	22.0
North Lanarkshire	123,063	82.6	26,010	17.4
South Lanarkshire	114,908	77.8	32,762	22.2
East Lothian	33,525	74.2	11,665	25.8
Midlothian	31,681	79.9	7,979	20.1
West Lothian	56,923	79.6	14,614	20.4
Moray	24,822	67.2	12,122	32.8
Perthshire & Kinross	40,344	61.7	24,998	38.3
East Renfrewshire	28,253	61.7	17,573	38.3
Renfrewshire	68,711	79.0	18,213	21.0
Stirling	29,190	68.5	13,440	31.5
Orkney	4,749	57.3	3,541	42.7
Shetland	5,430	62.4	3,275	37.6
Western Isles	9,977	79.4	2,589	20.6
SCOTLAND	1,775,045	74.3	614,400	25.7

Table A1.3: Votes cast on second question (tax-varying powers for a Scottish Parliament)

Local authority	YES		NO	
	N	%	N	%
Aberdeen	54,320	60.3	35,709	39.7
Aberdeenshire	50,295	52.3	45,929	47.7
Angus	27,641	53.4	24,089	46.6
Argyll & Bute	25,746	57.0	19,429	43.0
East Ayrshire	42,559	70.5	17,824	29.5
North Ayrshire	43,990	65.7	22,991	34.3
South Ayrshire	33,679	56.2	26,217	43.8
Borders	27,284	50.7	26,497	49.3
Clackmannan	16,112	68.7	7,355	31.3
Dumfries & Galloway	35,737	48.8	37,499	51.2
East Dunbartonshire	34,576	59.1	23,914	40.9
West Dunbartonshire	34,408	74.7	11,628	25.3
Dundee	42,304	65.5	22,280	34.5
Edinburgh	133,843	62.0	82,188	38.0
Falkirk	48,064	69.2	21,403	30.8
Fife	108,021	64.7	58,987	35.3
Glasgow	182,589	75.0	60,842	25.0
Highland	61,359	62.1	37,525	37.9
Inverclyde	27,194	67.2	13,277	32.8
North Lanarkshire	107,288	72.2	41,372	27.8
South Lanarkshire	99,587	67.6	47,708	32.4
East Lothian	28,152	62.7	16,765	37.3
Midlothian	26,776	67.7	12,762	32.3
West Lothian	47,990	67.3	23,354	32.7
Moray	19,326	52.7	17,344	47.3
Perthshire & Kinross	33,398	51.3	31,709	48.7
East Renfrewshire	23,580	51.6	22,153	48.4
Renfrewshire	55,075	63.6	31,537	36.4
Stirling	25,044	58.9	17,487	41.1
Orkney	3,917	47.4	4,344	52.6
Shetland	4,478	51.6	4,198	48.4
Western Isles	8,557	68.4	3,947	31.6
SCOTLAND	1,512,889	63.5	870,263	36.5

Table A1.4: Spoiled ballots on first and second questions

Local authority	First question		Second question	
	N	%	N	%
Aberdeen	436	0.48	962	1.06
Aberdeenshire	560	0.58	824	0.85
Angus	222	0.43	413	0.79
Argyll & Bute	234	0.51	306	0.67
East Ayrshire	307	0.50	474	0.78
North Ayrshire	327	0.48	571	0.85
South Ayrshire	233	0.39	409	0.68
Borders	273	0.50	382	0.71
Clackmannan	118	0.50	136	0.58
Dumfries & Galloway	317	0.43	566	0.77
East Dunbartonshire	266	0.45	487	0.83
West Dunbartonshire	234	0.50	340	0.73
Dundee	406	0.62	570	0.87
Edinburgh	847	0.39	1,525	0.70
Falkirk	342	0.49	484	0.69
Fife	840	0.51	991	0.59
Glasgow	1,909	0.78	2,765	1.12
Highland	466	0.46	720	0.72
Inverclyde	265	0.65	410	1.00
North Lanarkshire	883	0.59	1,281	0.85
South Lanarkshire	587	0.40	960	0.65
East Lothian	38	0.08	279	0.62
Midlothian	167	0.42	268	0.67
West Lothian	279	0.39	487	0.68
Moray	180	0.48	449	1.21
Perthshire & Kinross	320	0.49	473	0.72
East Renfrewshire	100	0.22	181	0.39
Renfrewshire	476	0.54	734	0.84
Stirling	169	0.39	268	0.63
Orkney	38	0.46	66	0.79
Shetland	37	0.42	65	0.74
Western Isles	110	0.87	167	1.32
SCOTLAND	11,986	0.50	19,013	0.79

Note: The percentages shown are of the total votes cast (including spoiled ballots themselves).

APPENDIX 2

The Survey of Electors

An integral part of our study of the Scottish referendum was a postal survey of a sample of the Scottish electorate which we began immediately after polling day. To the best of our knowledge this was the first-ever academic survey of voting in a referendum in Britain, although NOP undertook a short telephone poll of the electorate on behalf of the BBC in the week before the referendum and on polling day itself. In addition, a face-to-face survey was mounted by CREST after the referendum. The results of this research became available in November 1998 and we have been able to incorporate some of the data into the text.

Some social scientists have doubts about the wisdom of using postal surveys. These mostly relate to the possibility of a poor response rate, the difficulty of ensuring that the person selected is the one who answers the questions and the likelihood that some groups (the better-educated and middle-aged, for example) are more likely to respond. We were aware of these problems, of course, but decided to use this method for three reasons. Firstly it is relatively cheap as compared with telephone or face-to-face surveys. Secondly, the number of respondents can be sharply increased at relatively little extra cost and we thought it important to have a large number of respondents in order to enable the analyses of sub-groups that we wanted to undertake. Thirdly, in face-to-face surveys interviews normally have to be clustered in particular areas in order to control costs. Commercial firms are unlikely to want to interview in, say, the Shetlands or the Western Isles. A postal survey can cover the whole country without difficulty, however. For these sorts of reasons academics have increasingly found postal surveys an attractive alternative to face-to-face or telephone methods (see, for example, McAllister, 1992; Seyd and Whiteley, 1992; Denver and Hands, 1997a).

MECHANICS OF THE SURVEY

A random sample of the names and addresses of 4,500 Scottish electors was purchased from CACI Ltd and a first wave of questionnaires was despatched on the day after the referendum together with an explanatory letter and a pre-addressed, pre-paid envelope for reply. To encourage replies, the questionnaire was relatively short, comprising 37 questions printed on seven plain white A4 pages, and almost all questions were answered by the respondent ticking an appropriate box or boxes. Two weeks later a reminder card was sent to those who had not returned a questionnaire. After a further ten days a reminder letter and replacement questionnaire were sent to non-respondents. No further action was taken to increase the response rate.

RESPONSE RATE

A major objection that is frequently made of postal surveys is that they produce a very low response rate. This was not the case with our survey. Of the original 4,500 names in the sample we were informed of 13 who had died since the register was compiled (although the true figure is probably considerably larger). In addition, 105 envelopes were returned by the Post Office because the addressee was no longer resident at the address given. Again we suspect that this is likely to be an underestimate. Thus the effective sample was reduced to a maximum of 4,382. A total of 2,335 completed questionnaires were returned – a response rate of 53.3 per cent. This compares with a 62 per cent response rate for the 1997 Scottish Election Study survey (882 respondents) and a 68 per cent response rate (676 respondents) for CREST's referendum survey. Of our 2,335 respondents, 523 (22.4 per cent) completed the second (replacement) questionnaire.

GEOGRAPHICAL DISTRIBUTION OF RESPONDENTS

In Table A2.1 we show the geographical distribution of our respondents across 11 broad areas of Scotland. Comparing this with the actual distribution of the Scottish electorate (columns 3 and 4) shows that none of the areas is very sharply over- or under-represented in our sample. Moreover, the differences that do exist can largely be explained by deficiencies in the original sample supplied (see columns 5 and 6) since it contained proportionately too few names from the Borders, Glasgow, Perthshire and Kinross and the Northern and Western Isles, with consequent over-representation from other areas. The fact that there is little variation between the original sample and our respondents in terms of geographical distribution suggests that there is little difference from area to area in the propensity of electors to complete postal questionnaires.

THE REFERENDUM RESULT

We can compare results from our sample with the actual referendum result, with the figures found by a BBC/NOP telephone poll of 2,006 respondents which was undertaken during the day before the referendum and on referendum day itself, and with the CREST face-to-face survey. The figures are shown in Table A2.2. Firstly, 81.9 per cent of our respondents claim to have voted in the referendum although the actual turnout was only 60.4 per cent. There can be little doubt that genuine non-voters are under-represented in the sample. Non-voters, we would assume, will have been less interested in the referendum than those who voted and, therefore, less likely to complete our questionnaire. In addition, however, there are likely to be some among our respondents who did not vote but claim to have done so. This is a well-known phenomenon in electoral research and is also illustrated by the BBC/NOP poll figure, which found that 79.5 per cent of respondents said that they were 'certain to vote' or had voted, and the CREST survey which found 74.5 per cent of respondents claiming to have voted.

Our sample gives a slight overestimation of the proportions voting Yes to both questions — by 2.7 per cent and 2.3 per cent respectively — but these are within acceptable levels of accuracy. The BBC/NOP poll also slightly overestimated the Yes votes (+1.3 per cent and +0.7 per cent) as did the CREST survey (+1.4 per cent and +1.9 per cent).

GENERAL ELECTION VOTE

Our questionnaire asked respondents to indicate how they had voted (if at all) in the May general election and a similar question was asked of the NOP and CREST respondents. Responses are compared with the actual general election result in Scotland in Table A2.3. The NOP poll and our survey produced very similar results — both slightly overestimating Labour support. CREST was more in error in this case, overestimating the Labour share of the vote by more than eight percentage points. The fact that all three surveys overestimated Labour support is likely to be a consequence of the strong popularity of Labour at the time of the referendum. The new government was still enjoying its 'honeymoon' with the electorate and respondents may have mistakenly thought that they voted for them. Nonetheless, the distribution of party support among our respondents is not dramatically different from the distribution of votes in the general election.

SOCIAL CHARACTERISTICS OF RESPONDENTS

The main 'actual' comparisons we can make here are with the 1991 census but, of course, this is now seriously out of date. *Regional Trends* provides more up-to-date estimates, however. CREST seems to have too few men in their sample but our survey and the BBC/NOP poll are close to the figures for the Scottish population. All three surveys contained more owner occupiers and fewer council tenants than were recorded in the 1991 census. By 1994 the proportion of owner occupiers had increased quite sharply and that of council tenants decreased (as indicated by the figures from *Regional Trends*) and these trends probably continued thereafter. Even so, it is likely that there is a disparity in housing tenure between survey respondents and the actual distribution of tenures in 1997. Non-manual workers are clearly over-represented in our sample while, somewhat surprisingly, being under-represented in the telephone poll. In terms of age, our postal survey reveals a considerable under-representation of voters from the youngest age group. The same is true, although to a lesser extent, of the CREST survey. In social terms then, the respondents to our survey are more middle class and older than the electorate as a whole and, by implication, likely to have been more highly educated. The under-representation of young people is in part a consequence of the fact that many students will have moved from temporary accommodation between the compilation of the electoral register and our survey but, in general, it is simply the case that more established, middle-class people are more likely to respond to postal questionnaires. In this respect, however, our postal survey is no different from other forms of random survey which experience the same sort of response bias, as illustrated by the figures for the CREST survey.

The fact that there are disparities between our respondents and the population at large in terms of age, housing and occupation is not a substantial cause for concern, however. What matters for our purposes is that they are reasonably representative in terms of the vote for a Scottish Parliament. When we analyse the survey results in terms of the social characteristics of respondents each category is, in essence, an independent sub-sample and, providing that a sizeable number of cases is involved (which is usually the case given the large total number of respondents), its size relative to other categories is not an impediment to comparing the behaviour and attitudes of groups of voters.

Table A2.1: The geographical distribution of respondents

	Respondents N	%	Actual %	% Respondents minus % actual	Original sample %	% Respondents minus % orig. sample
Highlands & Islands	93	4.0	5.6	-1.6	3.8	0.4
North East Scotland	232	9.9	10.2	-0.3	10.0	-0.1
Perthshire & Tayside	145	6.2	7.7	-1.5	6.8	-0.6
Fife	195	8.4	6.9	1.5	8.4	0.0
Edinburgh & Lothians	387	16.6	15.3	1.3	17.0	-0.4
Central Scotland	145	6.2	5.3	0.9	6.1	0.1
Glasgow & Lanarkshire	529	22.7	24.1	-1.4	23.1	-0.4
Renfrewshire	176	7.5	6.9	0.6	6.8	0.7
Dunbartonshire & Argyll	138	5.9	5.6	0.3	5.6	0.3
Ayrshire	211	9.0	7.4	1.6	9.0	0.0
South of Scotland	83	3.6	5.0	-1.4	3.4	0.4
Missing	1	–				
Total	2,335	100	100		100	

Table A2.2: The referendum result

	Actual result %	Our sample %	BBC/NOP %	CREST %
Turnout	60.4	81.9	79.5	74.5
Yes to Q1	74.3	77.0	75.8	75.7
Yes to Q2	63.5	65.8	64.2	65.4

Note: The survey results reported are derived from unweighted data.

Table A2.3: General election vote

	Actual result %	Our sample %	BBC/NOP %	CREST %
Conservative	17.5	17	19	17
Labour	45.6	51	50	54
Liberal Democrat	13.0	10	10	8
SNP	22.1	20	20	21
Other	1.9	1	1	1

Note: The survey results reported are derived from unweighted data.

Table A2.4: The social characteristics of respondents

	Our sample	BBC/NOP	CREST	Census 1991	Regional trends 1994/5
	%	%	%	%	%
Male	49	47	43	48	48
Female	51	53	57	52	52
Owner occupier	67	70	63	52	57
Council tenant	26	23	29	38	33
Other	7	6	8	10	10
Non-manual	67	45	55	55	56
Manual	34	55	45	45	44
Aged 18-29	9		13	24	
Aged 30-49	39		41	35	
Aged 50-64	25		22	21	
Aged 65+	26		24	20	

Note: The figures for 1994/5 are from *Regional Trends 1996* (Central Statistical Office, 1996) pp. 46, 56, 98.

References

BBC (1997) *Independent Report on Review of News and Current Affairs Output*, BBC Glasgow.

Bennie, L., Brand, J. and Mitchell, J. (1997) *How Scotland Votes*, Manchester, Manchester University Press.

Black, C.E. (1966) *The Dynamics of Modernization: A Study in Comparative History*, New York, Harper & Row.

Blondel, J. (1990) *Comparative Government: An Introduction*, Hemel Hempstead, Philip Allan.

Bochel, J. and Denver, D. (1970) 'Religion and voting: a critical review and a new analysis', *Political Studies*, 18, pp. 205–19.

Bochel, J. and Denver, D. (1981) 'Local campaigning' in Bochel, J., Denver, D. and Macartney, A. *The Referendum Experience: Scotland 1979*, Aberdeen, Aberdeen University Press, pp. 43–55.

Bochel, J. and Denver, D. (1981) 'The local press', in Bochel, J., Denver, D. and Macartney, A. *The Referendum Experience: Scotland 1979*, Aberdeen, Aberdeen University Press, pp. 99–108.

Bochel, J. and Denver, D. (1981) 'The outcome' in Bochel, J., Denver, D. and Macartney, A. *The Referendum Experience: Scotland 1979*, Aberdeen, Aberdeen University Press, pp. 140–6.

Bochel, J., Denver, D. and Macartney, A. (eds) (1981), *The Referendum Experience: Scotland 1979*, Aberdeen, Aberdeen University Press.

Bogdanor, V. (1994) 'Western Europe' in Butler, A. and Ranney, A. (eds), *Referendums Around the World*, Washington DC, American Enterprise Institute Press, pp. 24–97.

Bradley, A.W. and Christie, D.J. (1979) *The Scotland Act*, Edinburgh, W. Green & Son Ltd.

Brand, J. (1978) *The National Movement in Scotland*, London, Routledge & Kegan Paul.

Brand, J., Mitchell, J. and Surridge, P. (1994) 'Social constituency and ideological profile: Scottish nationalism in the 1990s', *Political Studies*, 42, 4, pp. 616–29.

Brogan, B. and Campbell, D. (1997) 'Panorama clash avoided', The *Herald*, 10 September.

Brown, A. (1997) 'Scotland: paving the way for devolution' in Norris, P. and Gavin T.N. (eds), *Britain Votes 1997*, Oxford, Oxford University Press, pp. 150–63.

Brown, G. (1981) *The Labour Party and Political Change in Scotland, 1918–1929: The Politics of Five Elections*, Edinburgh University Ph.D., unpublished.

Budge, I. (1996) *The New Challenge of Direct Democracy*, Cambridge, Polity Press.

Budge, I. and Urwin, D.W. (1966) *Scottish Political Behaviour*, London, Longmans.

Butler, D. and Kavanagh, D. (1988) *The British General Election of 1987*, Basingstoke Macmillan.

Butler, D. and Kavanagh, D. (1992) *The British General Election of 1992*, Basingstoke, Macmillan.

Butler, D. and Kavanagh, D. (1997) *The British General Election of 1997*, Basingstoke, Macmillan.

Butler, D. and Kitzinger, U. (1976) *The 1975 Referendum*, Basingstoke, Macmillan.

Butler, D. and Kitzinger, U. (1996) *The 1975 Referendum* (2nd edition), Basingstoke, Macmillan.

Butler, D. and Ranney, A. (1978) *Referendums: A Comparative Theory of Practice and Theory*, Washington, DC, American Enterprise Institute Press.

Butler, D. and Ranney, A. (1994) (eds) *Referendums Around the World: The Growing Use of Direct Democracy*, Washington DC, American Enterprise Institute Press.

Butler, D., Adonis, A. and Travers, T. (1994) *Failure in British Government: The Politics of the Poll Tax*, Oxford, Oxford University Press.

Central Statistical Office (1996) *Regional Trends 1996*, London, HMSO.

Committee on Standards in Public Life (1998) *Funding of Political Parties in the UK*, Cmnd. 4057.

Constitutional Convention (1990) *Towards Scotland's Parliament*, Edinburgh, Scottish Constitutional Convention.

Constitution Unit (1996) *Report of the Commission on the Conduct of Referendums*, London, Constitution Unit.

Crewe, I., Fox, T. and Alt, J. (1977) 'Non-voting in British general elections 1966–October 1974', in C. Crouch (ed.) *British Political Sociology Yearbook*, vol. 3, London, Croom Helm, pp. 38–109.

Cronin, T. E. (1989) *Direct Democracy: The Politics of Initiative, Referendum and Recall*, Cambridge, MA, Harvard University Press.

Cunningham, G. (1989) 'Burns night massacre', The *Spectator*, 18 January.

Curtice, J. (1996) 'Who votes for the centre now?' in MacIver, D. (ed.) *The Liberal Democrats*, pp. 191–204, Hemel Hempstead, Prentice Hall.

Curtice, J. and Semetko, H. (1994) 'Does it matter what the papers say?' in Heath, A., Jowell, R. and Curtice, J. with Taylor, B. (1994) *Labour's Last Chance? The 1992 Election and Beyond*, Aldershot, Dartmouth, pp. 43–63.

Darcy, R. and Laver, M. (1990) 'Referendum dynamics and the Irish divorce amendment', *Public Opinion Quarterly*, 54, 1, pp. 1–20.

Denver, D. (1994) *Elections and Voting Behaviour in Britain* (2nd edition), Hemel Hempstead, Prentice Hall/Harvester Wheatsheaf.

Denver, D. (1995) 'Non-voting in Britain' in Font, J and Virós, R (eds) *Electoral Abstention in Europe*, Barcelona, Institut de Cièncès Politiques I Sociale, pp. 183–98.

Denver, D. (1997) 'The 1997 general election in Scotland: an analysis of the results', *Scottish Affairs*, 20, pp. 17–33.

Denver, D. and Hands, G. (1997a) *Modern Constituency Electioneering*, London, Frank Cass.

Denver, D. and Hands, G. (1997b) 'Turnout', *Parliamentary Affairs*, 50, 4, pp. 720–32.

Denver, D., Hands, G. and Henig, S. (1998) 'Triumph of targeting? constituency campaigning in the 1997 general election' in Denver, D., Fisher, J., Cowley, P. and Pattie, C. (eds) *British Parties and Elections Review*, 8, pp. 171–90.

DETR (1998) *Modernising Local Government: Local Democracy and Community Leadership*, London, DETR.

Ferguson, W. (1977) *Scotland's Relations with England: A Survey to 1707*, Edinburgh, John Donald Publishers.

Finlay, R. (1994), *Independent and Free, Scottish Politics and the Origins of the Scottish National Party, 1918–1945*, Edinburgh, John Donald.

Fitzmaurice, J. (1995) 'The 1994 referenda on EU membership in Austria and Scandinavia', *Electoral Studies*, 14, 2, pp. 226–32.

Fowler, J. (1981) 'Broadcasting – television' in Bochel, J., Denver, D. and Macartney, A., *The Referendum Experience: Scotland 1979*, Aberdeen, Aberdeen University Press, pp. 121–35.

Franklin, B. (1994) *Packaging Politics: Political Communications in Britain's Media Democracy*, London, Edward Arnold.

Franklin, B. and Murphy, D. (1991) *What News? The Market, Politics and the Local Press*, London, Routledge.

Franklin, M. (1985) *The Decline of Class Voting in Britain*, Oxford, Clarendon Press.

Franklin, M., van Der Eijk, C. and Marsh, M. (1995) 'Referendum outcomes and trust in government: public support for Europe in the wake of Maastricht', *West European Politics*, 18, 3, pp. 101–7.

Gallagher, M. (1996) 'Conclusion' in Gallagher, M. and Uleri, P. V. (eds) *The Referendum Experience in Europe*, Basingstoke, Macmillan, pp. 226–52.

Gallagher, M. and Uleri, P. V. (eds.) (1996) *The Referendum Experience in Europe*, Basingstoke, Macmillan.

Gamble, A. (1994) *The Free Economy and the Strong State*, (2nd edition), Basingstoke, Macmillan.

Harrop, M. (1987) 'Voters' in Seaton, J. and Pimlott, B. (eds) *The Media in British Politics*, Aldershot, Avebury Press, pp. 45–63.

Heath, A., Jowell, R. and Curtice, J. (1985) *How Britain Votes*, Oxford, Pergamon Press.

Heath, A, Jowell, R., Curtice, J., Evans, G., Field, J. and Witherspoon, S. (1991) *Understanding Political Change*, Oxford, Pergamon Press.

Hughes, C. (1994) 'Australia and New Zealand' in Butler, D. and Ranney, A. (eds) *Referendums around the World*, Washington, DC, American Enterprise Institute Press, pp. 154–73.

Huntington, S.P. (1971) 'The change to change: modernization, development, and politics', *Comparative Politics*, 3, pp. 283–322.

Johnston R.J. and Pattie C.J. (1992) 'Class dealignment and the regional polarization of voting in Great Britain, 1964–1987' *Political Geography*, 11, pp. 73–86.

Jones, P. (1997) 'A start to a new song: The 1997 devolution referendum campaign', *Scottish Affairs*, 21, pp. 1–16.

Keating, M. (1988) *State and Regional Nationalism*, London, Harvester Wheatsheaf.

Keating, M. and Bleiman, D. (1979) *Labour and Scottish Nationalism*, Basingstoke, Macmillan.

Kellas, J. ([1973] 1989) *The Scottish Political System* (4th edition), Cambridge, Cambridge University Press.

Kellner, P. (1996), *Report on Devolution Poll*, London, Political Context.

Kilbrandon (Chairman) (1973) *Report of the Royal Commission on the Constitution*, London, HMSO, Cmnd. 5460.

Lipset, S.M. and Rokkan, S. (1967) *Party Systems and Voter Alignments*, New York, Free Press.

Lowi, T. (1964) 'American business, public policy, case studies, and political theory', *World Politics*, 16, 4, pp. 676–715.

Macartney, A. (1981) 'The Protagonists', in Bochel, J., Denver, D. and Macartney, A. *The Referendum Experience: Scotland 1979*, Aberdeen, Aberdeen University Press pp. 12–42.

MacInnes, J. (1992) 'The press in Scotland', *Scottish Affairs*, 1, pp. 137–49.

MacInnes, J. (1993) 'The broadcast media in Scotland', *Scottish Affairs*, 2, pp. 84–98.

Magleby, D. (1994) 'Direct legislation in the American states' in Butler, D. and Ranney, A. (eds) *Referendums around the World*, Washington, DC, American Enterprise Institute Press, pp. 218–57.

Majone, G. (1994) 'The rise of the regulatory state in Europe', *West European Politics*, 17, pp. 77–101.

Marr, A. (1992) *The Battle for Scotland*, London, Penguin Books.

Marshall, G. (1997) 'The referendum: what, when and how?', *Parliamentary Affairs*, 50, 2, pp. 307–13.

McAllister, I. (1992) *Political Behavior: Citizens, Parties and Elites in Australia*, Melbourne, Longman Cheshire.

McAllister, L. (1998) 'The Welsh devolution referendum', *Parliamentary Affairs*, 51, 2, pp. 149–65.

McSmith, A. (1994) *John Smith*, London, Mandarin.

Midwinter, A., Keating M. and Mitchell, J. (1991), *Politics and Public Policy in Scotland*, Basingstoke, Macmillan.

Miller, W.L. (1980) 'The Scottish dimension', in Butler, D. and Kavanagh, D., *The British General Election of 1979*, Basingstoke, Macmillan.

Miller, W.L. (1984) 'The de-nationalisation of British politics: The re-emergence of the periphery' in Berrington, H. (ed.) *Change in British Politics*, London, Frank Cass, pp. 103–29.

Miller, W.L. (1988) *Irrelevant Elections*, Oxford, Clarendon Press.

Mitchell, J. (1989) 'The Gilmour committee on Scottish central administration', *Juridical Review*, pp. 173–88.

Mitchell, J. (1990a) *Conservatives and the Union*, Edinburgh, Edinburgh University Press.

Mitchell, J. (1990b) 'Factions, tendencies and consensus in the SNP in the 1980s', *Scottish Government Yearbook, 1990*, Edinburgh, Edinburgh University Press, pp. 49–61.

Mitchell, J. (1996) *Strategies for Self-Government*, Edinburgh, Polygon.

Mitchell, J. (1998) 'What could a Scottish Parliament do?', *Regional and Federal Studies*, 8, pp. 68–85.

Mitchell, J. and Bennie, L. (1996) 'Thatcherism and the Scottish question', *British Elections and Parties Yearbook 1995*, London, Frank Cass, pp. 90–104.

Mitchell, J. and Bennie, L. (1997) 'A very British affair? The 1997 general election in Scotland' paper presented at the 1997 EPOP conference, University of Essex.

Mitchell, J. and McAleavey, P. (2000) *Regionalism and Regional Policy in the European Union*, Basingstoke, Macmillan.

Moore, C. and Booth, S. (1989) *Managing Competition*, Oxford, Clarendon Press.

Nilson, S. and Bjorklund, T. (1986) 'Ideal types of referendum behaviour', *Scandinavian Political Studies*, 9, 3, pp. 265–78.

Parry, G., Moyser, G. and Day, N. (1992) *Political Participation and Democracy in Britain*, Cambridge, Cambridge University Press.

Pattie, C.J. and Johnston, R. (1990) 'Thatcherism – one nation or two? An exploration of British political attitudes in the 1980s', *Environment and Planning C: Government and Policy*, 8, pp. 269–82.

Pattie, C.J. and Johnston, R.J. (1998) 'Voter turnout at the British general election of 1992: rational choice, social standing or political efficacy?', *European Journal of Political Research*, 33, pp. 263–83.

Pattie, C.J., Johnston, R.J. and Fieldhouse, E.A. (1995) 'Winning the local vote: the effectiveness of constituency campaign spending in Great Britain, 1983–1992', *American Political Science Review*, 89, 4, pp. 969–83.

Pattie, C.J., Denver, D., Mitchell, J. and Bochel, H. (1999) 'Partisanship, national identity and constitutional preferences: an exploration of voting in the Scottish devolution referendum of 1997', *Electoral Studies*, 18, 3, pp. 305–22.

Rallings, C. and Thrasher, M. (1990) 'Turnout in English local elections – an aggregate analysis with electoral and contextual data', *Electoral Studies*, 9, 2, pp. 79–90.

Rose, R. (1982) *Understanding the United Kingdom*, London, Longman.

Rose, R. and Urwin, D. (1969) 'Social cohesion, political parties and strains in regimes', *Comparative Political Studies*, 2, pp. 7–67.

Rose, R. and Urwin, D. (1975) *Territorial Differentiation and Political Unity in Western Nations*, London, Sage.

Ross, W. (1978) 'Approaching the archangelic?', *The Scottish Government Yearbook, 1978*, Edinburgh, Paul Harris Publishing, pp. 1–20.

Sassoon, D. (1986) *Contemporary Italy*, Harlow, Longman.

Scottish Council Foundation (1997) *Scotland's Parliament ... a Business Guide to Devolution*, Edinburgh, Scottish Council Foundation.

Scottish Home Department (1948) *Scottish Affairs*, Edinburgh, HMSO, Cmd. 7308.

Scottish Office (1993) *Scotland in the Union – A Partnership for Good*, HMSO, Cmnd. 2225.

Scottish Office (October, 1998) Consultative Steering Group: CSG Decisions to Date, CSG(98) (83).

Seyd, P. (1987) *The Rise and Fall of the Labour Left*, Basingstoke, Macmillan.

Seyd, P. and Whiteley, P. (1992) *Labour's Grass Roots: the Politics of Party Membership*, Oxford, Clarendon Press.

Smith, A. (1976) 'Broadcasting' in Butler, D. and Kitzinger, U., *The 1975 Referendum*, Basingstoke, Macmillan, pp. 190–213.

Swaddle, K. and Heath, A. (1989) 'Official and reported turnout in the British general election of 1987', *British Journal of Political Science*, 19, pp. 537–51.

System Three (1997) *Political Poll on a Scottish Parliament*, Edinburgh, System Three.

Thatcher, M. (1993) *The Downing Street Years*, London, HarperCollins.

Trechsel, A. and Kriesi, H. (1996) 'Switzerland: the referendum and initiative as a centrepiece of the political system' in Gallagher, M. and Uleri P.V. (eds) *The Referendum Experience in Europe*, Basingstoke, Macmillan, pp. 185–208.

White, S. and Hill, R.J. (1996) 'Russia, the former Soviet Union and Eastern Europe: the referendum as a flexible political instrument' in Gallagher, M. and Uleri, P.V. (eds) *The Referendum Experience in Europe*, Basingstoke, Macmillan, pp. 153–70.

Index